Mr. Lincoln Runs for President

Mr. LINCOLN

RUNS FOR PRESIDENT

by MELVIN L. HAYES

✰✰✰

THE CITADEL PRESS   NEW YORK

MR. LINCOLN RUNS FOR PRESIDENT

Copyright © 1960 by Melvin L. Hayes
All rights reserved

FIRST EDITION

Published by The Citadel Press
222 Park Avenue South
New York 3, N.Y.

Manufactured in the United States of America

Library of Congress Catalog Card Number 60-15448

To
HELEN
PAT *and* SHERRY

CONTENTS

Preface   9

1   Out of the Tall Corn He Came   17
2   Chicago Bubbles Over With Excitement   35
3   The Convention Knuckles Down—But Not Much   44
4   Old Abe Is Shouted to Victory   52
5   Jubilant Republicans Rejoice Over Their
        Nominee   67
6   Four Candidates, One Issue, and No Holds Barred   82
7   Old Abram—Horribly Homely, Yet Handsome   99
8   The Rail-Splitters Harmonize   124
9   Wide-Awakes, Wigwams, and Whistle-Stops   137
10 Lincoln's Open-Door and Closed-Mouth Policy   167
11 The Fourth Estate Holds Forth   180
12 Ballyhoo Gives Way to Ballots   208
13 The Slave Issue Engrosses the Nation   222
14 The Union Begins to Crumble   242
15 Mr. Lincoln Goes to Washington   260
16 A Flight Through the Night   287
17 The Patriots Descend on D. C.   298
18 They Have a Capital Time   309

8   CONTENTS

19   "I Do Solemnly Swear . . ."   316
20   After the Ball Was Over   328

References   *333*
Index   *346*

*A sixteen-page illustration section
follows page 96*

PREFACE

A century ago, Americans liked their politics raw. But they also liked them garnished with the hoopla and ballyhoo that long has characterized our American institution, the national political convention, and the entire Presidential campaign.

This is the story of one of our most significant and colorful elections, one that recalled the "log cabin and hard cider campaign" two decades earlier with its "Tippecanoe and Tyler Too" slogan. It is the story of torchlight processions featuring Wide-Awake marching groups with caps and capes, stump speakers and barbecues, parodies and poems, wisdom and wit, verbal blasts in the press and cracked skulls on the street.

The book follows the fortunes of the Rail-Splitter candidate through the unusual four-sided political campaign of 1860 and the climactic inauguration of March 4, 1861.

As a blow-by-blow account of Honest Old Abe's first campaign and election, it pictures the rise to prominence, one hundred years ago, of one of America's greatest men. At the same time, it depicts the Republican party, now a centenarian, in its first national victory—its first chance at the Federal feed trough, as the opposition put it. It shows the rough-and-ready politics involved in electing a person who was, essentially, the first "Western man" in the Presidential chair, Ohio's William Henry Harrison having served only one month. It also is the story of slavery and secession, of a nation ripping apart, and of

9

the tall and homely rail-splitter of the Sangamon River valley who tried unsuccessfully to mend it.

This book is intended mainly for John Q. and his good wife, but may also be especially interesting to the journalist and the politician. It also is hoped that Lincoln scholars will find herein something of value.

The data has been garnered almost exclusively from the reports of the men who witnessed the events—the journalists of 1860-61.

The author examined thousands of issues of newspapers of those two years—the *Burlington* (Vt.) *Sentinel, Daily Omaha Nebraskan, Weekly Wisconsin Patriot, New Orleans* (La.) *Daily Delta, Worcester* (Mass.) *Daily Spy, Sacramento* (Calif.) *Daily Union, Albany* (N.Y.) *Atlas and Argus, Indiana State Guard, The Mississippian, National Intelligencer,* and scores of others. A number of periodicals of the nineteenth century also were drawn upon.

To a considerable extent, this book reflects the muscular "personal journalism" that still existed a century ago. It taps newspapers which were "the lengthened shadow of one man." As a prime example, it speaks through the pen of Horace Greeley, founder of the *New York Daily Tribune* and "Father of American Journalism." It voices the ideas of William Cullen Bryant, *New York Evening Post*; James Gordon Bennett, *New York Herald*; Thurlow Weed, *Albany* (N.Y.) *Evening Journal*; "Long John" Wentworth, *Chicago Democrat*; Joseph Medill, *Chicago Tribune*; and Samuel Bowles, *Springfield* (Mass.) *Daily Republican*. It also reflects the views of many other of the 3,000 newspapers of 1860-61, including Henry J. Raymond's *New York Times*, a pioneer in the new impersonal journalism.

Since newspaper items were reprinted and re-reprinted almost *ad infinitum* in the mid-1800's, the reader can assume that some items quoted in this book are several steps removed from their origin.

Many of the statements in this volume are from violently partisan journals, and the reader may conclude that the reporters' and editors' enthusiasm in trying to glorify their own candidates or to scalp the opposition led to inaccurate "facts" as well as exaggerated opinions. The author of this book cannot attest to the accuracy of most statements written a hundred years ago by journalists who were dug in on the front line of a raging political battle. He can only claim to have tried to select without bias from what they said about Lincoln. The result, he believes, is a picture of this historical period not too unlike the picture the reader might have received had he lived in 1860-61 and followed the press of that time.

This book in part concerns Abraham Lincoln before he had reached the pinnacle of greatness. Thus the reader may be jolted by the scathingly derogatory newspaper statements about this man who now "belongs to the ages." But the place of Honest Old Abe in the hearts of Americans is secure, and will not be shaken by echoes of the pot shots aimed at him along the road to fame.

The author wishes to thank employees of the newspaper reference room of the Library of Congress for assistance while he explored the "great game of politics" of a century ago.

MELVIN L. HAYES

"In all our rejoicing let us neither express, nor cherish, any harsh feeling towards any citizen who, by his vote, has differed with us. Let us at all times remember that all American citizens are brothers of a common country, and should dwell together in the bonds of fraternal feeling"

Lincoln's comments to Springfield neighbors and friends who gathered around his home in November, 1860, to celebrate his election.

Mr. Lincoln Runs for President

CHAPTER ONE

OUT OF THE TALL CORN HE CAME

Abe Lincoln, gangling Illinois lawyer, had just sat down "amidst the wildest demonstrations of enthusiasm." Then the chairman tossed out a teaser to the audience. "An old Democrat of Macon County, who has grown gray in the service of that party, desires to make a contribution to the convention," he announced. The puzzled Republican delegates awaited this surprise "contribution" by the foe. Then into the hall strode Democrat John Hanks with two gaily decorated old fence rails. They bore a banner inscribed:

ABRAHAM LINCOLN
THE RAIL CANDIDATE
For President in 1860
Two rails from a lot of three thousand made
in 1830 by Thos. [John] Hanks and Abe Lincoln—whose
father was the first pioneer of Macon County

"The effect was electrical," said the *Weekly Illinois State Journal* (Springfield). "One spontaneous burst of applause went up from all parts of the "Wigwam," which grew more and more deafening as it was prolonged and which did not wholly subside for ten or fifteen minutes after. The cheers upon cheers which rent the air could have been heard all over the adjacent country."

Old Abe, whose rail-splitting skill had gone largely unno-

17

ticed until now, rose slowly to explain. About thirty years ago, when he came to Illinois from Indiana, he said, he spent one season with his mother's family. There, near Decatur on the Sangamon River, he built a cabin, split rails, and cultivated a small farm. The two rails being paraded through the hall, he was told, were from a fence he had helped John Hanks build on that farm. He mauled many, many more rails—and much better ones—after growing up, he added.

This rail-splitter stunt worthy of a Madison Avenue mind, had been engineered by the convention chairman, thirty-five-year-old Richard J. Oglesby, candidate for the Illinois Senate and a future Major General, United States Senator, and Governor of Illinois. But the idea may have been hatched by farmer Hanks himself. The old Democrat explained, in the *Weekly Illinois State Journal,* that he had decided "to present some of them [the rails] to that convention as a testimonial of the beginning of one of the greatest living men of the age, believing they would speak more in his praise than any orator could."

Oglesby and Hanks, a relative of Lincoln's stepmother, had driven to the farm in a buggy and looked over the black-walnut and honey-locust rails Lincoln and Hanks had split. They picked out some rails and hauled them to Decatur for the state Republican gathering.

The dramatic episode at this convention on May 9-10, 1860, helped line up Illinois for Lincoln. The group instructed their delegates to the national convention, opening at Chicago one week later, to "use all honorable means" to capture the nomination for Honest Old Abe.

The stunt set the stage for the Republicans' national political slogan—"Abe Lincoln, the Rail-Splitter." It also launched a novel and, according to some reports, thriving business—the sale of wormy old fence rails. John Hanks peddled his two rails at the close of the Decatur convention, and before the political

season was wrapped up, many people had got into the act in a
financially profitable way.

The fence rail was the most conspicuous and striking feature of
the campaign of 1860. [*Century Magazine* said later.] It appealed
to the people almost irresistibly; it told of the candidate's rise from
a humble beginning; it was the emblem of his thorough democracy.
Nothing else, aside from the great principles for which he stood,
contributed so much to his election.

Anti-Republican newspapers sneered at the rail-splitter
campaigners. The *Daily Chicago Herald* suggested that the
rail may have been selected as the Republican symbol because
of the looks of "Long Abe" and his co-worker, "John *Shanks*."

The Washington *Constitution* declared that Lincoln's chief
recommendation was that thirty years earlier "he was able to
do what every farmer in the land can do as well, or better than
he." It asserted that if Lincoln deserved the top nomination,
farmer Hanks definitely merited the second.

But the detractors seemed merely to publicize this little-
known Lincoln. His being considered a most unlikely candidate by them didn't seem to slow down his bandwagon.

But this former Whig certainly did appear to own few of
the physical attributes for a tenant of 1600 Pennsylvania
Avenue in Washington. A rather stoop-shouldered, six-feet-
four, he was clothed in dark, loose, and leathery skin. Long
arms and huge hands hung carelessly at his sides. His wrinkled,
sallow face oozed melancholy.

But Old Abe looked plenty good to his buddies in Springfield. There on Eighth Street he lived in a frame house purchased sixteen years earlier for fifteen hundred dollars. Mary
Todd Lincoln and their sons, Robert, Willie, and Thomas
(Tad), shared the modest home.

A picture of this unpretentious Lincoln was penned a bit
earlier by humorist and satirist Petroleum V. Nasby, (pseu-

donym for David R. Locke, later editor of the *Toledo Blade*). After visiting Lincoln in a hotel, Nasby wrote:

He sat in the room with his boots off to relieve his very large feet from the pain occasioned by continuous standing, or, to put it in his own words, "I like to give my feet a chance to breathe." He had removed his coat and vest, dropped one suspender from his shoulder, taken off his necktie and collar, and he sat tilted back in one chair with his feet upon another in perfect ease. He seemed to dislike clothing, and in privacy wore as little of it as he could.

Other descriptions of this thin, wiry, raw-boned man who rose out of the tall corn of Illinois were less charitable. Later, one writer, perhaps with tongue in cheek, declared:

Mr. Lincoln stands six-feet-twelve in his sox, which he changes once every ten days. His anatomy is composed mostly of bones, and when walking he resembles the off-spring of a happy marriage between a derrick and a windmill . . . His head is shaped something like a rutabaga . . . His hands and his feet are plenty large enough, and in society he has the air of having too many of them. . . .

But it was not so much the way Lincoln stood, or the way he looked, that influenced Republicans in 1860. More important was what he *stood for* and the way he *looked at* crucial issues of the day.

It was the slavery issue that had set Lincoln's political blood racing through its extensive course. He had slipped out of politics in 1849 after one term as a Whig Congressman. But the repeal of the Missouri Compromise by the enactment of Stephen A. Douglas' Kansas-Nebraska Bill in 1854 provoked the lank lawyer back into the political arena.

The Missouri Compromise of 1820 had provided that Maine should be admitted to the Union as a free state and Missouri as a slave state, but that all the rest of the Louisiana Purchase north of 36 degrees, 30 minutes, should forever remain free. Instead, the Kansas-Nebraska Bill left it to the settlers to decide whether they would have slavery. Thus the Missouri Compromise was shoved aside by Douglas' "Squatter

Sovereignty." This principle was put to the test in a territory that became labelled "Bleeding Kansas."

Although Lincoln believed slavery was morally wrong, he did not favor disturbing it where it already was rooted. Nevertheless, he was bitterly opposed to allowing it to be transplanted to new areas.

Conflict seemed to be shaping up between the North and the South. The lines were more rigidly drawn in 1857 by the Dred Scott case. A slave, the decision declared, was always a slave, even though he had gone into and lived in free territory during part of his life. This jolting decision appeared to land a haymaker on the fledgling Republican party which had backed the policy of "fencing in" slavery.

Was a clash inevitable? The doctrine of the "irrepressible conflict" seemed to say so. And in bold strokes upon the wall! The *Daily Chicago Herald* quoted from a speech by William H. Seward, United States Senator and a former New York Governor:

It is an irrepressible conflict between opposing and enduring forces, and it means that the United States must and will, sooner or later, become either entirely a slave-holding nation, or entirely a free-labor nation. Either the cotton and rice fields of South Carolina, and the sugar plantations of Louisiana, will ultimately be tilled by free-labor, and Charleston and New Orleans become marts for legitimate merchandise alone, or else the rye fields and wheat fields of Massachusetts and New York, must again be surrendered by the farmers to slave culture and to the production of slaves, and Boston and New York become once more markets for the trade in the bodies and souls of men.

Opposition to the Kansas-Nebraska Bill and the Dred Scott decision brewed and bubbled and boiled across the North. In this turbulent climate the infant Illinois Republican party met in 1858 to choose a candidate for United States Senator "to fill the vacancy about to be created by the expiration of Judge Douglas' term of office."

At this gathering in Springfield, Abe Lincoln asserted:

⚓ "A house divided against itself cannot stand. I believe this government cannot endure permanently, half slave and half free. I do not expect the Union to be dissolved—I do not expect the house to fall; but I do expect it will cease to be divided. It will become all one thing, or all the other."

Lincoln, who was picked for the senatorial race, faced the most prominent and politically nimble of all Democrats—Stephen A. Douglas, the incumbent. "Little Doug" had scrambled to lofty heights. In rapid succession he had been a district prosecuting attorney, state legislator, U. S. Register of Public Lands, U. S. Representative, Illinois Supreme Court Judge, U. S. Senator, and candidate for Democratic nomination to the Presidency.

Douglas began pecking away at Lincoln's platform without squarely meeting the Rail-Splitter's arguments. So Abe challenged him to a series of debates. Dumpy, dwarfish Doug, and long, leathery Abe engaged in verbal tussles at Ottawa, Freeport, Jonesboro, Charleston, Galesburg, Quincy, and Alton, Illinois. This debate series was the most dramatic part of an energetic campaign in which Lincoln poured forth more than sixty speeches and Douglas not less than one hundred.

Douglas glided along this joint debate circuit through the seven Congressional districts in super-splendor. Often the "Little Giant" rode in luxurious private railroad cars. When his train arrived in town, a salute of thirty-two guns, for the thirty-two states, frequently was accorded him. Brass bands tooted up enthusiasm.

In contrast to this red-carpet treatment, humble Honest Abe, his meager finances further crippled by the drying up of attorney fees during his campaigning, journeyed in crowded railway coaches.

Holiday-happy crowds of up to 20,000 people gathered under the trees or in fields to hear the little judge and the tall attorney wage their battle of words. The people came down dusty roads on horseback, in wagons, or even on foot. Many brought grub. Some camped overnight, their flickering fires lighting the area.

As the crowds neared a debate town, they often formed into processions. Bands struck up lively tunes and banners were unfurled.

Commonly appearing in such parades was the political cheesecake of that modest day—thirty-two attractive girls in white, often on horseback, representing the thirty-two states. Sometimes there was also a somber-looking lass in black carrying a banner that proclaimed, "Kansas—I will be free."

The Charleston, Illinois, parade featured a float with the legend: "Westward the Star of Empire makes its way. We girls link on to Lincoln, as our mothers did to Clay."

The Republican and the Democratic processions sometimes judiciously chose different routes into town. Otherwise, their entry might have turned into a riot. But they merged peacefully for the speechmaking, and became all ears.

The crowds certainly could not have been favorably impressed by Lincoln's looks. He stood awkwardly before them, his legs and arms appearing unnaturally long, for only when standing did he loom above others. His face was marked by a lone mole. His cheekbones were high and prominent. Large ears flapped out. A shock of dark hair "lay floating," as his law partner William H. Herndon described it, "where his fingers or the winds left it, piled up at random."

When Lincoln spoke, his voice was often shrill and piercing, but when he came to a point that touched his emotions, it became musically soft.

The woe-struck rail-splitter apparently fared all right, even though he did not always steal the show from the polished orator, Steve Douglas. Said Carl Schurz, German-American Republican leader from Wisconsin:

I met him then, when he bearded the lion of demagogism in his den, when the brilliant sallies of his wit and sarcasm drew shouts of delight from the multitude, when the thunderbolts of his invectives rattled triumphantly against the brazen front of Stephen A. Douglas. . . .

Lincoln's platform performance was thus described by a reporter:

All the strings that play upon the human heart and understanding were touched with masterly skill and force . . . The tall, angular form with the long, angular arms, at times bent nearly double with excitement, like a large flail animating two smaller ones, the mobile face wet with perspiration which he discharged in drops as he threw his head this way and that like a projectile . . . After listening to him a few minutes, nobody would mind whether he was graceful or not. All thought of grace or form would be lost in the exceeding attractiveness of what he was saying.

"While I had thought Lincoln the homeliest man I ever saw," one listener remarked, "he was the handsomest man I ever listened to in a speech."

It was Freeport that became Douglas' eventual Waterloo. Lincoln asked the Little Giant, in effect, whether he believed the Dred Scott decision necessarily overthrew the idea of popular sovereignty. Douglas was bound to get burned by this hot potato—he would lose the North if he said the decision cancelled out popular sovereignty, the South if he said it did not.

Douglas asserted the decision did not necessarily overthrow popular sovereignty, for slavery could exist in a new area only if the local community decided to provide police protection. Poor Doug's name then became mud throughout the South, for not having taken an unadulterated pro-slavery stand.

What was the result of these historic debates? The *Delawarean* (Dover) expressed it this way during the campaign of 1860:

A speaker at a late Republican meeting stated that in the contest for the Senatorship between the Little Giant and Honest Abe, the former "bit the dust." For the benefit of benighted individuals who do not understand hyberpole, we would explain that the dust referred to was $3,000 a year and mileage.

And Douglas did win the Washington job, thanks to gerrymandered legislative districts, although Lincoln garnered the most *popular* votes. But Abe was playing for bigger stakes, perhaps. The debates made him more widely known, and chalked up some indelible marks in the cause of civil liberty. He jockeyed his long-time opponent, Stephen A. Douglas, into an uncomfortable position with the South, and diminished his chances for the Presidential victory in 1860, as the Northern Democratic nominee. Yes, Lincoln stumbled in the senatorial campaign, but he certainly did not fall.

The Rail-Splitter still was little known east of the Appalachians. An opportunity to become better-known there arose when he was invited to speak in Henry Ward Beecher's Plymouth Church in Brooklyn, N. Y., on February 27, 1860.

Clutching his odd-looking umbrella and bag, Abe Lincoln boarded the train for New York. There he was taken to the Astor House.

After arriving in Manhattan, Lincoln learned that the meeting place had been changed to Cooper Union, which was larger than the Beecher church. The Young Men's Central Republican Union had taken over the sponsorship.

Opponents really made political hay from the Young Republicans' admission charge to the speech. The *Fort Wayne* (Ind.) *Sentinel* announced that "the faithful were charged the regular circus rate of twenty-five cents' admittance fee." Lincoln was tagged the "two shilling candidate" because, said the Washington *Constitution,* "he's the fellow that charged his own friends two-shillin' apiece to hear him talk about politics." The New York Republican campaign club, after debating the issue nearly three hours, condemned the Young Men's Republican Union for charging admission, and "some rather severe things were said on both sides."

The fee apparently did not discourage too many people, for 1,500 gathered in the yellow gaslight and listened to the tall orator from way out West.

The Republican journals had helped whip up enthusiasm for the meeting. Horace Greeley's *New York Daily Tribune* announced that Lincoln's political addresses were marked by clearness and candor, chivalrous courtesy to opponents, and broad genial humor. It pointed out that "it is not probable that Mr. Lincoln will be heard again in our city this year if ever. Let us improve this present opportunity."

William Cullen Bryant of the *New York Evening Post* said, in introducing Lincoln:

I see a higher and a wiser agency than that of man in the causes that have filled with a hardy population the vast and fertile region which forms the western part of the valley of the Mississippi; a race of men who are not ashamed to till their acres with their own hands, and who would be ashamed to subsist by the labor of the slave. These children of the West, my friends, form a living bulwark against the advances of slavery, and from them is recruited the vanguard of the armies of Liberty. One of them will appear here before you this evening.

It was an awkward Abe, unschooled but not uneducated, a man from the rugged West, who stood that night before sophisticated and skeptical Easterners. He might have reminded one of an even more unpolished Abe who attended a cotillion party in Springfield many years before. Taking a shine to Mary Todd, who was to become his wife, he told her he wanted to dance with her "in the worst way."

But Lincoln was not planning to do the Cooper Union job "in the worst way." He had two important tasks: to become better known among eastern Republicans, and to try to sever his party from radical abolitionists who marched in the shadow of their martyr, John Brown, of Harper's Ferry fame—or infamy.

Draped in ill-fitting clothes, including an unruly collar that bobbled up and down as he spoke, Lincoln went laboriously to work. After having trouble finding one of the pages of his manuscript, he reportedly laid the sheets aside and then really warmed up to his subject. One reporter, borrowing from the poet, declared that Lincoln was "three parts sublime to one grotesque."

The Illinois lawyer emphasized that slavery was an evil and should not be encouraged. However, he stopped where his party had stopped—he would not tamper with slavery where it already existed. Thus he gave the Republican stand on slavery a conservative cast.

Although he came to Cooper Union with the reputation of being an "Aesop of the Prairies," the genial giant refrained from telling tales. In a logical way he put across his points to people who dealt in logic. "Let us have faith that right makes might," he concluded, "and in that faith let us to the end dare to do our duty as we understand it."

Did Abe achieve his goals in Gotham? Here is the *New York Daily Tribune*'s answer:

He was tall, tall—oh, how tall, and so angular and awkward that I had, for an instant, a feeling of pity for so ungainly a man. His clothes were black and ill-fitting, badly wrinkled—as if they had been jammed carelessly into a small trunk. His bushy head, with the stiff black hair thrown back, was balanced on a long and lean stock, and when he raised his hands in an opening gesture I noticed that they were very large.

He began in a very low tone of voice as if he were used to speaking out of doors and was afraid of speaking too loud. He said, "Mr. *Cheerman*" instead of "Mr. Chairman," and employed many other words with an old-fashioned pronunciation. I said to myself: "Old fellow, you won't do. It is all very well for the wild west, but this will never go down in New York."

But pretty soon, he began to get into his subject: he straightened up and made regular and graceful gestures. His face lighted as with an inward fire; the whole man was transfigured. I forgot his clothes, his personal appearance, and his individual peculiarities. Presently, forgetting myself, I was on my feet with the rest, yelling like a wild Indian, cheering this wonderful man. In the close [*sic*] parts of his arguments, you could hear the gentle sizzing of the gas burners. When he reached a climax, the thunders of applause were terrific.

It was a great speech. When I came out of the hall, my face glowing with excitement and my frame all aquiver, a friend, with his eyes aglow, asked me what I thought of Abe Lincoln, the rail-splitter. I said, "He's the greatest man since St. Paul!" And I think so yet.

The *Tribune* also noted that no one since the days of Clay and Webster had spoken to a larger assemblage of "the intellect and mental culture" of New York. It termed Lincoln "one of Nature's orators" who used his "rare power solely and effectively to elucidate and to convince, though their inevitable effect is to delight and electrify as well."

Not all journals waxed so enthusiastic. For one thing, the fact that Lincoln was paid the two-hundred-dollar fee provided political ammunition. The *Illinois State Register* (Springfield) commented sarcastically: "Subject not known, considered two hundred dollars and expenses. Object, Presidential capital. Effect, disappointment."

The "Border Ruffian" organs which had criticized the fee were answered in a *Weekly Illinois State Journal* item. It asked whether "these sapient journals would growl over this dry nut if Mr. Lincoln's speech were vulnerable to their weapons?" Then it answered "Assuredly not." It added that "the aggregate of decency and common sense in the whole crowd of Mr. Lincoln's assailants would fail to endow one respectable old Jackdaw."

Some Republicans farther west were disappointed in the speech, largely unleavened by jokes and anecdotes. But it apparently achieved its purpose in the East and perhaps set the stage for Abe's nomination.

Leaving New York, Lincoln went to New England to visit his eldest son, Robert, a student at Phillips Academy, Exeter, New Hampshire. In fact, the rather impecunious Lincoln had accepted the New York speech engagement partly because it would permit him to visit Bob and see how he was making out. The son had been unsuccessful in his attempt to enter Harvard College. Bob declared later that his failure in the Harvard entrance exams and his going to New England for preparatory work led to the Cooper Union speech and won the Presidency for his father.

At any rate, Lincoln's growing fame after the speech swept ahead of him to New England, where he made eleven speeches in twelve days.

Said the *Exeter* (N. H.) *News-Letter,* the Exeter Town Hall "was well filled with an enthusiastic audience, with a sprinkling of Ladies." Abe's speech at Woonsocket, Rhode Island, was supplemented by stirring campaign songs from the Du Dah Club. There wasn't even standing room in Harris Hall, one of the largest in the state.

Audience participation during the speeches was common. One wag yelled to tall Abe, "Didn't they want you any longer where you came from?" Spectators interrupted Lincoln to grill him or offer their own priceless views. If someone cried "put 'em out!" Lincoln replied, "No! I *want* you to jaw back."

Some New England newspapers were unimpressed. The *Dover Gazette* (N. H.) commented: "Mr. Lincoln, we have seldom seen your equal in adroitness at political jugglery."

Such, apparently, was not the attitude of most listeners. At Dover's city hall, Lincoln paused after speaking an hour and suggested he had talked enough. The audience urged him to go on. He did—for another hour.

As Lincoln concluded his address in New Haven, Connecticut, said the *Palladium,* "there was witnessed the wildest scene of enthusiasm and excitement that has been in New Haven for years." After the speech the people escorted Lincoln to the home where he was staying. There the crowd, eventually about a thousand strong, repeatedly cheered Lincoln.

Many New England journals gave high praise to the Pride of Illinois. The *New Hampshire Independent Democrat* said that his Concord speech was "masterly and massive, sweeping away every refuge of modern Democracy, as smoke is swept away before the wind."

A *Providence* (R. I.) *Journal* item lauded Lincoln on his speech there, saying:

He abounds in good humor and pleasant satire, and often gives a witty thrust that cuts like a Damascus blade. But he does not aim chiefly at fun. He strives rather to show by plain, simple, cogent reasoning, that his positions are impregnable, and he carries his audience with him as he deserves to.

For the first half-hour, said the *Weekly Illinois State Journal* concerning another of Lincoln's New England speeches, his opponents would agree with every word he uttered. From that point "he began to lead them off, little by little, cunningly, till it seemed as if he had got all into his fold."

By the time Lincoln boarded the train for Springfield, his political stock had climbed to a new high.

Lincoln's rise had begun, in a way, four years earlier at the Republican party's first national convention in Philadelphia. In fact, his name was presented for Vice President by John Allison, of Pennsylvania, who called him "the Prince of Good Fellows and an old-time Whig."

Abe's showing was somewhat less than spectacular, although he did come in second. John M. Palmer, who had been president of the Illinois State Convention that year, thanked the Lincoln supporters: "Illinois is devoted to the great cause that has brought us together here and in Abraham Lincoln she knows she has a soldier tried and true."

Lincoln mounted the stump about fifty times in behalf of the Republicans, especially Presidential candidate John C. Fremont, the "Pathfinder." Abe's oratory was even then a target for opponents just as it was, to a more exaggerated degree, years later. The *Cincinnati Enquirer* said of a speech there: "It is not worth reading. . . . Among public addresses from the stump, the speech of Mr. Lincoln belongs to the lowest order. . . . It is the speech of a pettifogging demagogue."

Nevertheless, Lincoln grew in political stature and eventually began to be considered by a few as Presidential timber. The *Sandusky* (O.) *Commercial Register* reported a meeting at Mansfield, Ohio, on November 6, 1858, saying, "An enthusiastic meeting is in progress here tonight in favor of Lincoln for the next Republican candidate for President." This appears to have been the first formal proposal of Lincoln for that exalted office.

The *Olney* (Ill.) *Times,* wanting "delivery from the bondage of a corrupt Administration," reported:

On the 12th of November, 1858, we placed the name of this eminent statesman [Lincoln] at the head of our columns as our choice for the Presidency in 1860, and it is with no little pride and satisfaction that we see the name has been gaining favor not only in Illinois, but throughout the whole nation.

The *Weekly Illinois State Journal* on January 11, 1860, announced an organizational meeting of a Lincoln Club. A letter in the *Journal* declared that "we cannot countenance Seward, because he is a scoundrel and avows it. We cannot countenance Douglas, because he is a scoundrel and denies it."

But more and more people could countenance Honest Abe, the Rail-Splitter of Illinois. Republicans meeting in Elizabethtown, Illinois, in February, 1860, announced Lincoln as their pick for President, describing him as "one of the brightest lights of the age."

Out here in Western Illinois, [said a Monmouth, Illinois, correspondent of the *Cincinnati Gazette*] many of us are of the opinion that our old and well tried steed Abraham Lincoln is as well calculated to pull in the Republican harness in the coming tug of political strength as any other the people have on the list of candidates subject to the decision of the Chicago convention.

An exchange item in the *Weekly Illinois State Journal* said:

My personal preference is for Abraham Lincoln, of Illinois; and my reasons therefore are—that he is, as I am, a Western man; that I think he is the only man, with the exception of Mr. Seward, who has looked the slavery situation in the face, and offered a practical solution of it; that he is a man of nerve; that there is no Lincoln clique, and no man who can say, "I am one of the advisors of Abe Lincoln;" and that he is a man of Southern birth, reared to manhood in the midst of the institution of Slavery.

For a time, Lincoln laughed off suggestions that he be a Presidential candidate. One such proposal came from Jesse W. Fell, Bloomington, Ill. Lincoln replied to Fell, a great-grandfather of Adlai E. Stevenson, Democratic Presidential nominee in 1952 and 1956, that there was "no use of talking of me for President while we have such men as Seward, Chase and others, who are so much better known to the people, and whose names are so intimately associated with the principles of the Republican party." Lincoln told another person, "I do not think I am fit for the Presidency."

But after a while, he admitted "the taste *is* in my mouth a little." He said, though, that "there is no such good luck in store for me as the Presidency of these United States." Nevertheless, he began to trim his political sails.

Lincoln wrote to Samuel Galloway, an Ohio politican: "My name is new in the field, and I suppose I am not the first choice set aside. . . ." It added that if "Honest Old Abe, the Giant Killer," were nominated, the wild enthusiasm his name would excite throughout the West would make it immaterial whom the Democrats might select.

So the stage was set for the great Chicago convention, one of the most colorful and significant in American history. All aboard the bandwagon of Honest Old Abe.

of a very great many. Our policy, then, is to give no offer to others—leave them in a mood to come to us if they shall compelled to give up their first love." He informed a friend Kansas he would send a hundred dollars for the trip to Chicago convention if the Kansan became a delegate.

Politicians, many of whom had practiced law with Linc became salesmen in his behalf in Pennsylvania, Ohio, Ind and other states.

Lincoln sought from Norman B. Judd, chairman of Illinois State Central Committee, a bit of help "in your of the vineyard." Judd, who later became Minister to Pr in Lincoln's administration, gave more than a bit—he h line up the National Republican Convention for Chica vitally strategic move.

The Lincoln boom kept growing. On April 28, in S field, the Republican County Convention resolved:

That our distinguished fellow-citizen, the tall pioneer of mon County, Abraham Lincoln, is our first choice for ca for President of the United States; and that we deem ou honored to be permitted to testify our personal knowl everyday life, as friends and neighbors. . . .

The following week, Abe Lincoln wrote to a political giving him the "lay of the land." "I think the Illinois tion will be unanimous for me at the start, and no oth gation will," Lincoln said. He noted, however, that ot egations apparently had no positive objection to him.

Lincoln's assertion that he probably would get Illir port was a gross understatement. That backing wa dramatically when Abe's and John Hanks' rails wer into the Illinois State Convention in May, 1860. Son nation of that enthusiasm was indicated in an earlier it *Journal:* "The West has never had a President excep short month in which General Harrison occupied tion, and she certainly has claims which it will be d

☆ ☆ ☆

CHAPTER TWO

CHICAGO BUBBLES OVER WITH EXCITEMENT

One week after Abe Lincoln was hailed as the mighty Rail-Splitter at the Illinois State Republican Convention, Chicago was in "a fever of excitement," as it opened its first national political convention. Said the *Daily Chicago Herald:*

In other places the fuss about a convention is usually confined to the place where it is to be held and the tavern to which the delegates resort. Here, however, the mania for politics is universal. . . . The population of Chicago seems a mercurial, restless one, always looking for a new excitement and plunging into it head-long. . . . Even the women and children talked politics along with their candy and crochet.

Chicago, then, was making ready for "The Greatest Show On Earth." Republicans of the Northwest looked to this convention on the shores of Lake Michigan as the "Northwest Passage" to the White House.

The convention's transactions, said *Scribner's* magazine in 1893, "overshadowed in importance, outreached in consequences, and transcended in results those of any assembly of men that was ever gathered on this continent."

Illinoisians who carried the ball for Lincoln were well aware of the convention's importance. At Chicago they would be playing on the home field.

Activity centered in the new Wigwam, a 100' x 180' structure at Lake and Market streets, reported to be the largest auditorium in the nation. This wonder, a large pine structure, would hold about 10,000 persons, nearly half of them standing. On its spacious stage would sit 460 delegates, identified by their state placards, and a group of about sixty newspaper correspondents. A gallery, stretching around three sides, was designated for "gentlemen accompanied by ladies." Because of the grade, the main floor provided a series of broad platforms or landings that accommodated the standees.

Opposition pundits were not exactly enthusiastic about the Wigwam. The *Daily Chicago Herald* remarked:

> It is called a Wigwam, probably because it does not bear the slightest resemblance to the style of dwelling affected by the red men. It . . . looks like a man who has got up in a terrible hurry to take an early train, and in his haste has overlooked some portion of his attire. It is an odd jumble. . . .

The *Albany* (N. Y.) *Atlas and Argus* declared that the building, "like the party for whose use it was erected, is unsubstantial and temporary—hastily put together by voluntary contributions—and full of cracks and flaws." Inhabitants of such Wigwams, the *Washington Constitution* suggested, must belong to the lost tribes.

On the inside, the Wigwam looked far from austere, mainly because of the skill and enthusiasm of Chicago Republican "girls"—a designation that embraced ladies with gray hair and rheumatism. The editor of the *Chicago Daily Journal,* visiting the Wigwam two days before the dedication, found "a bevy of ladies as busy as ants, decorating, sewing, and arranging wreaths and festoons."

Despite being unfranchised, these women were violent partisans. A writer commented that "one can't, I understand, commence the smallest bit of a flirtation without defining his position upon the question of the power of Congress over slavery in the territory."

One delegate at the convention's opening session proposed "three cheers for the ladies of Chicago." The men, restraining their gallantry, compromised with one cheer.

Evergreens and artificial flowers adorned the gallery, and banners and state coats of arms added to the color. The white columns also were decorated with evergreens, while red, white, and blue streamers were festooned between them. Among other decorations were portraits of all the Presidents, and an abundance of American flags.

Huge allegorical paintings decorated the wall behind the stage, which was divided into arched panels. One writer referred to "figures of the Goddesses of Liberty and Justice, and various other females of a rather coarse and bold exterior." Another painting symbolized the party's Cincinnati Platform. A critic in the *Daily Chicago Herald* said of it:

Like the schoolboy's drawing which required the words "a horse" to be written under it to assist the conjectures of the beholder, the caricature above mentioned was, of course, labeled "Cincinnatti Platform." Cincinnati with two *t*'s was a fitting accompaniment to such a brilliant conception.

Another "well wisher," the *Albany* (N.Y.) *Atlas and Argus,* said of one of the wall decorations:

Over the head of Gen. Gospel Nye was placed a little fat figure of Samuel searching the Scriptures. While above a little nest of Congressional and Legislative free-booters, stood a figure of Justice, blindfolded. And blind, indeed she must have been, to have occupied such a position without letting her sword fall on the necks of those beneath.

The *Daily Chicago Herald* mentioned the "emblematical devices, showing, as Brummell said about the Brighton Pavillion, a great deal of taste, and very bad taste at that."

But such poisoned journalistic barbs merely glanced off the impassioned Republicans, whose pride in the wonderful Wigwam was not to be pierced. Nearly 8,000 of them funnelled in for the formal opening on Saturday, May 12, 1860. The *Chicago Daily Journal* had said that day:

> The council fire will be lighted in the hut. . . . Come up and gather round for an old fashioned talk. Come all and put a shoulder to the wheel, for tonight the ball begins to roll and the signal guns of the approaching contest between Freedom and Slavery will be fired.

The inspiring sight, enhanced by the golden glow of gaslights, said another writer, was "a glorious omen of the future —a prophetic sign, large with golden promise of a glorious harvest of truth and right next fall . . ."

Speakers at this "glorification" included Ohio's old antislavery war horse, Joshua R. Giddings; Henry S. Lane, candidate for Governor of Indiana; Governor L. M. Morrill, of Maine; and an Iowa farmer who had walked a hundred and fifty miles to a railroad in order to get to Chicago.

Those who attended shelled out twenty-five cents admission by means of which, said the *Springfield* (Mass.) *Daily Republican*, "the Wigwam was not only paid for, but became henceforth hallowed with Republicanism."

The *Daily Chicago Herald* had heralded this admissions charge with the announcement that the "shining lights of the Republican party are really about to be exhibited with a rhetorical programme, at twenty-five cents per head! What will Barnum think now!" The *Washington Constitution* said that "We shall expect, if a Black Republican President is elected, that he will charge an admission fee to the White House."

Although some visitors already had arrived in the young Western metropolis, thousands more were packing their carpet-bags for the jaunt. The railroads were offering speedy transportation. The *Cleveland Weekly Plain Dealer* announced that the Cleveland and Toledo Railroad would make a special run to Chicago in *"less than 9 hours."*

The Michigan Southern Railroad, said the Chicago *Press and Tribune,* made the run from Buffalo to Chicago with delegates in fifteen hours and fifteen minutes despite a break-down between Toledo and Goshen. One reporter said this train "accomplished a feat in railroad annals that will long stand unsurpassed, if indeed it is safe and desirable" to repeat the performance. He asked, "what would the pioneers of less than a quarter of a century ago have thought of that?"

Rates were attractive. The *Appleton* (Wis.) *Crescent* said that "our numerous Shanghai (Republican) friends who desire to visit Chicago and witness the iniquity of a Republican convention . . . are hereby advised that . . . the Chicago and Northwestern Railroad will carry them at half fare to and from Skunk City."

During the days preceding the opening, delegates in high hats and high hopes poured into Chicago. With them were thousands of visitors in festive spirits. Arrivals of state or regional delegations triggered gala celebrations. Often the young men's political marching clubs, the torch-carrying Wide-Awakes, escorted the packs of visitors to their hotels. Many residents, and visitors who had arrived earlier joined the throngs that moved happily along the streets in the flickering torchlight. Bands blared. Rockets streaked upward into the sky from Michigan Avenue and Jackson Street.

A Pennsylvania delegation of about six hundred arrived during the wee morning hours. The Light Guard Band of Chicago, the "Sons of Pennsylvania," and other bands escorted them to the Briggs House.

The Chicago *Press and Tribune*, reporting the arrival of an Eastern delegation, said a large area "now was thronged with an eager crowd, all expectant. Very many ladies were there. . . ."

A girl who came West to Chicago at convention time described her arrival in *Putnam's Magazine* several decades later. "Terrified, I stared at the crowd pushing and pressing on us; but my uncle called upon our strong man, John C. Heenan, prizefighter and gentleman, to pilot me to the hotel. . . ."

All delegations, the magazine explained, brought along a

fighter to keep the peace. In those hot days, it said, men's opinions often cost them broken heads.

Train after train disgorged its load of visitors, resulting in the sudden doubling of the population of this city of 110,000, according to some enthusiastic Chicago reporters. Everywhere there was the rush and crush of crowds.

Could Chicago accommodate the hordes? newspapers had speculated. Some thought so. The Chicago *Press and Tribune* listed forty-two hotels including fifteen in the dollar-a-day class. At the top were $2.50-a-day hotels, among them the Briggs House, Richmond House, Tremont House, and Hyde Park House.

The newspaper noted that the city had done well in accommodating visitors to the United States Fair the previous season. "Of course on such occasions," it added, "the guests are stowed close, cots are placed wherever cots can stand and single-bedded rooms are the exception instead of any part of the rule."

The *Chicago Daily Journal* declared that when the hotels fail, "then without doubt our citizens will throw open their doors and extend their hospitalities cordially. The latch strings are all out and we can take care of all creation."

Nevertheless, Chicago's potential for accommodations apparently was heavily taxed. One witness who toured a hotel about midnight during the convention said he found a hundred and thirty persons sleeping on pool tables.

These hotels were nerve centers of the political pow-wow. A writer thus described one in the *Daily Chicago Herald:*

The great lobbying center is at the hotel from which I write. Here as many as a thousand people are packed in a hotel which would be full with half the number. . . . Probably as many as 20,000 persons have passed in and out of these doors within the last 24 hours. . . .

The hotel scenes are amusing at first, but tiresome. It is the same talk about the same men over and over again. Half of it is only buncombe, and the names of men are brought out as candidates without the smallest idea of anything more than a hoax for simple delegates or a verdant editor, which latter tribe is as numerous here as the locusts in Utah. If one wishes to see the provincial journalist in his full effulgence, let him go to a National Convention. . . . The more obscure his paper, the more ornate is his behavior, and the more expensive and superb his dignity. . . .

Included in these throngs were a few persons of great prominence, such as Carl Schurz, distinguished leader of the German-American Republicans, a politically significant group in the election of 1860. These "Dutch" delegates discussed having a separate convention at Chicago, but at informal meetings there, they decided to abandon the idea. Instead, the Germans concentrated upon a naturalization plank in the Republican platform.

Other celebrities included Thaddeus Stevens, a leader in the House of Representatives; Gideon Welles, Connecticut Republican leader and a member of the national committee; Joseph Medill and Charles H. Ray, of the *Chicago Tribune;* and Henry Villard, distinguished reporter who served on New York and Chicago newspapers. Tom Hyer, noted prize-fighter, was on hand too. The *Fort Wayne* (Ind.) *Sentinel* asserted that John Brown represented Lincoln at Harper's Ferry and it was fit that Tom Hyer should represent him at Chicago.

Also present was a Mr. Wye representing 100,000 "oppressed and downtrodden" disfranchised residents of the District of Columbia,—whose 800,000 inhabitants, a century later, were still voteless.

Attracting considerable attention in the Wigwam and in the hotels was a Mr. Buskirk, of Indiana, who was six feet eleven inches tall. With slavery a crucial issue, a slave-holding delegate was also an attention-getter. Said the *Daily Chicago Herald,* "We presume that delegate will be very eloquent and pathetic in his denunciation of slaveholders." After the convention, the newspaper declared, the Republicans probably would point to this slaveholder as evidence of their intense devotion to the rights and interests of the Southern states, and the Republican party's high regard for slavery.

Well in the limelight was the famous editor who had "gone West" to Chicago for a few days—Horace Greeley, editor of the *New York Daily Tribune.* A correspondent of the *New Orleans Daily Delta* said, "Horace Greeley and F. P. Blair (the latter universally conceded, I believe, to be the ugliest man in the United States) are both here, looking very knowing."

Most frequent exclamation at the convention, said *Scribner's* later, was "there's old Greeley!" It was not uttered with disrespect, but with "only a rough fondness in the adjective," the magazine added. To one writer, Greeley looked like a well-to-do dairy farmer, direct from his clover fields. He was full of business. And his business was that of vigorously opposing Senator William H. Seward, of New York, the "Mr. Republican" of 1860, and pushing for Edward Bates, Missouri political leader.

"Mr. Greeley has made a great sensation," said the *Springfield* (Mass.) *Daily Republican.* "He is surrounded by a crowd wherever he goes, who besiege him for a speech, and failing in that, seduce him into a conversation, which inevitably becomes a speech 'ere he closes."

On one occasion the great Greeley was the butt of jokesters. A wag pinned a Seward badge to Greeley's coattail. It was some time before the editor realized he was advertising the opposition on his ample behind.

This was good-natured bantering. But the joking from some quarters was less light-hearted. The *Republican Farmer* of Bridgeport, Connecticut, described the Chicago convention as composed of "rain-streaked, speckled, black, grey, and milk-and-molasses colored politicians." It asserted that "a more inharmonious, squabbling, unprincipled body of politicians never assembled." The *Albany Atlas and Argus* wasn't too impressed, either. It termed the convention "the rag, tag and bobtail of all the factions opposed to the Democratic party—a gathering of all the hungry (outs) who, under the name of Republicans, Know-Nothings, Choctaws, People's Party or Opposition, are eager for a taste of the spoils."

The *Daily Chicago Herald* made political hay out of the alleged case of an old and feeble Negro who came to Chicago to solicit money "from the bigger and lesser lights of Negro philanthropy" to purchase freedom for his only son. But, according to the *Herald,* he could collect only thirty-one dollars from "the tens of thousands of *genuine* abolitionists here gathered."

Choice of the title "Republican Party"—not "National Republican Party"—provided political ammunition for some editors. But charges of being a sectional party or of being penny-pinching abolitionists failed to puncture the pride and enthusiasm of these politicians of a century ago. They generated a contagious enthusiasm as they went after big game—the first Presidency for the six-year-old Republican party. They had never experienced a national victory, but as the opening of the convention approached, there was a mounting feeling that the Republicans soon would be eating high on the hog.

CHAPTER THREE

THE CONVENTION KNUCKLES DOWN—BUT NOT MUCH

It was noon on Wednesday, May 16, 1860. When the doors opened on this, one of the most historic meetings in the world's history, there was a terrific jam, as thousands attempted to work their way inside.

Always happy to find something about the Republicans to disapprove, the *Daily Chicago Herald* declared:

On no occasion have we ever witnessed such an utter disregard of every feeling of gallantry. . . . As soon as the doors were thrown open, men made a rush to gain admittance, jamming and crowding in the most reckless manner against ladies, in several instances inflicting severe injuries upon them.

Not all ladies were treated so unchivalrously. Men were admitted to some gallery sections only if they had feminine escorts. Schoolgirls, washerwomen, and novelty saleswomen outside the Wigwam engaged in a shuttle service at twenty-five cents or more a trip, one newspaper charged. But only a minority of the women in the audience were so occupied. Hundreds sat in the gallery, their flower-decorated bonnets and gay shawls and plaids adding color to the already colorful Wigwam.

Reporters and editors made up a sizeable segment of the audience. The *Springfield* (Mass.) *Daily Republican* said there were nine hundred applications for about sixty seats reserved on the stage for leading reporters. There were fifteen hundred applications for eight hundred other reserved editorial seats in the main hall.

For the press this was a great day. It was the seccond national political convention of the fledgling Republican party and perhaps the first in which it would choose a winning Presidential candidate. It was Chicago's first national political convention, held at a time when the Union was skidding into a national crisis. It claimed to be the first national political convention to provide telegraph instruments in the building for the use of reporters.

Crowding in and around the Wigwam were an estimated 25,000 persons when Governor Edwin D. Morgan of New York, chairman of the national committee, rapped the convention to order. David Wilmot, of Pennsylvania, author of the Wilmot Proviso, was chosen temporary chairman. Selected convention president was George Ashmun, of Massachusetts, an important figure among Republicans. *The Washington States and Union* declared that he was "eloquent at Chicago upon the subject of official morality" and asserted that this was "a living exemplification of the devil quoting Scripture."

At the Chicago conclave, Norman B. Judd, Illinois Republican leader, presented to Mr. Ashmun a gavel carved by a Chicago workman. Embellished with silver and ivory, it was made from the mast of Commodore Oliver Hazard Perry's flagship, the "Lawrence," which figured prominently in the Battle of Lake Erie in 1813. Judd expressed the hope that Perry's laconic message to General William Henry Harrison —"we have met the enemy and they are ours"—would become the slogan of the convention nominee.

On the stage was an unusual rustic chair made in Hillsdale County, Michigan. It featured thirty-four varieties of wood, symbolizing the thirty-three full-grown states and one—Kansas—in embryo. Kansas was represented by weeping willow wood. A gavel from this Lincoln convention was used a century later at the 1960 Republican Convention, also in Chicago.

Key figures in the Wigwam were the 465 delegates. They had journeyed to Chicago in response to an official invitation printed in the *Washington National Intelligencer* and other newspapers. It invited "the Republican electors of the several States, the members of the People's Party of Pennsylvania, and the Opposition Party of New Jersey, and all others who are willing to cooperate with them in support of the candidate which shall then be nominated and who are opposed to the policy of the present administration. . . ."

The *Chicago Times* conceded that the delegates were perhaps as "fine a looking body of men as ever assembled in the union." But one would not suspect, it quickly added, that they "entertained the extravagant and dangerous political sentiments that they pretend to believe in."

Represented were all eighteen free states; the slave states of Delaware, Maryland, Virginia, Kentucky, Missouri, and Texas; the territories of Kansas and Nebraska; and the District of Columbia.

Some conferees were paragons of virtue and some were— not. One eyewitness said of certain New York politicians who attended:

> They can drink more whiskey, swear as loud and long, sing as bad songs, and "get up and howl" as ferociously as any crowd of Democrats you ever heard or heard of. They are opposed, as they say, to being "too damned virtuous." . . . At night most of them who are not engaging in caucusing, are doing what ill-tutored youths call "raising hell generally."

A squabble over seating and giving fair representation to delegates from slave states and the territories marked the early part of the convention. The *Albany Atlas and Argus* contended it would have been as appropriate to have Arizona, Pike's Peak, and Nevada represented, but "as the Republicans lack States, they took up Territories." In defense of Republican delegates from slave states and the territories, one speaker declared that other delegations may have *done* more, but *dared* less. Backers of the controversial delegates pointed with pride to men such as H. W. Hawes, a Kentucky delegate who had freed his own slaves and sustained considerable loss in business "through the enmity of the ruling class."

After completing the roll of all states and territories known to be represented, someone suggested that the whole list of states in the Union be called.

Thereupon the residue of the Southern States "being solemnly called, came naught," whereupon the crowd expressed their mirth or disapprobation in proportion as the states were more or less under the ban of Republican opinion. When South Carolina was called, the hissing was very decided.

Some states were represented by proxy. Horace Greeley was announced as "Mr. Greeley, of Oregon or New York, I don't know which." He was actually a delegate for Oregon.

Such long-distance representation among Northern or Western states provided a touch of merriment. But the matter was different with slave states. "We say these states were represented," protested the *Daily Chicago Herald*, "but we should have said they were misrepresented."

A *New Orleans Daily Delta* writer said of the Republicans who represented slave states: "I may remark . . . that these Southern worthies are, by long odds, the most miserable-looking dogs of all the delegates that I have had the honor of beholding."

Texas delegates were the choice targets. A *Daily Chicago Herald* item claimed that not one of the men had been "within a thousand miles of Texas." It asserted that one edited a one-horse "Black Republican" paper at Allegan, Michigan; another ran a beer saloon in Grand Haven, Michigan; and another was a Canadian.

Some Texans didn't think too highly of these delegates,

either. Democrats in Freestone County, Texas, resolved later:

> That justice demands the immediate execution, by hanging, of those miserable deluded miscreants who at the late Chicago convention pretended to represent in that fanatical and unholy body the sentiments of our proud young State.

Nevertheless, a convention committee ruled that these delegates were entitled to represent the Republicans of the Lone Star State.

Another issue that touched off a minor skirmish was an invitation to a boat ride on Lake Michigan, tendered by the Chicago Board of Trade. After accepting it, the convention discovered that the date conflicted with one of its own sessions. "A fierce debate ensued, in which the previous action of the convention in accepting the invitation" was censured, the *Daily Chicago Herald* reported. To complicate matters, hungry Norman B. Judd, of Illinois, was "vociferous upon a question of dinner."

The controversial boat-ride issue was referred to a committee and a more acceptable time decided upon. Many persons took the gay ride in four vessels, lashed together. The Garden City band provided music. In the evening there was a snappy drill in the Wigwam by the famous Chicago Zouave Cadets.

Instead of watching parading cadets, some political powers were at hotel headquarters looking over the prospects for their candidates. In the Tremont House were the headquarters for Lincoln, with David Davis, Illinois circuit judge, at the controls. Here one might also see Judge Stephen T. Logan, an outstanding Illinois attorney; William H. Herndon, not a delegate but, as Lincoln's law partner, one of the group that had Abe's interests in hand; and Jesse W. Fell, another ardent Lincolnite.

Murat Halstead, of the *Cincinnati Commercial,* pictures the scene at the Tremont:

There are now at least a thousand men packed together in the halls of the Tremont House, crushing each others' ribs, tramping each others' toes, and titillating each other with the gossip of the day; and the probability is, not one is possessed of a single political fact not known to the whole, which is of the slightest consequence to any human being.

A correspondent for the *New Orleans Daily Delta* wrote more acridly. "The Tremont House, which is the headquarters of the leading delegations, is thronged with every variety of woollyhead, from the lank Down-easter to the burly Germans of the West, who have suddenly attained a wonderful insight into the horrors of Southern slavery."

Despite differences of opinion on the quality of the politicians at the Tremont, there could only be agreement on the capacity to stow away the grub. During convention week, the Tremont's commissariat revealed, there were consumed 5,220 pounds of beef; 1,620 pounds of hams; 1,229 pounds of chickens; 880 pairs of pigeons; 1,400 pounds of fresh fish; 166 bushels of potatoes; 2,102 dozen eggs; 1,630 gallons of milk; 1,260 pounds of butter; and 1,380 pounds of sugar. The bartender had not reported.

On exhibit at the Tremont House was one of the convention's best conversation pieces—a seven-foot bowie knife. Earlier, in Congress, Roger A. Pryor, of Virginia, had challenged John F. Potter, of Wisconsin, to a duel. Potter ended the matter and amused much of the nation by accepting the challenge and selecting bowie knives as the weapon. The Tremont bowie knife was presented to Potter by Missouri Republicans. On one side was the inscription, "Will always meet a Pryor engagement."

There were other diversions, too. Murat Halstead wrote:

Many of the delegates kept up the excitement nearly all night. At two o'clock this morning, part of the Missouri delegation were singing songs in their parlor. There were still a crowd of fellows caucusing—and the glasses were still clinking in the barrooms—

and far down the street a brass band was making the night musical.

New York's famous Dodworth's Brass Band, Gilmore's Band from New England, and other bands were pouring music into the night. There were parades that included fireworks, illuminated posters, and other festive features. The flag-waving processions frequently passed street-corner rostrums where orators were holding forth for their favorite candidates.

According to the *Republican Farmer* (Bridgeport, Connecticut), some of the Chicago crowd found less political pastimes:

> The mayor of Chicago, Long John, took it into his head to raise something to pay the expenses of entertaining his friends, made a descent upon a number of houses of prostitution and nabbed a number of the delegates, who were taken to the station, a magistrate called up at four o'clock in the morning, who let them go on payment of about $25.00 each.

Reports on the amount of hard liquor imbibed are conflicting. One reporter said he had observed little drinking, perhaps because of the bad repute of Chicago liquor. A politician said the beverage was so strong he could not tell whether it was brandy or a torchlight procession going down his throat. Perhaps Chicagoans were peddling a whiskey which the *Olympia* (Wash.) *Pioneer and Democrat* described as "tangle-leg," a concoction of diluted alcohol, nitric acid, boot-legs (upper parts of boots) and tobacco. The newspaper declared this potent booze would upset a man four hundred yards from the jug.

Regardless of the wallop, apparently, plenty of people were ready to become bottle-scarred veterans. Halstead, *Cincinnati Commercial* reporter, wrote concerning his roommates at the convention:

> They were irrepressible until a late hour. And this morning I was aroused by a vehement debate among them, and rubbing my eyes, discovered that they were sitting up in bed, playing cards to

see who should pay for gin-cocktails all around, the cocktails being an indispensable preliminary to breakfast.

Another *Cincinnati Commercial* report said:

Whiskey flows like water. . . . Some New York fellows on a spree last night, alarmed the moral Republicans. They sung several songs not found in the hymn book, and . . . threw the Western Reserve into prayers and perspiration.

Whiskey was readily available to any Republicans who wanted to wet their whistles. Near the Wigwam a whiskey shop displayed a large sign informing arid passers-by that it was the "Republican Depot."

Many delegates came well-heeled, ready to participate in their favorite pastimes. One Philadelphia delegate lost four hundred-dollar bills when he accidentally yanked them from his watch pocket. Some lost money to pickpockets, who were thicker than flies at a church picnic.

Through all this the leaders were busy at their task—among them the supporters of a man who disapproved of riotous celebration and political chicanery, Honest Abe, the Rail-Splitter of Illinois.

CHAPTER FOUR

OLD ABE IS SHOUTED TO VICTORY

Who would capture the Republican Presidential nomination? A correspondent commented that "the amount of idle talk that is done is amazing. There are a thousand rumors afloat, and things of incalculable moment are communicated to you confidentially, at intervals of five minutes."

Col. John C. Fremont, chosen the party's first Presidential candidate at the Philadelphia convention four years earlier, had already notified the Chicago delegates from his California home that his hat was not in the ring.

Would the nominee be Salmon P. Chase, Ohio Governor and former U. S. Senator, who represented the culture of the West? Or Edward Bates, of Missouri, a skillful attorney and friend of free labor? Or perhaps the shrewd and bold Simon Cameron, U. S. Senator from Pennsylvania? Or even Abe Lincoln, the dark horse from Illinois?

But the early favorite was Sen. William H. Seward, of New York, acknowledged chief in the Republican camp. This former New York Governor symbolized the wealth and culture of the East.

With tongue-in-cheek, the *Daily Chicago Herald* said it just couldn't write off Old Abe, though. "We think those rails which he mauled," said the *Herald*, "are superior stuff to Seward's 'Labor States and Capital States.' It is a matter, however, of indifference to us, which we beat."

Although Seward carried the odds, his having held office for many years meant that he had acquired some close enemies. One was Horace Greeley, who worked tirelessly at Chicago to derail the New York Senator. Greeley denied that his opposition was because Seward had once brushed off America's most famous editor as "the editor of a certain newspaper." But regardless of the reason, he was doing all he could to dismantle the Seward machine.

Backing Seward was Henry J. Raymond, editor of the *New York Times*. Furthermore, there was plenty of cash backing Seward. A correspondent for the *New Orleans Daily Delta* expected Seward's men to gather the required votes since they commanded such a supply "of music, whiskey, and cigars."

The Seward men have been in high feather this second day of the convention. [The *Cincinnati Commercial* reported.] They entertain no particle of doubt of his nomination in the morning. They have a champagne supper in their rooms at the Richmond House tonight, and have bands of music serenading the various delegations at their quarters. Three hundred bottles of champagne are said to have been cracked at the Richmond.

However, the nomination was not yet in the bag for Senator Seward. By the second day the contest had narrowed down to, as Lincoln's partner Herndon later described it, "a neck and neck race between the brilliant statesman of Auburn and the less pretentious, but manly, rail-splitter from the Sangamon bottoms."

The badge-bedecked Seward delegates were far from tears, however, when they marched from the Richmond House into the packed Wigwam on Thursday as a band played "Oh, Isn't He a Darling!"

Outside the Wigwam was another vast horde of humanity. A note was passed inside asking the convention president to send out speakers to entertain 20,000 Republicans and their wives outside the building.

Some persons charged that the Lincoln leaders had packed the Wigwam with their own crowd, having taken advantage of their local connections, to distribute the tickets in such a way as to pack the gallery with Lincoln rooters. It was even charged that Lincoln's backers had printed their own big batch of tickets. Thus, when the Seward paraders arrived at the Wigwam they found it already crammed with supporters of Honest Old Abe. If this was true, it certainly had not been done with Lincoln's blessing.

At any rate, tickets were at a premium. The *Daily Chicago Herald* reported that the convention had to purge itself at one time because "members of the convention had passed tickets to outsiders, through the windows and over the railings."

Political strategists realized the Chicago convention would be controlled to no little degree by a voice "vote." The previous evening Illinois delegates at the Tremont had decided that the West must be heard. They were on their own grounds and there was no reason to lose the battle of lungs. There was a sort of state pride in not being out-yelled.

Then living in Chicago, said a writer in 1885, was—

A man whose voice could drown the roar of Lake Michigan in its wildest fury; nay, it was said that his shout could be heard on a calm day, across the lake; Cook, of Ottawa, knew another man living on the Illinois River, a Dr. Ames, who had never found his equal in his ability to shout and huzza. He was, however, a Democrat.

Shunting aside such a minor barrier, the Illinois political engineers rushed these two cheerleaders to the Tremont House. There they mapped plans for out-shouting the opposition at the Wigwam.

But there was to be business before the tumult and the shouting. Starting at the bottom, the Republicans began nailing down the planks in their platform. They had two major goals: admitting Kansas as a free state, and building a fence around slavery.

There was general agreement on policy. And, anyway, as the *Daily Chicago Herald* said, the prospect of spoils would "act like a charm" in bringing harmony.

Like all such documents, the Chicago platform of 1860 promised all good things to all good people. At the suggestion of Ohio politician Joshua Giddings, it even incorporated a part of the Declaration of Independence, reasserting "that all men are created equal. . . ." Giddings' contribution was first turned down, after an Indiana delegate had argued that, while all Republicans favored the Declaration of Independence, he thought it unnecessary to make it part of the platform. But another speaker warned, "I have to ask this convention whether they are prepared to go upon the record and before the country as voting down the words of the Declaration of Independence?" They heeded that warning and the convention quickly voted in the sanctified phrases.

Since the Republican party had not had a chance to flex its muscles in office, it could hardly "point with pride." However, it was not handicapped in "viewing with alarm." The platform said that "the people justly view with alarm the reckless extravagance which pervades every department of the Federal Government."

The Republican platform contained planks on the defense of the Union, prohibition of slavery in the territories, and condemnation of the Dred Scott decision. It denounced the recent illegal reopening of the African slave trade. It sought to dissociate itself from John Brown supporters by condemning lawless invasions of any state. And, of what it had once termed "those twin relics of barbarism, polygamy and slavery," it ignored the first.

The platform advocated a railway to the Pacific, and river and harbor improvements, a higher tariff, and a homestead act. It called for generous treatment of aliens, aiming at the immigrant vote.

Some anti-Republicans probably were ready to assert that the party had followed the poetic advice of the *Daily Chicago Herald:*

> Resolved, by all these Wigwam braves
> Who now in counsel loudly figure
> This rule alone from death can save—
> Ignore John Brown, *but hug the nigger!*

When the seventeen-plank platform was adopted, the people in the Wigwam tested their vocal prowess. The *Chicago Daily Journal* said:

> In an instant, as if all hearts in the vast hall had been linked by an electric cord, that immense concourse of people, delegates and spectators, numbering in all not less than 15,000 souls, stood to their feet, and cheers upon cheers, deafening, tumultuous, and rapturous, went up from every throat. Men waved their hats, ladies their handkerchiefs, reporters their written pages and all screamed with very [sic] joy. It was . . . a spectacle that was worth a man's lifetime to witness.

By the party's friends the new Republican platform was hailed as a well-built structure. The *Toledo Blade* later reported that many independents saw in the Chicago platform and the "noble character of our candidates the certain and only relief of the nation from demoralization, political and moral. . . ."

Editorial writers of opposing political camps set to work dismantling the Republican platform, plank by plank. The *Daily Chicago Herald* termed it "a mass of glittering generalities . . . [showing] the flesh marks of the struggles between the old Whigs and the old Democrats."

Congressman Lewis D. Campbell, of Ohio, said "spit upon it." To which the *New York Evening Post* retorted that Campbell was a rather "fishy" Congressman "with a dwelling place politically on the confines of three different parties, but always so near the borders that he could escape before he could be served with process" from any of them.

The *New Orleans Daily Delta* pointed to the "wonderful moderation" of the Chicago delegates in declaring themselves opposed to John Brown invasions. This, said the *Delta* writer, was also prudence, for "there is probably more hemp in the Old Dominion!" The writer continued:

The ill-assumed moderation of the platform of the Black Republicans is bosh and nonsense, and can deceive no one, although it is in perfect keeping with the hypocrisy of their leaders, of whom "Tis too much proved, that with devotion's visage and pious action [they] do sugar o'er the Devil himself."

"We have become quite accustomed to Republican tergiversation and falsehood," said the *Olympia* (Wash.) *Pioneer and Democrat*, "but this naturalization resolution is a *coup d'essai* so unexpected and so remarkable for its effrontery that it almost challenges our admiration." It termed the Republican party a merely ephemeral spoils organization whose adherents had nothing in common except a blind hatred of Democrats.

One newspaper mentioned a seven-year-old girl who had memorized the entire "Chicago Platform." The newspaper commented it didn't believe there was a Republican in the whole party who could repeat a quarter of it—and it knew that not one could make the platform consistent with Republican history or objectives.

The *Springfield* (Mass.) *Daily Republican* termed Lincoln "the Republican platform in boots." "A most unprepossessing platform truly," the *Daily Chicago Herald* responded, "and exhibiting more length than breadth."

One cartoon pictured Horace Greeley and a Negro carrying Lincoln on a rail—the Republican platform. "It's the hardest stick I ever straddled," the "Rail Candidate" commented in the cartoon. Another showed Lincoln on top of a woodpile labeled the Chicago Platform. Beneath him, a Negro was sheltered. At the side, Horace Greeley was trying to convince "Young America" that the Republicans had no connection with the abolitionists. The youth countered with "I can see the nigger peeping through the rails."

It was after the convention had adopted this platform, even after the Wigwam had been deserted for the day, that the course of history really began to be traced. For it was in hotel rooms, during the late-evening and early-morning hours, that one of America's greatest Presidents was maneuvered into the candidacy.

There were hundreds of small-time politicians, of course, who believed they were writing the history. The *Daily Chicago Herald* said of them:

> Of all the things in the world, the small politician at a National Convention is the most entertaining. Attired in solemn black, he stalks gloomily along, as if the fate of the Nation rested on his shoulders. He affects the diplomatic, and pretends to be acquainted with sundry terrible schemes which are hatching. When one is aware that two or three quiet, pleasant fellows behind the scenes work matters as they please, and that our ponderous friend is to them clay in the hands of the potter, the effect is comic beyond measure.

Thursday evening, the second day of the convention, a straw vote indicated that Seward was way ahead in the opinion of these small-potato politicians. Had the vote been taken in the convention that day, Seward probably would have won. But behind the scenes in the smoke-filled rooms that night, "two or three pleasant fellows" worked away.

So, the popping of corks and the serenading of bands in the Seward faction was like the Christmas-night revelry of the Hessians at Trenton. Lincoln backers, knowing that time was on their side, were preparing to cross the Delaware. Many Lincoln supporters did not retire at all that historic Thursday night.

What were wealthy Judge David Davis, Lincoln's campaign

manager, and Norman B. Judd, Illinois Republican boss, up
to? They were striving to rally around the Rail-Splitter all who
opposed Senator Seward. More specifically, they were attempting to get united action among delegates from the key states
of Pennsylvania, New Jersey, Indiana, and Illinois.

According to several reports, it was David Davis' promises of cabinet positions that put doubtful states in the Lincoln column.

The strings were pulled and the package tied in nocturnal
caucuses. Shortly before midnight, Horace Greeley popped
his head into a caucus room, asked if anything had been done,
then sent a telegram that turned out to be a classic blunder.
It reported to his *New York Daily Tribune*—and to the nation—that Seward's nomination on Friday seemed inevitable.

Meanwhile, Lincoln had been told of the plan to swap
horses and win support. Some accounts emphasize that he immediately advised his backers to do nothing that would bind
him. Nevertheless, they strode ahead with their political bargaining and set up the nomination for Abe.

While these dozen moguls were molding the destiny of the
convention, lesser lights were making plans to join one of several railway excursions into Wisconsin, Iowa, and other areas
immediately after the convention.

On Friday morning, the last day of the Chicago meeting,
the spirits of Abe's friends were high, for the Lincoln boom
had prospered. If they could only squelch any movement to
nominate Lincoln for Vice-President, success on the higher
level seemed within reach.

Lincoln was much more than "an accessible candidate,"
the beneficiary of shrewd manipulators. The *Chicago Press
and Tribune* enumerated his qualities as a candidate. They
were, in part:

1. By his own motion he is not a candidate. The movement in
his favor is spontaneous.

2. He occupies the happy mean between that alleged radicalism

which binds the old anti-slavery men to Mr. Seward and the conservatism which dictates the support of Judge Bates.

3. He has no new record to make. Originally a Whig, though early a recruit of the great Republican party, he has nothing to explain for the satisfaction of New Jersey, Pennsylvania, or the West.

4. He is a Southern man by birth and education.

5. He is a man of the people. . . . He has that sympathy with the men who toil and vote that will make him strong.

6. Without the stain of Know-Nothingism on his skirts, he is acceptable to the mass of the American party.

7. He is an honest man.

Seward supporters on Friday morning were still confident of victory. To strengthen his cause they marched and counter-marched through the streets, serenaded delegates whose favor they hoped for, set off rockets and waved banners, and supplied large measures of music and noise.

Seward's nomination as a Presidential candidate that day brought an ovation. Then Norman B. Judd, standing near some Lincoln-split logs, said: "Mr. President, I beg leave to offer as a candidate before this convention for President of the United States the name of Abraham Lincoln of Illinois." (A different 26-word version is sometimes quoted.) Another ovation shook the Wigwam. The seconding of Seward's nomination unleashed another thunderous demonstration. Lincoln was seconded as the man "who knows better how to split rails and to maul Democrats than any other man living." Then, said one witness, "a thousand steam whistles, a tribe of Comanches, headed by a choice vanguard from Pandemonium, might have mingled in the scene unnoticed."

Several other candidates were also nominated, and then balloting began.

On the first ballot, Seward plunged ahead, with Lincoln second, followed by Cameron, Chase, and Bates. On the second ballot, Seward and Lincoln were really the only contenders, with Seward only a few votes ahead of the Illinois candidate. On the third ballot, Lincoln leaped into the lead, but lacked a few votes of the necessary number.

Meanwhile, on the Wigwam roof, near the skylight, men waited to relay to the outside throng the results of the voting. While waiting for the finals, a rooftop announcer shouted to the overflow crowd: "Gentlemen, give me your attention! I have received an interesting report from the Chamber of Commerce. You will all be glad to know its contents. Dent corn, 62; flint corn, 66; pop corn, 71; sweet corn, 78; Lincoln, 181, and going up!"

In the Wigwam, a deep stillness had enveloped the crowd at this critical moment during the third ballot. One could hear the scratching of pencils and the ticking of telegraph instruments at the reporters' tables, said witnesses. Then David K. Cartter, chairman of the Ohio delegation, rose and changed four votes from Governor Chase to Lincoln, swinging the nomination to Abe. "There was a silence for a moment and the next instant," wrote Murat Halstead, of the *Cincinnati Commercial*, "there was a noise in the Wigwam like the rush of a great wind in the van of a storm, and in another breath the storm was there. Thousands were cheering with the energy of insanity."

What had brought about this strategic Ohio change? Joseph Medill, of the *Chicago Tribune*, was quoted thus in the *Saturday Evening Post* in 1899:

After the second ballot, I whispered to Cartter of Ohio, "If you can throw the Ohio delegation for Lincoln, Chase can have anything he wants." "H-how d-d'ye know?" stuttered Cartter. "I know, and you know I wouldn't promise if I didn't know," Medill declared.

When the chairman announced that "Abraham Lincoln of Illinois is selected as your candidate for President of the United States," pandemonium tore loose again.

Cannons on the roof boomed and the throng below took up the shout. The *New York Daily Tribune* reported:

The first roar of cannons soon mingled itself with the cheers of the people and the same moment a man appeared in the hall bringing a large painting of Mr. Lincoln. . . . Two cannons sent forth roar after roar in quick succession. Delegates torè up the stakes and boards bearing the names of the several states and waved them aloft over their heads, and the vast multitude before the platform were waving hats and handkerchiefs.

Reporters strained their vocabularies in trying to describe the demonstrations set off by Lincoln's nomination that Friday, May 18, 1860. A report in the *Springfield* (Mass.) *Daily Republican* said:

The audience, like a wild colt with a bit between its teeth, rose above all cry of order, and again and again the irrepressible applause broke forth and resounded far and wide. . . . The Illinois, Indiana and Ohio delegates seemed wild. They acted like madmen. One smashed his hat on another's head, who returned the compliment, which was followed by a mutual embrace. Henry S. Lane, Republican candidate for Governor of Indiana, teetered up and down on a chair, not saying a word, but grinning all over his expressive countenance, while he waved in a huge circumference a tile, damaged somewhat from its frequent contact with the head of a fellow delegate.

One prominent delegate, said another reporter, executed a war dance with another dignified delegate as partner. Black hats "circled over heads like a mass of hornets." Ladies were "throwing up their handkerchiefs." The screaming masses stomped until the Wigwam's planks and pillars quivered. The wild enthusiasm became so raucous, newspaper reports said, that some people covered their ears to prevent pain.

Was all such shouting in the Windy City a waste of wind? Not according to the *Daily Chicago Herald*. It claimed Lincoln owed his nomination in large degree to the outside pressure made possible by holding the convention in Northern Illinois. "It was perfectly amazing to see the effect of 5,000 voices, yelling in mad fury, upon the small band of delegates," said the *Herald*. "They fairly quailed before the stentorian power of the people and the majesty of physical force."

So there may have been method in their madness as the Republicans produced what was, according to the *Chicago Tribune*, applause which had "never been equaled on the American continent nor since the day that the walls of Jericho were blown down." Some delegates may have had especially strong motivation. For, said the *Daily Chicago Herald*, these men seemed to sniff the possibility of being left out in the cold when the future President "made up his jewels." So they stampeded to Lincoln. The *Herald* continued:

> The contagion now became epidemic, and there was a mad struggle to change the anti-Lincoln votes before the ballot should be announced [third ballot]. They deserted the "Irrepressible Conflict" like rats would a sinking ship. They fled from Seward as if the fiery "plague spot" was already visible upon him. No raw militia regiment ever fled in such a panic before the charge of grenadiers. There was one universal spirit of "Tom Walker-take-the-hindermost."

After the tumult subsided, Lincoln's nomination was made unanimous. Caleb B. Smith of Indiana then addressed the convention. He observed that "thirty years ago on the Southern frontier of Indiana might have been seen a humble, ragged boy, barefooted, driving his oxen through the hills." This ragged boy was now the Presidential choice of the Republican party.

To the mourners over the party's great leader, Smith said ". . . It is not that we loved Seward less but because we loved the great Republican cause more."

When the convention reconvened later in the afternoon, it voted on candidates for Vice-President. Sam Houston, of Texas, hero of the Battle of San Jacinto, was among those who garnered some votes. Hannibal Hamlin, of Maine, won on the second ballot. The convention then adjourned, "to meet at the White House on the 4th of March next."

What of the successful Republican candidate on this historic Friday? He had been tossing ball part of that day and had played a bit of billiards to tone down his excitement. The *Springfield* (Mass.) *Daily Republican* thus described his receipt of the glad tidings:

When Cartter of Ohio announced the change of four votes, giving Lincoln a majority, and before the great tumult of applause in the Wigwam had fairly begun, it was telegraphed to Springfield. The telegraphic superintendent immediately wrote on a scrap of paper, "Mr. Lincoln, you are nominated on the third ballot," and gave it to a boy, who ran with it to Mr. Lincoln, who was in the office of the *State Journal*. He took the paper in his hand and looked at it long and silently, not heeding the noisy exultation of all around, and then rising and putting the note in his vest pocket, he quietly remarked, "There's a little woman down at our house who would like to hear this. I'll go down and tell her."

Back in Chicago, when Lincoln's nomination was announced, the enthusiasm spread outward like rings from a stone tossed into a pond. When one little boy, who had heard nothing but "Seward-Seward-Seward" for days, learned that Old Abe had been nominated, he ran off shouting, "Three cheers for Old Abe Seward!" Another lad, when told Lincoln and Hamlin were the teammates, reportedly began yelling, "Hurrah for Lickem and Hangem!"

Opportunists took occasion to do some extra elbow-bending. One lubricated fellow became so overenthusiastic about the nomination, the *Daily Chicago Herald* reported, he "squared the circle" and invited everyone to come in. Only the police accepted.

According to a *Washington Constitution* item, the Chicago telegraph office was busy filling in Lincoln's name on blank messages that had been deposited there before the convention. More than fifty such messages, which required the name and

address of the nominee to be supplied, had been deposited.
An example: "To——: Terrible struggle . . . but fidelity
and devotion have pulled you through. We would not be beat-
en! George Johnson."

It didn't take long for all Chicago to learn the voting results. Factory whistles blew, locomotives tooted, church bells
pealed, and cannons boomed. One hundred guns were fired
from the top of the Tremont House. In the evening, bonfires
blazed and rockets made fiery trails across the sky. Wide-
Awakes, with gleaming torches and glistening caps and capes,
marched through the streets to the music of bands. Many
buildings were illuminated from "turret to foundations." Especially bright was the *Press and Tribune* building. At the
doors and inside the building were Lincoln rails, brilliantly
lighted with tapers. Outside, between the second and third
stories, was a large transparency: "For President, Honest Old
Abe, For Vice-President, Hannibal Hamlin."

The Democratic *Daily Chicago Herald* also hauled out its
guns. Thus it described the response to Lincoln's nomination:

There was a Republican jubilee last night, and a horrible waste
of powder. Bands of music paraded the streets with those liveried
wet-weather fellows called the "Wide-Awakes," tagging at their
heels. Minute, half-minute and quarter-minute guns were fired—
the State supplying the cartridges. An old fashioned Abolition
pow-wow was held at the Wigwam, at which Mr. Giddings of
Ohio and a score of striplings launched forth with flowery rhetoric.
This was interlarded with songs by the inevitable Lumbards. At a
late hour, the fandango broke up and the tired people went home.

Earlier, the *Herald* had described how the Republicans
"went into hysterics" when Lincoln's nomination was announced:

The guns that had been loaded to the muzzle with Seward, Weed
and Co.'s cartridges were brought into requisition, and were made
to belch forth in honor of the winning man. Processions were

formed, headed by a band, and led by an enthusiastic individual who carried a huge stock of cordwood upon his shoulders for about two hours. Various devices were called into use by those imaginative individuals. One fellow had a rake with a hook dangling from it as he bore it aloft. Another had an axe deeply imbedded in a chunk of wood, which he untiringly bore aloft, while a dozen or so rushed into a store and invested eighteen pence apiece in brooms, which they brandished about in a most desperate manner, evidently trying to sweep an imaginary Democratic candidate out of their way. After yelling themselves hoarse and dry, they adjourned to the Randolph Street lager beer cellars and partook of some refreshments, fortifying themselves for what was to follow in the evening.

To thousands of ardent supporters, most of them more sober than the *Herald* would admit, the selection of the humble Pride of the Prairies was a heaven-sent choice. Except for the brief month's administration of William Henry Harrison, the West had not had a President—and they felt they were long overdue. So they whooped it up for Honest Abe and put their shoulders to the bandwagon, to roll it from the Wigwam to the White House.

☆☆☆

CHAPTER FIVE

JUBILANT REPUBLICANS REJOICE OVER THEIR NOMINEE

The news of the Rail-Splitter's nomination set off a prairie fire of enthusiasm across the nation. Murat Halstead, of the *Cincinnati Commercial* reported the scene he witnessed as he returned from the convention city, on the Fort Wayne and Chicago railroad:

At every station where there was a village until after 2 o'clock, there were tar-barrels burning, drums beating, boys carrying rails, and guns, great and small, banging away. The weary passengers were allowed no rest, but were plagued by the thundering jar of cannon, the clamor of guns, the glare of bonfires, and the whooping of boys, who were delighted with the idea of a candidate for the presidency who thirty years ago split rails on the Sangamon River—classic stream now and forever—and whose neighbors named him "Honest."

Along other railroads, cars of returning delegates and convention visitors received rapturous greetings all along the way. In Winnebago, Illinois, a woman standing near the tracks, finding she had no handkerchief to wave, dexterously hoisted the rear of her skirt, slipped off a petticoat, and waved it in circles above her head.

In Albany, New York, the "wildest excitement" prevailed, said the *Worcester* (Mass.) *Palladium.* "State Street is a perfect sea of fire from burning tar-barrels. The whole heavens are illuminated with a red glare, while cannon is firing, music is playing, and the people are shouting on State Street and Broadway."

Keene, New Hampshire, enjoyed a plentiful and much-needed rain immediately following the announcement of the nomination. The grateful townsmen fired a hundred guns for Lincoln and Hamlin.

At Dayton, Ohio, a large circular rail fence was erected at the junction of Main and Third Streets, enclosing a huge bonfire. High Street in Columbus was a blaze of bonfires, and bands poured out patriotic airs. The ratification celebration, said the *New Hampshire Statesman* (Concord), excelled any other ever given a candidate in Ohio's capital. At Troy, Ohio, according to that city's *Times,* the gray heads cut "pigeon wings" in the streets. "There were whoops and hurrahs—hats whizzing up, and hats banged down—congratulations and cavortings," the *Times* said.

But it was in Abe's home town that the celebration reached its height that Friday, May 18. Firing of cannon continued through most of the afternoon and evening, and bells pealed in the evening, fireworks were shot off and bonfires blazed. Springfield's public buildings, stores, and many private homes were brightly illuminated.

Jubilant Illinois Republicans roamed the main streets. Only a few Democrats were seen and these, reported the *Weekly Illinois State Journal,* "wore countenances of unusual length."

Enthusiasm rose even higher Saturday night. About 7:30, a large delegation of citizens at the railroad station greeted the official committee which had come to notify Lincoln that he was the pick of the lot. George Ashmun, Convention president; Norman B. Judd, Illinois Republican boss; Henry J. Raymond, editor of the *New York Times;* Francis P. Blair, of Maryland, who had been a member of Jackson's "Kitchen Cabinet"; Edwin D. Morgan, Governor of New York; and

David K. Cartter, the Ohioan who had clinched the nomination for Abe, were in the group.

Led by the Young America Silver Band and the German Saxhorn Band, and surrounded by a throng, the committee was escorted to the Chenery House. To the boom of cannons and the light of bonfires and rockets the triumphal march began.

Having performed this high-level delivery service, the crowd marched to the Hall of the Illinois House of Representatives, many men carrying their hats atop old rails. They stacked their rails on the speaker's stand and took their places for a rip-roaring ratification meeting.

The official committee, meanwhile, after a sumptuous supper at the Chenery House, headed toward Lincoln's home. They took streets, said one item, that would allow them to escape the crowd. The men found that Abe's home was, according to the *New York Daily Tribune,* "an elegant two-story dwelling, fronting west, of pleasing exterior, with a neat and roomy appearance, situated in the quiet part of the town, surrounded with shrubbery."

As they entered the gate, wrote a correspondent of the *Chicago Daily Journal,* two handsome lads of seven and nine met them. "Are you Mr. Lincoln's son?" William M. Evarts, New York attorney, asked Willie, the older one. "Yes, sir," said the boy. "Then let's shake hands." The committee began greeting the boy so warmly that the younger boy, Tad, who had stood silently by the opposite gate-post, sang out, "I'm a Lincoln, too!" Then several delegates, amid considerable laughter, greeted the younger Lincoln.

Receiving the delegation in the parlor Lincoln, following his custom, asked the height of the tallest member, Judge Kelly, of Pennsylvania. Kelly, six-feet-three, was an inch shorter than Lincoln. "Then," said Judge Kelly, "Pennsylvania bows to Illinois. My dear man, for years my heart has been aching for a President that I could look up to, and I've found him at last in the land where we thought there were none but *Little* Giants."

Several delegates introduced themselves to Abe, then Ashmun urged others to step forward. Judd added, "Come up, gentlemen, it's nobody but old Abe Lincoln."

Cartter recited a tribute to "Glorious Old Abe, the Rail-Splitter and Douglas mauler." The refreshment Lincoln served his distinguished guests, the *New York Daily Tribune* reported, was "plentiful draughts of delicious and pure ice water." Earlier, Lincoln had courteously refused liquors offered him for the occasion by his neighbors, choosing to serve "the only beverage I have ever used or allowed in my family."

A *Chicago Daily Journal* writer turned some attention to Mary Todd Lincoln, declaring "she adorns a drawing room, presides over a table, does the honors on an occasion like the present or will do the honors at the White House with appropriate grace." She appeared petite, he noted, while standing by her almost gigantic husband, although she really was about the average height of ladies.

Having notified Lincoln of what he already knew—that he was the Republican standard bearer of 1860—the committee returned to the hotel, shook a host of Springfield hands; then, about midnight, headed out of the city on their special train.

A *Jacksonian* (Rushville, Indiana) item reported this official notification quite differently:

The Official Committee arrived in Springfield in dewy evening and went to honest Old Abe's house. Mrs. Honest Old Abe said Honest Old Abe was out in the woods splitting rails. So the Official Committee went to the Woods, where sure enough they found Honest Old Abe splitting rails with his two boys. It was a grand, a magnificent spectacle. There stood Honest Old Abe in his shirt sleeves, a pair of leather home-made suspenders holding up a pair of home-made pantaloons, the seat of which was neatly patched with substantial cloth of a different color. "Mr. Lincoln, Sir, you've been nominated. Sir, for the Highest office, Sir—" "Oh don't bother me," said Honest Old Abe, "I took a stent this mornin' to split three million rails afore night and I don't want to be pestered with no stuff about no conventions till I get my stent done. I've only got two hundred thousand rails to split before sundown. I kin do it if you'll let me alone."

Later, he accepted, the article explained, then cracked a few jokes.

And as an evidence that he is a statesman as well as a wag, it may be stated that during the evening he profoundly observed that "governments were governed too much," and that "an honest man was the noble work of God."

While the committee carried out its official mission—either at Lincoln's house or out in the woods—the ratification meeting at the State House roared on. At the close, the throng trooped to Lincoln's home. There, with burning tar-barrels in the street providing illumination, the Home Town Boy addressed them briefly. He explained that he would invite the entire crowd into the house if it would hold them. (Someone yelled, "We will give you a larger house on the fourth of March.") Lincoln added he would, however, welcome as many as could find room.

Deafening cheers greeted the invitation [reported the *Weekly Illinois State Journal*] and in less than a minute Mr. Lincoln's house was invaded by as many as could "squeeze in!" The invaders were warmly received and many of them had the pleasure of shaking the right hand of their hospitable host.

The Republican men were so well pleased with the day's work, said the *Journal,* that they could not make up their minds to go home until after midnight.

Not all newspaper editors were so favorably impressed by the celebrations which highlighted Honest Old Abe's triumphal entry into higher politics. The *Daily Chicago Herald* reported that in Buffalo there were "extravagant demonstrations of joy, the like of which has not been seen since the Atlantic

Cable affair." The comparison, said the article, was "not very happy as a prognostic" since the cable turned out to be "one of the greatest failures of the age."

The *Fort Wayne Sentinel* described a torchlight procession and "frothy speeches and other noisy demonstrations" as Fort Wayne Republicans greeted returning Chicago delegates to "congratulate them on their success in nominating a man they did not want."

The *Republican Farmer* (Bridgeport, Connecticut) quoted the *New York Times* as comparing the Republican celebration in Manhattan with "blowing through horrible tubes the most dissonant and far-resounding notes . . ." by "the Fejee Islanders whenever they had secured a particularly fat family of foreigners for one of their national feasts."

While the jubilation continued in many cities, Abe Lincoln was busy drafting an important letter. He had asked the convention committee for a bit of time to respond to their official notice that he was the Republican Presidential candidate. He told them he was "deeply and even painfully sensible of the great responsibility which is inseparable from this high honor —a responsibility which I could almost wish had fallen upon some one of the far more eminent men and experienced statesmen."

After Lincoln finished a brief letter of acceptance, he asked Newton Bateman, his close friend and state superintendent of public instruction, for suggestions. The Illinois schoolmaster merely pointed out that the Rail-Splitter had split an infinitive.

Lincoln's letter, dated May 23, was sent to Hon. George Ashmun, President of the Republican National Convention. It began, "Sir: I accept the nomination tendered me . . ." and wound up with "Your obliged friend and fellow-citizen, A. Lincoln."

A *Buffalo Courier* item claimed the letter was remarkable for what it did *not* contain. The note really said, asserted the

Courier, "My friends, I'll take the Presidency if I can get it—meanwhile, keep shady." The *New Hampshire Patriot* charged that "as one hundred dollars is his lowest price for a political speech, it is probable that he will not take less than that for the letter. He contrives to make politics pay."

As the tar-barrels burned and Abe concluded the formalities of the nomination, newspapers responded to the surprising choice at Chicago in words that blessed or blistered.

Lincoln, still to become the legendary figure of history, was then comparatively unknown. He had long been out of political circulation; he had not even been in the nation's capital for eleven years.

But the fact that backwoodsman Abe Lincoln "was one of them" carried more weight with many voters, a century ago, than if he had been a polished statesman. To many, his nomination was a triumph of the people over politicians. The *Bucyrus* (Ohio) *Weekly Journal* said, "He has summered and wintered with them, slept on their couches, shared their toils and come up through the paths of honest labor to an honorable position and fame." This was the man who, a quarter century earlier, had *walked* a hundred miles from the State Legislature at Vandalia and still could take a joke about how cold he became because "so much of him is on the ground."

Yes, Lincoln was a plain man. The *Washington Constitution* quipped: "Montcalm commanded the Citadel at Quebec, and, like Seward, fell on the *plains* of Abraham."

There was enough romantic interest connected with Lincoln's early life to set up a half a dozen candidates in business, the *Springfield* (Mass.) *Daily Republican* commented. This, combined with evangelistic anti-slavery ardor, was first-rate political equipment for the Republicans.

Said the *Newark Daily Advertiser:* "A nobler speciman of the honorable, clear-headed and excellent in humanity is nowhere to be found." Lincoln left Congress, declared the Washington correspondent of the *New York Tribune,* with the reputation of an able, genial, and worthy man of unquestioned integrity and great popularity.

Lincoln was a guileless, incorruptible patriot, an honest, fearless champion of liberty, said the *Weekly Illinois State Journal,* which then continued with a ninety-one word sentence extolling his virtues.

The *Newark Daily Advertiser* thought his name should no longer be spelled "Abram" [properly, it wasn't], but have another syllable "like that of the great founder of the Hebrew nationality." A Kansas delegate to the Chicago conclave declared, "We simply put our trust in God, and He who makes no mistakes gave us Abraham Lincoln."

In headlines and articles, Republican papers shouted for joy. "Hurrah for Old Abe!" cheered the *Alton* (Ill.) *Courier.* "Let the Welkin Ring . . . Down with the Party which Has Its Foot on the Neck of Man . . ." And, declared the *Kansas State Record* (Topeka, Kansas Territory), "We hail the return to the age of purity."

Republican journals saw the future through rose-tinted spectacles. The *New York Tribune* prophesied that Lincoln would make a clean sweep of the Northwest. And the *New-Hampshire Statesman* predicted that "Honest Old Abe" is the man "destined to warm the cushion of the Presidential chair the coming four years."

While some Republicans were applauding Lincoln, those who had backed Seward had to look far for consolation.

"In St. Paul, where Seward has hosts of friends, curses both loud and deep were hurled at the Convention, for cowardly rejecting the great apostle of Republicanism, for a man whose political record consists in his defeat by Douglas for U. S. Senator," declared the embittered *St. Paul Pioneer.*

Many persons agreed with an Illinois Republican who concurred in "the higher claims of William H. Seward . . . as the acknowledged leader of our party from the days of its infancy."

Some newspapers reacted with real acrimony. A *Jonesboro* (Ill.) *Gazette* item commented:

Alas! Poor Seward! The pride and glory of the Republican party —the master-spirit, by which this piebald association of odd ends and worn-out elements of old political organizations was spoken into existence—is immolated to make place for Abram Lincoln, of Illinois. . . .

Seward's fall inconvenienced his supporters in more ways than one. At Chicago, for instance, delegates reportedly had an eight-hundred-dollar banner bearing his likeness ready to unfurl following his nomination. It remained furled.

The *New York Tribune* of May 16, 1860, carried this premature ad of a Boston publishing firm:

THE NEXT PRESIDENT OF THE UNITED STATES
Now Ready:
"The Life of William H. Seward,"
by a Jeffersonian Republican.
30c
Agents wanted to sell this work throughout the country.

Some Seward sufferers, having licked their wounds, looked for the silver lining. Gen. James W. Nye, of New York, an ardent campaigner for Seward, said "I suppose the blow was struck in love. I will try to find honey on the end of the rod." He was going back home, he said, on a night train—he didn't dare return in daylight. Plucking a few sour grapes, the *Washington National Intelligencer* pointed out that "In our country the highest civic honors are not always awarded to the most eminent competitor."

Despite the varied responses, there were no two ways about it. The Seward men were, as the *Cleveland Weekly Plain Dealer* put it, like Jonah—down in the mouth. A *Jonesboro* (Ill.) *Gazette* item said the Seward supporters accepted Lincoln's nomination like a convicted criminal accepts his sentence—as something that cannot be helped.

The *Council Bluffs* (Iowa) *Bugle* quoted an exchange paper's assertion that Lincoln's nomination was the meanest specimen of "availability" ever attempted.

In Lockport, New York, the American flag was hoisted upside down as a signal of distress when Seward's defeat was learned, reported the *Rochester Union and Advertiser*. Some newspapers noted that Lincoln was nominated on Friday, "Hangman's Day." The *Cleveland Weekly Plain Dealer* printed a cartoon showing Lincoln about to strike a bull (Seward) with a maul in the "Wigwam slaughter house."

The Seward-loving *Auburn* (N. Y.) *Advertiser* merely announced Lincoln's nomination, explaining sorrowfully that "we have no time nor heart for comment." The *Albany Atlas and Argus* borrowed this description from an exchange:

Silently and sadly the Doctor delivered the message [of Seward's fall]. His woe-begone face told that the "Defender of the Rights of Man" was sacrificed on the altar of expediency—Sacrificed for Abraham Lincoln, a barroom politician . . . then was each Republican heart filled with woe, and with horror did each Republican "hair stand on end like quills upon the fretful porcupine."

The house of joy was turned to the house of mourning. Meanwhile the cannoneers were waiting impatiently for the signal. The Doctor approached them—his face as long as one of the rails that "Honest Abe Lincoln" used to split—and ordered the cannon back to the armory. He "would not fire for a democratic victory" and was so little a soldier that he could not see the utility of firing at a funeral.

The "black funeral smoke" from a few tar-barrels in Albany and the firing of a few guns, declared the *Argus*, were entirely in keeping with "the funeral."

At least a few persons, said one newspaper, felt about the nomination like the man who came to a fork in the road, and asked a farmer which branch he advised him to take. "It don't matter much which," the man replied. "Take either and you'll wish you'd taken t'other before you're half over it."

But most Republicans who grieved over the Seward loss were soon drying their tears and getting ready to do battle for Honest Abe. They knew that Seward was bypassed for good reasons—because of his rather extreme views on certain questions and his accumulation of enemies during his long public service. They knew that Republicans had rallied to Lincoln not because they loved Seward less but a Republican victory more. They looked for the honey on the end of the rod.

So the weeping and wailing of Seward men soon ended and they buckled on their armor and rode forth to battle for Honest Abe. But the responses of anti-Republican journals immediately following the Chicago meeting were only warm-ups for a six-month assault.

The *Washington Constitution* declared that the nomination of Lincoln and Hamlin was immediately followed by a severe frost in Maine. The situation must have been even more critical in Massachusetts if we are to believe a *Boston Courier* item reprinted in the *Constitution:*

Friday, May 18, will long, long be remembered by the men of Massachusetts as the day on which the Republican party was executed. . . . Had the Capitol on Beacon Hill, from some hidden cause, sunk into the crust of the earth—had the Court House turned around—had the City Hall and the old State House moved arm-in-arm on a visit of ceremony to the Custom House—all these unnatural things combined could not have produced so profound a sensation as did the unlooked-for announcement that Abe Lincoln, of Illinois, had received the nomination of the Republican convention at Chicago. Such was the intense sadness of the Republicans—so real was their depression and woe that Democrats could not find it in their hearts to make light of their affliction.

The laboring mountains have truly produced a most ridiculous mouse!

In Concord, said the *New Hampshire Patriot,* the "Black Republicans" fired one hundred guns but the reports were very feeble, "the calibre of the gun used corresponding to that of the candidates."

A large sketch of a rat was used by the *Cleveland Weekly Plain Dealer* to illustrate an article about a "Great Republican

RAT-ification meeting!" Another article was headlined "Lincoln and Circumcision." It reported a speech in which the speaker quoted, "Neither shall the name be called Abram, but Abraham; for a father of many nations have I made thee. For I will make thee exceedingly fruitful . . ." The paper asserted that Lincoln's responsibility, then, was having children, not rulership.

The Republicans descended to low water for a candidate, charged an *Albany Atlas and Argus* item. There, the paper asserted, the party will stick in the mud and be engulfed in the advancing tide. The *Washington Constitution* termed the nomination "A disgraceful burlesque." A *Daily Chicago Herald* article called Abe a third-rate lawyer without tact, talent, or ordinary discernment, and concluded that "the day of humbugs has not gone by."

A touch of Shakespearean ridicule was used by the *Constitution*: "Hamlet—'What news from Chicago, Horatio?' Horatio—'None, but the black republicans have nominated an "honest" candidate.' " A *New York Herald* item pointed to "Profitless incubation at Chicago." Another *Herald* item declared:

The conduct of the Republican party in this nomination is a remarkable indication of small intellect, growing smaller. They pass over Seward, Chase, and Banks, who are statesmen and able men, and they take up a fourth-rate lecturer who cannot speak good grammar, and who, to raise the wind, delivers his hackneyed, illiterate compositions at $200 apiece. Our readers will recollect that this peripatetic politician visited New York two or three months ago on his financial tour, when in return for the most unmitigated trash, interlarded with coarse and clumsy jokes, he filled his empty pockets with dollars coined out of Republican fanaticism. If, after he becomes President of the United States, the public finances should fail, he can set out upon a lecturing mission, through the country, taking Horace Greeley along with him. He may thus replenish a collapsed Treasury.

Lincoln's nomination smothered Republican zeal like putting green wood on the remaining embers in the kitchen stove on a wintry morning, said the *Prairie du Chien* (Wis.) *Courier*. An Ohio Congressman, in a speech reported in the *Daily Chicago Herald,* declared the Chicago convention bypassed able statesmen and "have gone West, and found a fellow lying on a rail, like a coon with his belly full of grapes, and they have taken him up and nominated him for the Presidency."

One newspaper said Lincoln looked like a baboon; another termed him a "third-rate slang-whanging lawyer;" still another characterized him as a narrow-minded demagogue of the disunion stamp." The *Floridian and Journal* (Tallahassee) suggested, "A. Lincoln appears to be a man after Joshua R. Giddings' own heart—vile and brutal abolitionist as he is." Hamlin, the Vice-Presidential candidate, was given a left-handed compliment by the *New London* (Conn.) *Daily Star*. "Weak as the ticket is, it is a kangaroo ticket," said the *Star*. "The strength is all in the hind legs." However, a *Washington Constitution* item declared that New England delegates were seeking to punish both Hamlin and Lincoln when they tacked on this "additional element of weakness" to the Lincoln ticket and "let the head go with the tail."

Lincoln's relative obscurity was hit at by the *Rochester* (N.Y.) *Union and Advertiser* which declared that selecting him was "going it blind," or buying "a pig in a poke." A *Washington Constitution* item described an alleged incident in Buffalo when a prominent New York state official of German background stopped Judge Stevens on the street just after the Chicago nominations to ask why all the excitement:

"Shudge Stefens," said the ponderous official, "vat ish all dis excitement apot?" "Why," replied the Judge, "the Chicago nominations, to be sure. Have you not heard that Abraham Lincoln has been nominated for President?" "No!" exclaimed the Honorable Dutchman. "Ish dat so? Coot! Very coot inteed! Who vash it you say?" "Old Abraham Lincoln." "Lincoln—Lincoln—" repeated Mr. ——, "Vell, now dat ish a shtrong nomination! Shudge Stefens, how you spell dat name?" "L-i-n, lin, c-o-l-n, coln," explained the Judge. "Ah, yes! dat ish recht 'L-i-n, lin, c-o-l-n—lincoln! Vell, now dat ish a very coot ticket. Dat vill run well! Now dat can be elected sure!" —and our German friend started to continue on his way down the street; but suddenly recollecting himself, he turned back "Shudge Stefens, vare dosh dat man live?"

Recalling that Lincoln was defeated by Douglas for the U.S. Senate, a *Detroit Free Press* item, reprinted in the *New York Tribune,* asserted that Lincoln's only claim to fame was as the man who was beaten, and "his reputation will not desert him this year." The *New Orleans Daily Delta* claimed that Lincoln was a sectional candidate "with the odor of defeat already about him." And the *Jonesboro* (Ill.) *Gazette* quoted Lincoln as saying "nobody has ever expected me to be president" and added that six months later he could conclude "nobody has been disappointed."

Lincoln's stand on the slavery issue was pounced on by many journals. A *Daily Chicago Herald* item termed Abe the representative of "the deadliest and most determined sectionalism." It called on voters to "tear off the flimsy disguise, and strike the devilish aggressor to the earth." According to a Pennsylvania newspaper, Lincoln was "personally one of the bitterest Abolitionists in the country."

How did members of the Fourth Estate on the other side of the political fence view the response of Republican newspapers? Said the *Louisville* (Kentucky) *Journal:*

We hardly know from the sounds emitted by the Republican organs whether they are happy or miserable over Lincoln's nomination and Seward's defeat. They are like the boy who got his mouth puckered by a green persimmon and couldn't make his companions understand whether he was crying or whistling. "If you are crying," said one of them, "you do it tolerable well; if you are whistling, it is a decided failure."

The Chicago nominations fell like a lump of lead upon the "Black Republicans," declared a *Trenton True American* item reprinted in the *New York Tribune*. It charged that "Mr. Hamlin is as black as Mr. Lincoln, and they are both as black as—need be." The *Daily Chicago Herald* declared the convention attempted to put the "1840 touch on the whole affair, substituting fence rails for log cabins and hard cider, and 'Honest Old Abe' for 'Tippecanoe and Tyler Too.' But it was a sad failure."

What effect did Lincoln's nomination have upon Democratic ardor? According to a *Herald* article, the news was received with tremendous joy. The *Jonesboro* (Ill.) *Gazette* declared that "over this light team any good, conservative Democrat who might receive the nomination could achieve an easy victory." Election of a Democrat could now be "regarded as certain," the optimistic *Washington States and Union* remarked.

☆☆☆

CHAPTER SIX

FOUR CANDIDATES, ONE ISSUE, AND NO HOLDS BARRED

Even before Lincoln's name had been hoisted aloft at Chicago, the Democrats were struggling to select a standard bearer. In late April they had packed their valises and journeyed to Charleston, South Carolina, for their great conclave.

The Squatter Sovereigns, under Stephen A. Douglas, had boasted they would descend on Charleston a thousand strong, said the *Weekly Illinois State Journal*. They would turn the convention into a political beer garden and achieve the Little Giant's nomination by outside pressure, it was argued. According to advance rumors, though, the Charleston hotel-keepers—perhaps at the instigation of the "Fire-Eaters" of the deep South—were prepared to curb this threatened invasion of the carpetbag faction of Democrats. While official delegates were to enjoy Southern hospitality at reasonable rates, the tariff for room and grub reportedly would be jacked up sky-high for the myriad hangers-on.

The convention opened in normal convention style. Some irrepressible persons persisted in popping up every few minutes, apparently just to show their faces. This prompted the suggestion that daguerrotypes be taken of them and passed around, thereby making this annoyance unnecessary.

Much less annoying was the plentiful presence of gaily-dressed ladies, God bless 'em! Many were standing in the stairway of the hall entrance at convention opening, prompting chivalrous Mr. Cochrane of New York to announce: "The delegates upon this side of the house wish to inform the ladies that there is ample room here for those who cannot get seats elsewhere." The correspondent for the *New Orleans Daily Delta* explained (not complained) later:

> The ladies who at first confined themselves to the galleries, have now taken formal possession of about one-quarter of the floor. They have even encroached upon the space alloted to the press, and I am now writing amid a bevy of distractingly charming South Carolina beauties.

The men enjoyed these fancy dishes at the convention. About as attractive for some was the abundance of tasty drinks nearby. Said a *Weekly Illinois State Journal* item:

> Huge bowls of claret punch, brandy punch and other luxurious concoctions of the balmy south are loading down the counters. About ten expert blacks assist the white bar princes in turning out cocktails, sherry cobblers, mint juleps, smashes, and all sorts of those things. The weather is hot; the people are thirsty . . . There are drinkers from the frozen North, drinkers from the crafty East, drinkers from the luxuriant West, drinkers from the fiery South—drinkers from everywhere. The conversation is heated although the drinks are cooling. . . .
> And so it is for hours and hours. They talk and talk—jabber and jabber—bet and bet—and drink and drink!

Tippling was also featured when "the faternity of the quill" got together during the convention. "A great many funny things were said"—all off the record, of course. Among those attending was an unfortunate luminary who craved sympathy, he having sunk, a reporter explained, from the editorial chair to the humble position of a Member of Congress.

More characteristic of the Charleston conclave than such fun fests were confusion, bitterness, and even violence. However, the press, sometimes, even tried to laugh this off. The *New Orleans Daily Delta* carried an article purporting to be telegrams received from Charleston by "Bullyrag Telegraph Line":

Mr. Douglas telegraphed his friends to go so far and no farther.

Mr. Douglas's friends telegraphed back that they can't go any farther because their board bill isn't paid.

The majority of the Southern delegates at the Mills House refused rice pudding for dinner, and it is now said that the South Carolina delegation, incensed thereat, have threatened to bolt for Douglas.

Mr. Yancey has knocked Mr. Pugh down and is sitting on him.

It is now said Mr. Pugh is sitting on Mr. Yancey and thereby interfering with his digestion.

The delegations from Indiana and Illinois have just marched in armed with Minie rifles and taken possession of a corner.

The delegations from Mississippi, Alabama, Louisiana and Texas have just rushed in armed with Howitzers, and fortified themselves in the Southern corner.

At this moment a window blew open and the wind carried Mr. Barksdale's wig into the middle of the Hall. He rushed to secure it, when a dozen Minie rifles were discharged at him by the Illinois sharpshooters. Mr. Barksdale exclaimed "Gentlemen, you certainly won't shoot me with my wig off." By this incident, good humor was restored.

But such lightheartedness only occasionally shone through the oppressive pall of deadly seriousness. The *Washington Constitution* noted that both the Northern and the Southern factions of the Democracy, as the party sometimes was called, realized that a decisive struggle was at hand. The Democrats had been divided to some extent ever since Douglas, with Lincoln nipping at his heels during the Lincoln-Douglas debates, refused to ditch Popular Sovereignty and become a straightaway slavery man. To a significant extent it also reached back to Douglas' opposition to the pro-slavery Lecompton Constitution in Kansas, which President Buchanan supported adamantly.

Building a platform was one of the big orders of the day. Platforms at Charleston were as plentiful as blackberries. Everyone thought he had discovered the magic formula to reconcile the Southern Rights men and the Squatter Sovereigns. The final platform tended to be fashioned more along Northern Democratic lines, although some claimed that Douglas almost choked, trying to swallow it.

Perhaps it was dislike of Douglas even more than the platform that was the trouble, suggested the *Washington States and Union.* At any rate, the chances for compromise between the Northern Douglasites and the Southern Fire-Eaters did not appear promising. Missourians pleaded for mediation, but when William L. Yancey, of Alabama, rose to reply, "a wild storm of applause for five minutes rang through the hall." This pro-slavery fanatic argued that the only rock of safety which they could now stand upon was that "slavery was right and therefore ought to be."

In a similar vein, a convention leader asserted: "We must strangle this serpent, Squatter Sovereignty. . . . The Northern Democrats have gone in pursuit of a false God that the South cannot worship and we must endeavor to bring them back to the true faith." One Southern Senator charged that Douglas Democrats were talking "Black Republicanism" at Charleston where avowed Republicans were not allowed.

Northern Republicans didn't see much "Black Republicanism" in Stephen Douglas or any other Democrats. Republican Horace Greeley wrote of a Southern slave, tired of working for hog and hominy, who decided to stow away on a ship leaving Charleston. The ship happened to be carrying New England Democrats returning from the Charleston conclave. Greeley said he had heard of jumping "out of the frying pan into the fire," but to attempt to escape from slavery by hiding among Democrats "goes ahead of any absurdity within our knowledge."

But to the deep South, Douglasites were radicals. Tension between the two convention groups kept piling up, partly over the sharp division on the platform and partly over the proposed choice of Douglas as chief. Then something snapped. An historic point in the historic campaign of 1860 had been reached. The Alabama delegation strode out of the hall and was followed by the delegations from most of the slave states. The convention was thrown into a disorder that "beggars all description," said the *New Orleans Daily Delta.* Three of the South Carolina delegates temporarily stuck with the convention, and violent hostility was manifested against them in the South.

The bolters reconvened in St. Andrews Hall to organize and to keep an eye on the other body. Given half a chance, predicted the *Philadelphia North American and United States Gazette,* they would endorse the nominee of the regular group. The proposition became theoretical, for no nomination was reached on fifty-seven ballots. The necessary two-thirds majority couldn't be cornered.

The *Jonesboro* (Ill.) *Gazette* said that a Washington, D. C., group had raised $60,000 to back Douglas at Charleston. Money will accomplish wonders, it added, but "it won't restore the dead to life." Douglas' comment at the close of the Charleston affair, said the *Daily Chicago Herald,* might well have been "Save me from my friends!"

Why did the states secede at Charleston? Mainly because they demanded a platform and a candidate that would call upon the Federal government to protect, throughout the land, that special "species of property recognized in fifteen sovereign states"—slaves.

Mississippi delegates declared they were unwilling to adopt a Janus-faced platform that simultaneously looked to the North and the South. "The living and the dead are separated at Charleston," said the *New Orleans Daily Delta.* "The real, breathing, true and unconquerable Democracy, with seventeen sovereign States at their back, will meet the niggerites of the North on their own ground." The *Daily Delta* hoped the Northern Democrats would learn that "the way of the transgressor is hard."

The South said to its bolters, "Well done, ye good and faithful servants." The Washington *Evening Star* declared every exchange newspaper it read was rejoicing over the Charleston secession and that the South was "fairly on fire" with enthusiasm. In one Georgia town, ten delegates who did not withdraw at Charleston, said the *Star,* were hung in effigy, then stoned and brickbatted, and their remains, bearing the signs "Georgia Traitors," burned at the liberty pole. A cannon was fired once toward the ground, signifying submission by the delegates.

New Orleans staged a huge mass meeting to approve the action of its delegates. A 100-gun salute was fired. One hundred guns also were fired in Savannah in honor of all Southern states that withdrew. On his return from Charleston, William L. Yancey, chief of the Fire-Eaters, as the pro-slavery fanatics were called, was met in a coach drawn by four white horses and escorted by "costly and dazzling" vehicles filled with admiring friends. The *Huntsville* (Ala.) *Democrat* put out a black-bordered edition as mourning for the "degeneracy" and "traitorous audacity" of the Douglas Democrats.

Some saw the Southern bolt in a different light. A New Englander, said the *Mississippian,* remarked he didn't "keer so much about the delegates themselves, but there go four million bales of cotton with them."

The "anarchical" act, a Washington *States and Union* item claimed, met favor principally with a few sore-headed politicians. One newspaper asserted that the secession was a deliberate stroke aimed at wrecking the Democratic party. Another article in the *States and Union* rejoiced that the Fire-

Eaters were gone. "If we could, by our votes, bring them back, we would not do so. We would rather be defeated without them than triumph with them. Let them go—

> Fare thee well! and if forever,
> Still forever, fare thee well!"

Some Republicans were especially happy about the Charleston debacle. At one meeting a Republican called for three cheers for Douglas, for "busting up" the Democratic party.

The *Philadelphia North American and United States Gazette* puzzled over the Democrats' having adjourned without adopting any plans to save the Union and divide the spoils. "Is it possible that the National flesh-pot," asked the newspaper, "rich and steaming with an annual sustenance of 60-100 million dollars, has ceased to be savory in Democratic nostrils?"

Differences of opinion over the dramatic walkout were contrasted by the *Gazette* when it printed together two items from Savannah, Georgia, and Columbus, Ohio. The first reported a salute fired in honor of the Southern withdrawal; the latter applauded the Douglasites. The combined item was headed "The Irrepressible Conflict."

So the divided Democrats crept out of Charleston empty handed, but with separate plans to reconvene in June to renew their "Irrepressible Conflict." Would a change of venue do the trick? A *Daily Chicago Herald* item suggested that the Douglas Democrats sing this song when they reconvene at Baltimore:

> So when a raging fever burns,
> We shift from side to side by turns;
> But 'tis a poor relief we gain
> To change the place but keep the *pain.*

The Northern Democrats, shuffling along on one limb, still could find the lighter touch as their second convention opened. For example, they chuckled over a Texas delegate whose beard reached nearly to his waist. Fifteen years before, he had vowed he would not clip his whiskers until Henry Clay was elected President.

Some flooring collapsed shortly after the opening prayer, and this caused great excitement. In the stampede toward the exits chivalry was forgotten and some women were almost trampled underfoot. This unscheduled flight prompted considerable joking later.

An eccentric old fellow with a dazzling red vest kept several thousand in stitches after one session while they waited for a rain to let up. The oratorical fun-fest rippled on until the lights were turned out by the building's economical superintendent.

But even more than at Charleston, sizzling controversy rather than humor characterized the Baltimore convention. At one session two angry men rushed at each other after one commented "Is the impertinence of that old man to be tolerated?" The crowd prevented fisticuffs. Later that day, however, the son of one of the assailants met his father's adversary on the street and a blood-splattering fight followed.

In the Maltby House a Delaware Congressman and the competitor for his office engaged in battle. One, after being struck a jolting blow, dragged his opponent across the room by the necktie. The Congressman reached for his pistol but it fell to the floor. It was appropriated by his adversary who resisted the temptation to use it.

Some "boyish good fun" was carried out on a grander scale in Monument Square. There Douglas and anti-Douglas wings —the seceders were now also in Baltimore—held adjacent "confusion meetings," and rival orators kept orating. However, as the Washington *Evening Star* reported, they could seldom be heard above the noise and confusion. At one time, a Douglas man boldly invaded the opposing speaker's balcony and proposed three cheers for Douglas. He was ejected rather promptly.

At another time, according to a *Star* item, a band marched into the crowded square "throwing rockets and bombs to open their way, and discoursing most discordant sounds. When nearly in front of the Gilmore House [where the anti-Douglas group held forth], the cry of 'put them back,' and 'take their instruments,' was raised and in a moment . . . surging waves of humanity swept upon the band, knocking their instruments right and left, and blows were struck promiscuously."

The newspaper added that "the excitement around the hotels and headquarters is as great as ever, and the discourses are carried on with a bitterness that increases hourly." Newspapermen at Baltimore, on the other hand, were "like an oasis of peace in a desert of strife," declared the *Star*. And this in spite of the *Louisville* (Ky.) *Journal's* having asserted that Democratic papers recently were "uncommonly decent" because their editors had all gone to Baltimore. The *Star* said of the "happy family" in the Maryland city:

> We see the *New York Tribune* and *Charleston Mercury* batting over the current news in the most friendly manner; The *Boston Post* and the *New Orleans True Delta* drowning Douglas and dissension in a Brandy punch; the *Herald* and the *Constitution* exchanging cigars; while the *Times* and the *Richmond Enquirer* walk arm-in-arm down the street as though they were better friends than Damon and Pythias.

To no one's surprise, the convention finally got around to nominating Stephen A. Douglas as the candidate for President, with Herschel V. Johnson, former Georgia Governor, as running mate. "Cheers for the Little Giant, were responded to by the people outside until all was a perfect roar inside and outside the building," said the *Daily Chicago Herald*. Once again Abe Lincoln, who was waiting quietly in Springfield, and Steve Douglas were to be political competitors.

The *Herald* had Lincoln saying, "My political grave is 'DUG!' " A *Washington Constitution* item declared, though, that the cannon fired over the nomination of Douglas reverberating "throughout the length and breadth of the land" indicated "the Douglasites have gone to thunder." Some delegates, said the *Troy* (Ohio) *Times,* had promised their states to Douglas, but the pledge was "subject to a slight incumbrance held by Abraham Lincoln." Much of the South was in open arms against Douglas. And, if we are to believe some Republican reports, not all of the Northern Democrats were too happy over him. Said the *Weekly Illinois State Journal* concerning the "Bob-tail" convention and the "double-headed democracy":

The Douglas worshippers of our city finally raised their spirits to the noisy point, and attempted a formal demonstration in the evening. It was however more like a funeral occasion than anything else. A large bell was put upon a dray and wheeled about the streets tolling mournfully the while. A few guns were subsequently fired in the vicinity of the cemetery. The funeral oration was pronounced by V. S. Edwards on the courthouse steps, after which the benediction was offered by Ben Bond. . . .

We have no desire to dwarf its proportions, however, (which would indeed, be difficult, on account of its limited character) but are willing to let our Douglas friends enjoy themselves, without molestation as much as they can—satisfied, as we are, that there will be no fun for them after election.

The *Jonesboro* (Ill.) *Gazette* furnished this inscription for a proposed monument over the remains of a "certain Western Senator":

Here Lyeth ye Remanes of ye Little Giant,
Who was kilt in ye Irrepressible Conflict for ye Presidency,
At Charles Town, May the two, 1860.
Ambitious youths take warning by his fall
And never try to fill a place for which you are too small.

Just before the Douglas convention in Baltimore, the Southern seceders met in Richmond, Virginia, but failed to accomplish their mission. Then some of them gravitated to Baltimore, where, after another futile try with the Douglasites, named thirty-nine-year-old John C. Breckinridge, of Kentucky, then Vice-President, as Presidential nominee. Joseph Lane, U. S. Senator from Oregon, was nominated for Vice-President.

The *State Gazette* (Texas) declared: "Never have we seen a presidential ticket receive from the masses such warm, fervent, and enthusiastic welcome. It seized at once the hearts of the people, and seems to come with the wild fury of the tornado, sweeping before it every obstacle in its path." " 'Breckinridge and Lane' is our battle cry," said another newspaper article. "Heroes in war, statesmen in peace, and the favorites of a free people, it is with pride we nail them to our masthead." A Barnstable, Massachusetts, paper said it put the Breckinridge-Lane names on its masthead within thirty minutes after receiving the news. "We march with them to victory," it proclaimed.

Anti-Democratic newspapers were quick to publicize the Democratic split. And some Democratic journals reminded their colleagues "I told you so." The Washington *National Intelligencer* held that the Breckinridge Democrats had laid the egg which would be hatched as Lincoln's election. It declared it had "heard the cackle of the political hens who dropped it."

In the walkout of the South at Charleston, the *Worcester* (Mass.) *Daily Spy*, was reminded of a captain who was about to launch a bloody battle. He told his company: "Boys, this fight is going to be bloody; there's no telling who'll get whipt; we may have to retreat, and as I'm a little lame, I'll leave now!"

In their efforts to stimulate hatred toward the Southern faction, the Northern Democrats, said the *Daily Chicago Herald*, resembled "the wolf who was silly enough to get his tail cut off in a steel trap and then endeavored to persuade others that it was fashionable."

Many writers and campaigners went happily to work at widening the Democratic split. *Walton's Daily Legislative Journal* (Montpelier, Vt.) recommended that the American Eagle be removed from the Democratic party's banner since it was not a double-headed bird. In its place, the newspaper suggested, should be two Kilkenny cats, symbolic of discord. The *Weekly Illinois State Journal* commented that "the two factions, hards and softs, have fought each other until, like the Kilkenny cats, there is nothing left of them . . . except their tails."

Douglas was referred to by the *Mississippian* as "the rock of the Democratic party"—that is, the rock upon which the Democratic party was split. And the *Weekly Illinois State Journal* noted that Lincoln was once a rail-splitter and that Douglas has always been splitting hairs, and had now split his party. The *Baltimore Sun* ran this little side-splitter:

> Quoth Abe to Steve, "I cannot fail,
> I'm bound to fill that station;
> Long—long ago—I split the rail
> To fence this mighty nation."
> "Of what you've split, don't talk to me,"
> Quoth Steve, with chuckle hearty,
> "I've split old Jackson's hickory tree,
> The Democratic party."

The *Sacramento* (Calif.) *Daily Union* quipped that the Republicans are called Rail-Splitters and the Democrats, since Baltimore, are known as the Split-Railers.

The idea of two Democratic teams in the field was played upon by many newspaper writers and would-be humorists. The *Manhattan Express* (Kansas Territory) noted that flying machines had proved unsuccessful but that the Democratic party might now "go up" since it had two "wings." Democrats had a lot to excite their enthusiasm—say two candidates for President, commented an item in the *New Albany* (Ind.) *Daily Ledger*. The *New-Hampshire Statesman* (Concord) quoted an Irishman as exclaiming "It's all over wid ye now, sir! It's baten ye are sure, for the Dimmycrats can nominate two tickets to yer one."

An item in the *Troy* (Ohio) *Times* was intended to illustrate why the Democratic party should run one of their candidates a little while, then the other. "Why, Jimmy," said a man to a professional beggar, who was unbuckling his crutch, "you are going to knock off for the day so early?" "No, you mutton-head, I'm only going to put my crutch on t'other knee. You don't suppose a fellow can beg all day on one leg, do you?"

Someone suggested the two Democratic factions be called the "Blacks" and the "Mulattoes" to distinguish their stands on slavery. An Ohio newspaper gave up trying to figure out this "double-headed Democracy" and ran both tickets at the top of its editorial columns.

A favorite journalistic claim was that the Democratic party had become a dead duck. "The Death of Democracy," was one newspaper headline, illustrating this approach. The *Weekly Illinois State Journal* declared that Douglas' "backers and bottle holders" came sneaking back from Charleston "with an immense flea in their ear," having wound up both Mr. Douglas and the Democratic party. The *Manhattan Express* (Kansas Territory) asserted that "The Invincible—the immutable—the harmonious—the united—the real *E Pluribus Unum*—the immortal—thus succumbs and passes off the stage of action . . . The curtain of oblivion comes down . . ."

The Democratic affair reminded the *Weekly Illinois State Journal* of an old man who solemnly carried a small coffin down the street under his arm. He was headed to the cemetery to bury a deceased grandchild. When some boys snickered at the old fellow, he turned and remarked: "Hush, boys, hush; stop dat laffin' dar; I'se a funeral."

The *Bucyrus* (Ohio) *Weekly Journal* ran this obituary: "Died—at Charlestown, S. C., on the 23d inst., the old and well known horse, *Democracy*. The above named horse was sired by Thomas Jefferson, dam(n)ed by Stephen A. Douglas."

This was the *Weekly Illinois State Journal* interpretation of the Democratic debacle:

> The journals of the country are holding a post-mortem examination over the Democratic party. All sorts of opinions are expressed as to the cause of death. The verdict of the majority appears to be, "died of Douglas." One journal, however, thinks that it died of the 19th century; another says it died of old age and general imbecility. A very religious journal suggests that it died of a visitation of God—for its manifold sins. A Yankee says "The Little Giant sot on it, and killed it." A wag insinuates that it tumbled off the platform and broke its neck. A Southerner says it was strangled while trying to swallow Squatter Sovereignty. A Northerner declares that its insides were burnt out by an injudicious attempt at fire-eating. A lawyer says that it died of the Dred Scott Decision. A delegate to Charleston says it became insolvent, owing to the hotel extortions of that city, and concluded to commit suicide. Another delegate says they went to Charleston with the motto "Douglas or Death," and as they couldn't get Douglas, they had to "kick the bucket" as a matter of course.

Another *Journal* item announced the "delightfully mournful" news that the Democratic party had departed this life from a complication of loathsome diseases. It suggested that the carcass be buried before it bred a pestilence. It gleefully concluded:

> Lay down de shovel and de hoe.
> And hang up de fiddle and de bow
> For there's no more work for de ole party now—
> It has gone where all bad things do go.

While not asserting that the Democratic party was stone dead, the *Troy* (Ohio) *Times,* explained that it was in an awkward situation. One half of the Democrats declare that Douglas could not possibly be elected; the other half argue that no other Democrat can. Putting the two together, chuckled the *Times,* one has that *rara avis,* a Democratic truth.

Meanwhile, Democratic editors scrutinized the Republican revelry. One newspaper noted that a certain Republican editor daily predicted Democratic failure, "after writing which the editor doubtless throws up his hat and turns a complete somersault to relieve his exhilarated spirits." It beseeched the gentleman of the press not to rend his linen at this early stage of the campaign.

Regardless of which side of the political fence they were on, all agreed that an unusual creature had been born at Baltimore. But this Maryland city had done more than give birth to twin Democratic tickets. It had also produced a third pair of candidates in the now four-way race—John Bell, of Tennessee, a former U. S. Congressman and Secretary of War, with Edward Everett, former Unitarian clergyman who had been a U. S. Congressman, Governor of Massachusetts, Secretary of State, and president of Harvard University, as running mate. Bell and Everett represented the Constitutional Union Party which waved the motto: "The Constitution of the Country, the Union of the States, and the Enforcement of the Laws." This party was pieced together from remnants of the Old Whig party and the southern wing of the American or Know-Nothing party.

A grandson of Patrick Henry thanked the convention for honoring his state, Tennessee, by the nomination of Bell. Then, according to the *New Orleans Daily Delta,* "the ancient optimists and fossils quietly wended their way home by slow stages, in the full consciousness of having saved the republic."

What did the anti-Bell newspapers think of the nominations? The announcement fell still-born upon the world, declared the *Albany Atlas and Argus.* A Southern Congressman, said the *New York Tribune,* asserted that Choate (Rufus Choate, Massachusetts lawyer and statesman) should have

Slogans of the 1860 Republican campaign are incorporated in this lithograph. At a time when the nation was about to crumble, the motto "The Union must and shall be preserved" carried considerable significance. (Below) The grand Republican conclave in the Wigwam at Chicago during May, 1860.

FREE SPEECH · FREE SOIL · FREE MEN ·

This is to Certify that

is a member of the

WIDE-AWAKE CLUB.

1860

Pres.

Sec.

Capt.

Orderly.

"Nobody ever expected me to be President. In my poor, lean, lank face, nobody has ever seen that any cabbages were sprouting out."

I come to see and be seen.

Honest old Abe on the Stump.
Springfield 1858.

Honest old Abe on the Stump,
at the ratification Meeting of
Presidential Nominations.
Springfield 1860.

Young Republican groups called Wide-Awakes marched and demonstrated in Lincoln's behalf in cities all over the North. This membership certificate shows Wide-Awakes with their regalia of torches, caps, and capes. (Left) Lincoln's detractors based this concept of a two-faced stump speaker on comments made by Lincoln in 1858 and 1860. After the campaign got underway, Lincoln did not make speeches on his party's behalf.

"I'm not to blame for being white, sir," a white child pleads, as an abolitionist hands some coins to a Negro child. An example of anti-Republican caricatures that attacked supposed abolitionist discrimination in favor of Negroes. (Below) Stephen A. Douglas and Abe Lincoln have at it, with a trip to the White House as the prize.

THE UNDECIDED POLITICAL PRIZE FIGHT.

A Political Earthquake!

THE PRAIRIES ON FIRE FOR LINCOLN!

THE BIGGEST DEMONSTRATION EVER HELD IN THE WEST!

75,000 REPUBLICANS IN COUNCIL!

IMMENSE PROCESSION!

Speaking from Five Stands by Trumbull, Doolittle, Kellogg, Palmer, Browning, Gillespie, etc., etc.

MAGNIFICENT TORCHLIGHT PROCESSION AT NIGHT.

MEETINGS AT THE WIGWAM AND THE REPRESENTATIVES HALL.

Lincoln's home-town newspaper, the "Illinois State Journal" (Springfield), reports a rip-roaring Republican rally there. The "Journal" even indulged in a sketch, at a time when newspaper illustrations were rare. (Below) A Currier & Ives caricature in which Lincoln ponders "which one to swallow first"—Douglas on the soft shell or Breckinridge on the hard. (Opposite page) A disgruntled politician lets the "Spirit of Discord" out of the bag. Horace Greeley, extreme left, complains that "she ain't to be let out until after Lincoln is elected."

HONEST ABE TAKING THEM ON THE HALF SHELL.

LETTING THE CAT OUT OF THE BAG!!

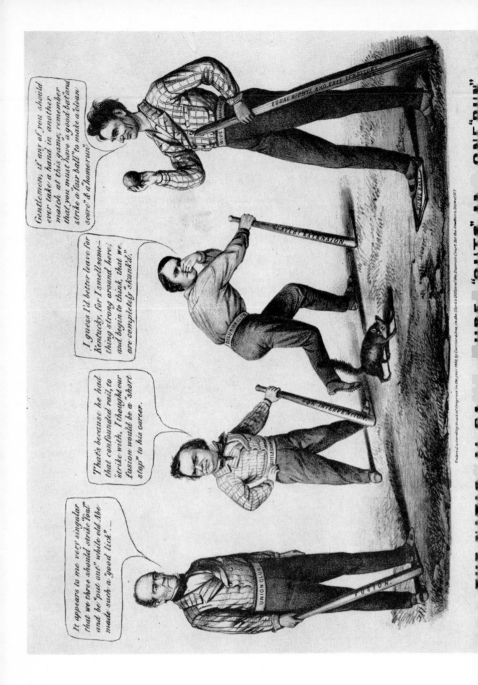

The unusual four-sided campaign of 1860 seen in terms of a baseball game. The players, left to right, are Bell, Douglas, Breckinridge, and Lincoln. (Opposite page) Horace Greeley carries Lincoln on a rail into a lunatic asylum. Abe babbles, "the millennium is going to begin, so ask what you want and it shall be granted. (Currier & Ives print.)

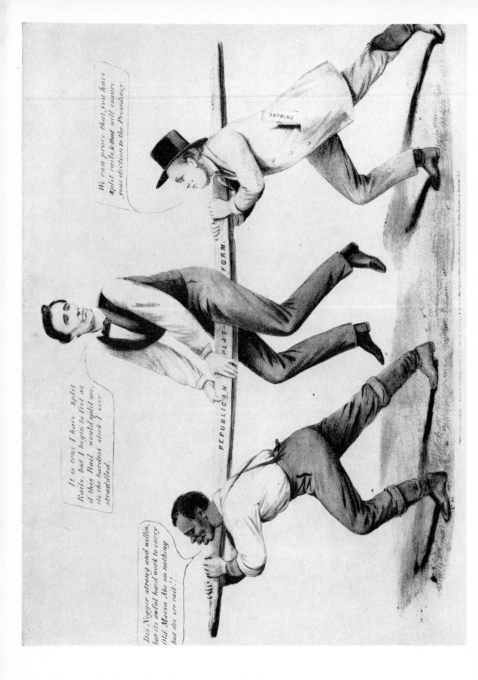

Horace Greeley and a Negro carry Lincoln on a rail, representing the Republican platform. "It's the hardest stick I ever straddled," complains Abe. (Opposite page) Senator William Seward of New York, the "Mr. Republican" of 1860, was tossed overboard at the Chicago convention. Here Horace Greeley does the tossing, while Lincoln takes the helm.

"THE IRREPRESSIBLE CONFLICT".
OR THE REPUBLICAN BARGE IN DANGER.

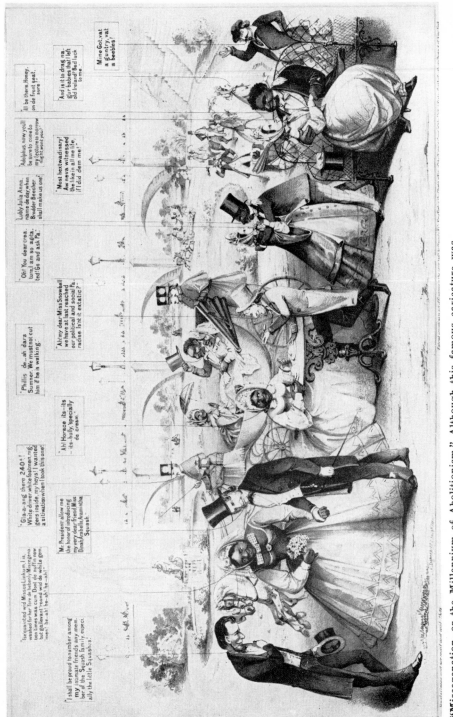

"Miscegenation or the Millennium of Abolitionism." Although this famous caricature was

THE GREAT EXHIBITION OF 1860.

Lincoln, with padlocked lips, capers about on the Republican platform, while Greeley grinds the Republican organ, the "New York Tribune." Seward holds a Negro baby and says "It's no use trying to keep me and the 'Irrepressible infant' in the background."

Bucyrus Journal

Thursday, Nov. 8, 1860.

D. R. LOCKE AND J. G. ROBINSON,
Proprietors and Editors.

The Journal has a Circulation of 1,400.

THE THING IS DID!

The Most Glorious Triumph Ever Achieved!

Lincoln Elected!

DISUNION REBUKED!

DOUG. NON EST!

BRECK. NO WHERE!

BELL,——

THE COUNTRY SAVED!

A Chance for a Big Yell.

It is with feelings of unmixed pleasure that we announce to the gallant Republicans of Crawford the entire success of our party at the election on last Tuesday.

Lincoln has carried EVERY NORTHERN STATE! by tremendous majorities, larger than the most sanguine dared to hope for, and has received a respectable vote in the border Slave States. We refer our readers to the returns in another column.

P. S.—New Jersey has gone fusion by a small majority.

(Above) Lincoln's alleged flight through the night in Scottish garb is caricatured in this cartoon. Because of a suspected "Baltimore Plot" to assassinate him, the President-elect hurried to Washington from Harrisburg on a night train instead of the announced day train. (Left) Some Republican newspapers were uninhibited in announcing Lincoln's victory. The "Bucyrus (Ohio) Journal" piled up quite a stack of one-column heads and subheads to herald the event. (Opposite page) Abe implores the southern states to get out of the secession mud hole. "Only think what a bad example you show the other boys," he reminds them. In his hand he holds South Carolina, the Palmetto State, which led the secession movement.

Entered according to Act of Congress, in the Year 1861, by Harper & Brothers, in the Clerk's Office of the District Court for the Southern District of New York.

ABRAHAM LINCOLN, THE PRESIDENT ELECT, ADDRESSING THE PEOPLE FROM THE ASTOR HOUSE BALCONY, FEBRUARY 19, 1861.—[See Page Four.]

En route to Washington, Lincoln stayed at the Astor House in New York. In this "Harper's Weekly" illustration he addresses a crowd from the hotel balcony. (Below) Office-seekers at Washington during Lincoln's first Inauguration. The satirical legend declares, "These Gentlemen, who are ready, like good Patriots, to serve their Country, are all ORIGINAL LINCOLN MEN."

OFFICE-SEEKERS AT WASHINGTON DURING THE INAUGURATION.

These Gentlemen, who are ready, like good Patriots, to serve their Country, are all ORIGINAL LINCOLN MEN. 'Tis true, they voted for PIERCE and BUCHANAN; but this was a deep game to insure the Election of LINCOLN in 1860.

The Inaugural procession approaches the Capitol, with its unfinished dome. (Below) The scene at the Capitol, from a sketch by Thomas Nast, the famous cartoonist.

"Diogenes his lantern needs no more,
"An honest man is found!—The search is o'er."

Illustrations in this section courtesy of the Library of Congress.

been nominated. When reminded that Choate was dead the Congressman added, "Oh I know it; but he hasn't been dead a very long time."

Bell's party called for compromise at virtually any cost. Or better yet, it preferred to duck the slavery issue by ducking its own head in the sand. The platform, declared a New York newspaper, was "no North, no South, no East, no West, no Anything." It defined Bell as "a hollow metallic vessel for giving a sound on being struck."

Relatively few newspapers, however, made personal attacks on Bell and Everett, who were both generally considered gentlemen. The *Daily Chicago Herald* said the Constitutional Union Party was a respectable party, with respectable purposes, and respectable candidates. The only respect in which it was not respectable, concluded the *Herald*, was in numbers. And a *Washington Constitution* item, declared that the candidates were as "eminently respectable as their chances of being elected are slender."

In a minor way, there was a fifth candidate—Sam Houston, a former Governor of Tennessee and hero of the Battle of San Jacinto in Texas, who had once lived for several years among the Cherokee Indians in Arkansas. His zealous supporters had labored valiantly but unsuccessfully to promote his candidacy at the other conventions. Not willing to say die, they pushed him as a Union candidate in Texas.

The *Weekly Illinois State Journal* ran a column-long article entitled "The Five Platforms." After describing the platforms of the Republican party, the "Douglas Faction of the Sham Democracy," the "Breckinridge Faction of the Sham Democracy," and the Constitutional Union Party, it concluded with:

THE SAM HOUSTON PARTY

Candidates: For president—Sam Houston, of Texas.
Platform: The candidate's old Indian blanket.

Also, in a minor way, there was a sixth candidate—Gerrit Smith, New York philanthropist and reformer. Some voters and politicians with abolitionist sentiments rallied around him.

Essentially, though, the lines had been drawn for a four-way battle—Breckinridge and Bell, mainly in the deep South and border states, and Douglas and Lincoln, in the North and West.

CHAPTER SEVEN

OLD ABRAM—HORRIBLY HOMELY, YET HANDSOME

Folks in 1860 were interested in other things besides politics. They chatted about the amazing telegraph, the third unsuccessful Atlantic cable, horse railroads, the Pony Express, Pike's Peak, patent medicines, smallpox, bloomer girls, and the muscle movement and gymnasiums.

Talked-about celebrities included John Brown, fiery abolitionist raider recently hanged at Charles Town, Virginia; Horace Greeley, crusading editor of the *New York Tribune;* Garibaldi and Italian independence; the young Prince of Wales then on tour in the United States; visiting dignitaries from that hermit kingdom, Japan, recently opened by American enterprise; Charles Sherwood Stratton, better known as Tom Thumb; P. T. Barnum; and Charles Blondin, French tight-rope walker who did gymnastics on an eleven-hundred-foot rope stretched above swirling Niagara River. Readers also were interested in baseball, duels, the stock market, and the erection of the Washington Monument. There were also newspaper sensations about reckless speeders in buggies, about Yale and Harvard students who stole Bibles from each other's chapels and mailed them to rival officers; and about John C. Heenan who had battled English pugilist Tom Sayers thirty-seven rounds.

People were also intrigued by odometers, which registered the mileage of carriages. One woman suggested that someone invent a similar instrument to tell how far husbands had been in the evening when they just "went to attend a political caucus."

But in the summer and fall of '60, political meetings—did draw huge attendances. In fact interest in the four Presidential candidates, and the single question that divided them, was intense. Curiosity about the Republican candidate, particularly, was keen.

Immediately after his nomination at Chicago, the newspapers catered to the interest in this relatively unknown fifty-one-year-old Springfield attorney. They told how Abe's ancestors had migrated from Massachusetts to Pennsylvania, to Virginia, to Kentucky, and focused on the highlights of Abe's life in Kentucky, Indiana, and Illinois. And, of course, the Republican journals never neglected to capitalize on Abe's humble beginnings. Said the *New York Daily Tribune:*

> He was in turn a farm laborer, a common workman in sawmills, and a boatman on the Wabash and Mississippi Rivers. Thus hard work and plenty of it, the rugged experiences of aspiring poverty, the wild sports and rude games of a newly and thinly peopled forest region—the education born of the log cabin, the rifle, the axe, and the plow, combined with the reflections of an original and vigorous mind, eager in the pursuit of knowledge by every available means, and developing a character of equal resource and firmness —made him the man he has since proved himself.

One item asserted that Lincoln's ancestors fled to Hingham, Massachusetts, for their part in chopping off the head of Charles I of Great Britain.

Some journals were not very charitable in their biographical sketches. The *Vermont Patriot* (Montpelier) said that Lincoln was descended directly from "Old Abraham and the ram, some account of which may be found in a book not much in vogue, we are afraid, among our Republican friends." Lincoln's birthplace was ridiculed by the *Daily Chicago Herald:*

Current report has it that he was born in Hardin County, Ky. The Hardin people do not seem, however, to be overwhelmed with the honor, and lay the blame of his production on Nelson County; while Nelson County insists that he first saw the light of day across the line in Washington County from the top of Possum Ridge. We have not heard what the Washingtonians have to say in their defense.

Newspapers that smiled benignly upon Lincoln's struggle for an education printed complimentary anecdotes. For example, the *Cincinnati Gazette* recalled how Lincoln had sat by the crackling fire at night while others were asleep, and wrote and ciphered on a board he had smoothed with a drawing knife. When the board was filled, he shaved off the writing and continued his schooling.

The story of Abe's volunteering to cut fodder for an Indiana neighbor to pay for a borrowed book which had become damaged was printed in many newspapers, among them the *Washington* (Ohio) *Herald*. Three days of hard work were said to have made Lincoln the owner of a "Life of Washington" which had been soaked by rain seeping into the cabin.

Some papers preferred to show how Lincoln *did not* get an education. The *Topeka Tribune* (Kansas Territory) declared that if ignorance of schools and an absence of other educational advantages fitted a man for the Presidency, then Topeka had a better prospect than Lincoln. This Topekan, who had never attended school a day and could not read a word, never let "an opportunity pass unimproved to denounce all Democrats and proclaim himself a Republican."

In a society predominantly rural it was politically popular to play up the country angles. Thus the *Jerseyman* (Morristown), referring to Lincoln and Hamlin, declared, "Two farmer boys of 1809 will be at the head of the National Government in 1861." Other papers pointed out that Lincoln had groomed his own horse, chopped his wood, and tended his cow in Springfield. To this the *Weekly Wisconsin Patriot*

(Madison) retorted that the only respect in which Lincoln was a "leading man" was in leading cows to water.

Hard work was another theme popular with Lincoln supporters. The Newburyport (Mass.) *Daily Herald* noted that Lincoln found few opportunities for mental cultivation, but that persons such as Abe "make their own opportunities, as rivers are said to form their own channels."

The antagonists went to work with a will on this new theme, Lincoln's hard labor. The *Cleveland Weekly Plain Dealer* ran sketches and comments parodying Lincoln's life. One said: "He emigrates to Illinois, engages on a farm and is set to work splitting bass-wood rails. He *sets* about it at once." The illustration showed him "setting" idly on the log, his maul beside him. In a *New London* (Conn.) *Daily Star* item, a Chicagoan asserted Lincoln never split the number of rails he was reputed to have, for "he was too confounded lazy." It asserted he got experience as a flat-boatman only by taking a trip to shirk husking corn for his father.

A letter by Charles Hanks, brother of John Hanks, Lincoln's rail-splitting partner, attempted to deflate the Lincoln stories which flourished after the rail episode at the Illinois Republican Convention in May. In the letter reprinted in the *Daily Chicago Herald* Charles Hanks said, "I think . . . that the rails that are now being worshiped all over the North as Lincoln rails, were made by poor Bill Strickland, who is now poor, blind, helpless, and in the Macon county poorhouse." He conceded that John and Abe had split a few rails but contended all these had burned.

Thus the Republicans strived to build up the story of a lowly man who had grown tall in wisdom. His opponents worked hard, on the other hand, to sell the "mud-sill" theory: that the laboring man could never be educated.

Some newspaper stories ridiculed Lincoln's abilities as a wrestler, fighter, and warrior. The *Jonesboro* (Ill.) *Gazette* printed an anecdote about Lincoln and his opponent for a Sangamon County office, Dr. Cartwright, a pioneer Methodist minister. Lincoln allegedly said that "Peter Cartwright was a d—d rascal, and so were all Methodist preachers. They would all steal horses. . . ." He intended to whip Cartwright the first time he met him, the article declared. Some time later, Cartwright met Lincoln and a group of other men. The clergy-man inquired which of the men was going to whip him. Lin-coln, not recognizing Cartwright, declared "I am the lark that is going to thrash him well. I can whip any Methodist preacher the Lord ever made." When Cartwright identified himself, Lincoln began crawfishing. "Now, Sir, you have got to whip me as you threatened or quit cursing me," said the Methodist preacher, "or I will put you in the river, and bap-tise you in the name of the devil, for surely you belong to him." That settled the matter, said the *Gazette*, and the two men became friends.

The *Fond du Lac* (Wis.) *Weekly Commonwealth* told of the case in which Lincoln allegedly was to fight a duel with General Shields. Lincoln, according to the item, had chival-rously assumed responsibility for an article in the *Sangamon* (Ill.) *Journal* in which the General was good-naturedly ribbed. The article was actually written by a young lady. Shields challenged and Lincoln accepted, with broadswords the weapons. However, a third party, said the *Commonwealth*, appeared on the field of honor and talked them out of the duel.

Lincoln's experiences as a military captain were frequently ridiculed in the journals. The *Washington* (Ohio) *Herald* de-clared that he, "unfortunately for the country, escaped the tomahawk and scalping knife." A story in the *Toledo Times* during the 1860 campaign purported to describe Lincoln's *first* campaign—during the Black Hawk War. As a sentry one dark night, he imagined he heard Indians approaching. Seeing a horse nearby, he jumped on it and dashed away. Unfor-tunately, the horse was tethered. When it came to the end of its rope, the story explained, the horse stopped abruptly, but Lincoln did not.

Abe's skill as a raconteur was publicized during the '60

campaign. For instance, the *Salem* (Mass.) *Register* revived the story which Lincoln had once told: A committee named to erect a bridge over a rapid and dangerous river had been unable to find an engineer to do the job. Finally they called in a man who assured them that he "could build a bridge to the infernal regions, if necessary." The conservative committee was horrified. After the engineer left, his friend on the committee who had recommended him said in his defense, "If he states soberly and positively that he can build a bridge to Hades, why I believe it. But I have my doubts about the abutment on the infernal side." Lincoln added that when Democrats asserted they could harmonize the Northern and Southern wings of the party, he believed them, although he had his doubts about the abutment on the Southern side.

According to the hostile *New York Herald,* Lincoln was best known in Illinois as a teller of smutty stories. His reputation for wit was satirized by the *Saint Anthony Weekly Express* (Hennepin County, Minn.) with this story: Lincoln and some friends were crossing a small stream when he asked its name. "It is called the 'Weeping Waters,' " said one. Lincoln replied, "You remember the laughing waters up in Minnesota, called Minnehaha. Now I think, this should be Minnebobo." The newspaper added: "The guideboard to the wit in it is missing . . . , and we cannot tell for the life of us where the laugh comes in. Can't some of our Republican friends help us out of our unpleasant predicament?"

The fact that Lincoln was not widely known was pounced on by many publications. The *Oregon Sentinel* (Jacksonville) applauded *Vanity Fair's* term for Lincoln as the "nameless candidate of an aimless party." Another paper labeled him "a first-rate second-rate man." Said the *Cherry Valley* (N. Y.) *Gazette* Honest Abe's "highest claim to distinction is based— if it has any basis at all—upon an unsuccessful and brief political career, a hideous nickname, and a certain adroitness in the primitive business of rail-splitting in a wilderness." The *Albany Atlas and Argus* likened Lincoln and the Republican party to the mushroom—"soon up, soon rotten." It declared that Lincoln was "first heard of in politics a year ago last Fall, when limping with wounds and howling with anguish, he was driven through the state of Illinois by Douglas." But when one Chicago paper called Lincoln "a nonentity," the *Weekly Illinois State Journal* replied that if a nonentity gave Douglas such a terrific fight in 1858, beating him by several thousand *popular* votes, "we wonder what an entity would have done."

Lincoln's character was a matter of pride to Republicans. "He is a man of stainless purity—his whole life is spotless as the driven snow," said the *New York Daily Tribune;* and added he was the type of man "this sorely swindled and disgraced nation needs for President." Another *Tribune* eulogy declared:

Abe Lincoln, combining the intellectual power of a giant with the simple habits of a backwoods farmer; the genuine whole-souled manliness of a Kentucky-born, Western-raised, self-educated, and self-made man, will be hugged to the people's hearts like a second Andrew Jackson. He has the magnetism of genius in him; his mien is genial and dignified; his wit is natural and unaffected, and he drops in the most casual way some of the more terse and epigrammatic expressions that ever fell from human lips.

Lincoln's armor, proclaimed the *New Hampshire Statesman* (Concord), is without a hole; his escutcheon without a stain. A friend of Lincoln, said an item in the *Portsmouth* (N. H.) *Journal,* declared he would as soon have expected Samuel Adams to submit to the Stamp Act as Abraham Lincoln to dishonor himself.

The *Statesman* gave Lincoln this build-up:

He never drinks intoxicating liquors of any sort, not even a glass of wine. He is not addicted to tobacco in any of its shapes. He never uses profane language. He never gambles. We doubt if he ever indulges in any games of chance. He is particularly cautious about incurring pecuniary obligations for any purpose whatsoever, and in debt, he is never content until the score is discharged. We presume he owes no man a dollar. He never speculates . . . He would be a bold man who would say that Abraham Lincoln ever wronged any one out of one cent, or spent a dollar that he had not honestly earned.

Many Republican papers exhumed earlier tributes to Lincoln by his adversary, Douglas, who had described him as "The ablest lawyer in Illinois; and the smartest stump speaker in the Union; an earnest and honest man who believes what he professes, and who will carry out what he undertakes."

Trying to destroy this image, the *Topeka Tribune* asserted that the "party claiming to monopolize all the morality, honesty, and virtue of the nation," was running a second-rate man who was a fourth-rate politician and statesman. A letter in the *Saint Anthony Weekly Express* (Hennepin County, Minn.) termed Lincoln a "good clever pettifogger and a superlative demagogue." In the *Charleston* (S. C.) *Mercury* Lincoln was labeled a "bigot and extremist." The *Democratic Republican* (Haverhill, N. H.) asserted that some Democratic newspapers were lying when they claimed "that honest Old Doctor Abe takes half a pound of tobacco at two chews. He never exceeds six ounces."

In addition to such brief items the newspapers carried biographies of Lincoln. The first published life of Lincoln was in the *Chester County* (Pa.) *Times* early in 1860. It was from Lincoln's own laconic account, written at the suggestion of Jesse W. Fell, political associate of Lincoln and great-grandfather of Adlai E. Stevenson. The biography began, "I was born Feb. 12, 1809, in Hardin County, Ky. . . ." Accompanying the article was a brief note from Lincoln explaining "there is not much of it, for the reason, I suppose, that there is not much of me. If anything be made out of it, I wish it to be modest. . . ."

Many exaggerated or satiric accounts of Lincoln's life were spread by the opposition. For instance, the *Weekly Wisconsin Patriot* (Madison) said:

He cast his lot with one as celebrated as himself, named Hanks. He feels the inspiration of his talent, spits upon railsplitting, tears himself from Hanks, and turns lawyer. He is just budding into manhood. An extraordinary convulsion of nature casts him into the State Legislature. A still more extraordinary convulsion lands him in Congress. . . . He goes home and is driven into obscurity by an indignant constituency.

The *Bellows Falls* (Vt.) *Argus* told how Lincoln rid Southern Indiana of Indians in less than one week after he arrived. To prevent their return he spent nine days, five hours and fifteen minutes erecting a fifty-foot-high rail fence around the whole Hoosier state.

A biography in the *New-Hampshire Patriot* (Concord) said Lincoln was "long enough to be tedious, his head is said to 'defy description' . . . that he is of a religious turn of mind is shown by the fact that 'his wife is a member of the Presbyterian Church.' . . . As for swearing, which is both an immoral and ungentlemanly practice . . . he is free from that vice, and in his most irascible moments never says anything more emphatic than 'damn him.' "

An article reprinted in the *Washington Constitution* said "all we can find out about Mr. Lincoln is that

he is sixteen feet high, and fifty-one years long; that he is as thin and angular as a split rail; that he was born a Hoosier, but finally became a Sucker; that he has been in turn a farm laborer, a top-sawyer, a flat-boatman, a counter-jumper, a militia captain, a lawyer, a Presbyterian, and a politician; that he beat Douglas over the left in Illinois, and drove him into the U. S. Senate; that his favorite motto is "two shillings are better than one." And that he is spotless in everything but his linen.

A biography in the *Jonesboro* (Ill.) *Gazette* began: "The

subject of our biography was born at Bunker Hill on the fourth of July, 1776, and was one of the original signers of the precious document which sealed our liberties on that day. . . . At the age of two years, young Abraham began splitting rails for a living, singing beautiful hymns while so engaged, and displaying all those noble virtues for which he has since become distinguished."

Long after this campaign was history, one of Lincoln's colleagues allegedly called him a "damn fool" and Lincoln reportedly replied that if this associate thought he was a "damn fool," then "I must be one, for he is usually right in these matters." The opposition newspapers during the '60 campaign pictured Lincoln as this particular kind of a fool. But thousands of people would have none of such characterizations of this man of the people. And many were ready to spend their hard-earned cash to buy books which described his rise from poverty, from the log cabin to—they hoped—the White House.

A real workhorse in the campaign of 1860 was the book, *Political Debates Between Honorable Abraham Lincoln and Honorable Stephen A. Douglas in the Celebrated Campaign of 1858 in Illinois.* It reprinted Lincoln's speeches from the *Chicago Press and Tribune* and Douglas' speeches from the *Chicago Times.* Published at Columbus, Ohio, the book opened with Lincoln's famous "House-divided-against-itself" speech. Since Lincoln did not make many political addresses in 1860, voters looked to sources such as this book to determine his stand on critical questions.

Horace Greeley and John F. Cleveland, both of the *New York Daily Tribune,* compiled *A Political Text Book for 1860.* Murat Halstead, of the *Cincinnati Commercial,* provided a complete record of all the national political conventions in *The Caucuses of 1860.* Among other books featured in the campaign were *Lives and Speeches of Abraham Lincoln and Hannibal Hamlin, Memorabilia of the Chicago Con-*

vention, Speeches of Abraham Lincoln, Republican Pocket Pistol (five cents, postage paid), *The Case of Dred Scott, The Kansas Narrative, The Barbarities of Slavery, Land for the Landless,* and *The Democratic Leaders for Disunion.*

Publicity about Lincoln's life prompted numerous journalistic retorts. The *New Albany* (Ind.) *Daily Ledger,* noted that six lives of Abe Lincoln were said to be in the course of publication at Boston. Others would follow, it added, so that "Abe may yet rival the most ancient of the feline tribe by having nine lives." Lincoln had received fifty-two applications to write his biography, according to the *Troy* (O.) *Times.* Should he survive this extraordinary number of "attempts on his life," said the *Times,* the Democrats would certainly be unable to kill him in November. The *Albany Atlas and Argus,* having seen a new "Life of Lincoln," suggested it was well that Lincoln had "so many lives." "The only 'Life' of 'Old Abe' yet known to the public," the *Argus* argued, "has nothing in it to recommend him to the people's confidence." The *Chicago Daily Journal,* having observed a "new life of Lincoln," asked if the "old rail-splitting, flat-boating, whisky-distilling one" wasn't new enough for a Presidential aspirant?

Although there was much publicity about Lincoln's life, he did not go about authorizing biographies. The Columbus publisher of the Lincoln-Douglas debates was about to issue an "authorized biography of Lincoln" by William Dean Howells, *Ohio State Journal* writer who later won fame as a novelist. "How dare I to send forth, by my authority," Lincoln wrote a friend, "a volume of hundreds of pages, for adversaries to make points upon without end?" Lincoln stressed that in the present crisis it was not discreet of him even to write or speak publicly.

Opposition forces were painfully aware that Lincoln got plenty of favorable publicity, nevertheless. The *Washington States and Union* pointed to the vast distribution of political tracts and especially the Republican handbook, popularly known as "Helpers book," which had had a circulation of several hundred thousand. "It is useless to deny," said the newspaper, "the influence of such sheets of mischief, and the only way to counteract the *poison* is by the circulation of Democratic papers." The *States and Union* was announcing its own new weekly antidote, *The Campaign.*

While Lincoln's "lives" and other books figured in the campaign, it was in the newspapers that the running battle occurred. One of the earliest skirmishes was over Lincoln's first name. Many newspapers during the weeks immediately following the Chicago convention referred to him as *Abram* Lincoln.

The masthead of the *Troy* (Ohio) *Times* proclaimed: "For President, Abram Lincoln, of Illinois. 'Fear not, Abram: I am thy shield and thy exceeding great reward.'" (Genesis 15:1) The name later was corrected to Abraham and the Scriptural quotation dropped. The *Kansas State Record* (Topeka) also carried in bold letters on its masthead, "For President, Abram Lincoln." It, too, hurriedly made a correction.

By mid-June, many newspapers were quoting the *Chicago Daily Journal:* "We have Mr. Lincoln's authority for saying that his name is Abraham." In a letter signed "A. Lincoln" and sent to George Ashmun, National Republican Chairman, Abe sought to get the matter settled on the top level.

"What a sad commentary on a political party that selects for the highest office in the gift of a nation, a man so little known, that his own partisans do not know even his name!" cried the *Cleveland Weekly Plain Dealer.* The *Cheshire* (N. H.) *Republican* also asserted this was a strange situation for a party "claiming all the intelligence." The *Rochester Union and Advertiser* suggested that the *bra* was necessary in A*bra*ham. "Nothing can be more appropriate," said the *Advertiser,* "than the shouting of *bra(y)s* by the Lincolnites during the coming campaign."

Actually, it didn't matter whether he was first called Abram and afterwards Abraham, like his patriarchal namesake, said the *Fayette and Union Telegraph* (Connersville, Indiana). "He must wait for the fulfillment of his Presidential hopes till he is older than Abraham was when Sarah bore him his promised son; say, till he is about a hundred and twenty." The *Cleveland Weekly Plain Dealer* declared, "It's of no consequence. The name of Lincoln will figure conspicuously in stud-horse type for a few months, to be sure, but it will never be signed to a White House document."

The Republican journals tried to squeeze some good out of the "name-calling." Said the *Exeter* (N. H.) *News-Letter:* "Abraham . . . means 'father of a great multitude.' So Mr. Lincoln's name indicates that he is drawing a great multitude after him, and is destined to become the head of this great and multitudinous nation, as Abraham of old was the father of Israel."

Old Abe's name made splendid promotion copy—it recalled weatherbeaten log cabins, split rails, homespun clothes, and old family Bibles. However, the *Republican Farmer* (Bridgeport, Conn.) asserted in late summer that many Republican journals were dropping "like hot potatoes" "endearing names" such as Honest Old Abe. "Has the upward tendency of the public nose been influential in the matter?" asked the *Farmer*. The answer might well have been that of a Republican speaker at Beverly, New Jersey, who declared that Lincoln's name "can't be rubbed out; we'll rub it in from now till next November."

There was a question, said the *Weekly Illinois State Journal,* whether Abe's name was pronounced Link-on, Link-um, or Ling-kun. In Illinois, said the *Journal,* he was "Old Abe Linkem." A toast to bachelors at a jubilee in New York State recommended that they "add a Link-on."

In view of Abraham's length, the *Albany Atlas and Argus* thought his name should be spelled Lank-un. The *Republican Farmer* noted that Republicans called their Illinois candidate the "tall Sucker" but that these voters would be the tall suckers if he were elected.

To the *State Journal*, there was a singular "fitness of things" in the names of Lincoln and his running mate, Hamlin. It noted that the last syllable of Abraham Lincoln's first name and the first syllable of his last name made the name of the Vice Presidential candidate—that is, "Abra (Hamlin) coln." It was impossible at Chicago to have Abraham Lincoln's name on the ticket, observed the *Springfield* (Mass.) *Daily Republican*, without Hamlin's being there also. A Kentucky paper asserted Lincoln's name really was Linkhorn. If this should prove true, said another newspaper, "what becomes of the 'first syllable of the last name and the last syllable of the first name' that we have heard so much about?" The Republican team was referred to by some papers as the Chinese ticket— Lin-con and Ham-lin.

So the corny punning went on and on. One newspaper noted that both Abraham Lincoln's and Hannibal Hamlin's names each contained just fourteen letters. A correspondent for the *Portsmouth* (N. H.) *Journal* pointed out that the name of Abraham Lincoln contained the letters which make Hamlin's first name, Hannibal, and left six letters—O. A. L. R. M. C. These, of course, signified "Old Abe Lincoln, Rail Maker Candidate."

The *Cherry Valley* (N. Y.) *Gazette* poked fun at such name games by noting that in Abraham Lincoln's name alone "we can find the words ham, ram, lam, calm, cram; and the words, man, ban, clan, and nan; to say nothing of ball, call, mall, and Hall!" If this does not prove Lincoln "peculiarly fit for the Presidency of the United States, why nothing else does, that's all."

Playing with the name of the Vice-Presidential candidate, Hamlin, the *New Albany* (Ind.) *Daily Ledger* noted that *Ham* was the name of the first colored man. It added that "there is a disposition often seen in the human race to preserve family names, and the Republicans seem to follow the old custom." The *Daily Chicago Herald* also asserted that the Republican devotion to the interest of Ham's descendants, seemed apparent in the fact that in "Abra*ham Ham*lin" the Republican Party begins and ends "with its index finger pointing to the colored race." The *New Albany* (Ind.) *Daily Ledger* noted that the last syllable of Abraham Lincoln's first name and the first syllable of Hamlin's last name suggest swine. "We trust," said the *Ledger,* "this important fact won't induce them to make hogs of themselves because they got the nomination for nothing."

A particular target of the newspaper jesters was the name "Abe." The *Boston Courier* had claimed it was impossible for Lincoln to attain the Presidential chair because *Abe* lacked an *l* of being *able*. In rebuttal, the *Weekly Illinois State Journal* pointed out that he had the *L*—Abe L-incoln. A Boston journal charged that "Old Abe" was deficient in *Abe-ility*. Another newspaper retorted that with "Abe" Lincoln at the head of the Government and "Bill" Seward as a cabinet officer, the government would be conspicuous for *Abe-Bill-ity*. A *Columbian Weekly Register* (New Haven, Conn.) item suggested that if Lincoln were elected, the Presidential office probably would be Abe-used. Lincoln's alleged—but unproven—sympathy with anti-slavery radicals prompted a recommendation that Honest Abe be rechristened Abe-olition.

Considerable attention was focused on the "Honest" part of the "Honest Abe" nickname. Lincoln was called "Honest" Abe, said the *Washington Constitution,* to distinguish him from the rest of his party. The *Dover* (N.H.) *Gazette* declared that the label itself created suspicion. "How many gulls do they expect to catch with that kind of chaff?" asked the *Gazette*. Lincoln acquired the appellation, declared the *New Albany* (Ind.) *Daily Ledger,* when he carelessly ruined a book he had borrowed, and then agreed to pay for it by pulling fodder.

"What a description is this for the Chief Magistrate of thirty millions of people—he is an 'honest man,' " cried the *Topeka Tribune*. "Wonderful! Just so might a fool be 'honest,' and yet would this entitle him to the office of President?" The *Republican Farmer* (Bridgeport, Conn.) asserted that many of the Republican papers were dropping the title of "honest" when speaking of their candidate because "his acts and pilfering when in Congress showed that he never was deserving of having that word prefixed to his name."

The Republicans, nevertheless, were mighty proud of the title "Honest," which represented a quality they thought exceedingly rare in Democratic circles. The *New-Hampshire Statesman* (Concord) declared that honesty could not possibly be carried to a market where it was more needed than in Washington. A Springfield clergyman, after pointing to the political corruption in the Illinois capital, noted that virtually all public men seemed to be liars, but that he had never heard anyone accuse Lincoln of intentional dishonesty and corruption. Lincoln, the *New York Daily Tribune* declared, was "sterling stuff, which may always be relied upon for perfect integrity, and constant fidelity to duty."

A few papers also philosophized about the "Old" in "Honest Old Abe." The *Newark Daily Advertiser* emphasized that it was a term of endearment for the fifty-one-year-old candidate. It carried mellow and affectionate recollections as in the words "should auld acquaintance be forgot?"

Some journals dug up other ways to dangle the name of Lincoln in the spotlight. For instance, the *Jerseyman* (Morristown) reported a Republican Club with seven men named Lincoln as officers and committeemen. The *New York Evening Post* told a story of General Washington's deputing General Lincoln, who the *Post* said was a relative of Abe, to receive the sword of Cornwallis at Yorktown in 1781, "which you know was the last of George the Third." It added that Lincoln, representing the principles of Washington, would receive the staff of office from James Buchanan, and this "will be the last of the Democratic party for centuries to come."

Seven of the fifteen Presidents of the United States had surnames ending with "N", a Massachusetts newspaper reminded. This fact, it added, must be N-couraging to Lincoln and Hamlin.

Newspaper writers played merrily with the names of other Presidential candidates, too. The *Painesville* (Ohio) *Telegraph* noted that an Illinois editor termed Douglas "The Pitt of America." It added that "the American Pitt is *Dug.*" *The Easton* (Pa.) *Times* said of Stephen A. Douglas:

> Little Dug will be sadly affected
> Whate'er his political lot;
> He'll remain S.A.D. if elected,
> And be S.A.D. if he's not!

The Southern Democratic team was rated O. K. by their supporters, since Lane was from *O*regon and Breckinridge from *K*entucky. The *Exeter* (N.H.) *News-letter* declared, on the other hand, that "if the Douglas Democrats have a hard road to travel, the other sort have a hard Lane to run."

Bell, the Constitutional Union entry, suffered his share of jibes. His party was said to be so small it had to be *Bell-ed.* A compromise group straining to straddle the Mason-Dixon line, this party was compared to an old cow eating grass on one side of a little brook and switching her tail on the other side. Party leaders were termed "dumb-Bells" and "Bell-zebubs."

Concerning a Washington item about the purchase of a "new bell" there, the *Painesville* (Ohio) *Telegraph* remarked: "We know of a certain Old Bell that wants to ring in there, but we're afraid he'll be tolled to stay out."

Thus was waged the war of words.

Lincoln's physical appearance, especially his height and "homeliness," was a factor of particular interest in the campaign. A speaker in Boston's Faneuil Hall, according to the *Weekly Illinois State Journal,* said that "A man 6 feet 4 inches high is found seldom except on a prairie. It is a way they have of looking up and peeping over, for they are always aspiring to look beyond the horizon."

This speaker was referring to the longest of "The Long Nine." These were nine representatives from Sangamon County to the Illinois Legislature in the 1830's. Each was more than six feet tall.

Lincoln took considerable pride in that lengthiness, and he rarely passed up an opportunity to measure. When a long, lanky Missourian visited him during the campaign, the Presidential aspirant suggested, "Let us measure." The Missourian was backed against the wall and warned to be honest and stand flat on his heels while his height was measured with a stick.

Lincoln and Hamlin together, the *Topeka Tribune* explained, were twelve feet five inches tall. The Republican standard would not be lowered in their hands, one newspaper declared. Another journal, however, reflecting on the height of Lincoln and his six-foot, eleven-inch Indiana supporter, Mr. Buskirk, exclaimed, "What a fall they'll have!"

Abe was somewhat stooped and, said the *Delawarean* (Dover), "if a line were let fall perpendicular from the crown of his head to the sole of his foot, it would cut him in two about three times." A *Springfield* (Mass.) *Daily Republican* item was more harsh. It said:

Lincoln is the leanest, lankest, most ungainly mass of legs, arms, and hatchet-face ever strung upon a single frame. He has most unwarrantably abused the privilege which all politicians have of being ugly. . . . We would regard his election as a national calamity.

Newspapers differed on Lincoln's dimensions as well as his name. The *Republican Farmer* (Bridgeport, Conn.) declared Lincoln "is now said to stand six feet four inches in his stock-

ing feet. A month ago he was only six feet three. This shows
the effect of a presidential nomination upon physical growth.
It is more rapid than ordinary guano." The *Fayette and Union
Telegraph* (Connersville, Ind.) said Lincoln was understood
to be six feet three before the election, was declared to be six
feet four immediately after the election, but recently was described as "a little less than six feet four." In continued:

So from stretching an inch on hearing the news of success, he is
now, under the poor prospects of success, shrinking back to his
former dimensions—still he is more than half as long as the fence
rails split by him, and now sold in the market at $10 each. We
hope the Republican papers will keep the public posted of his expansion and contraction under the alternating prospects of the
campaign.

The *Albany Atlas and Argus* was surprised "to hear Lincoln's grown," but wouldn't be surprised "to hear Lincoln's
groan" in November.

The *New London* (Conn.) *Daily Star* compared Lincoln,
the American splitter of rails, with Tom Sayers, the English
splitter of noses. Lincoln was also compared with his opponent, Stephen A. Douglas, who reached only half-way between
Lincoln's elbow and shoulder, according to the *Norfolk
County Journal* (Roxbury, Mass.). An alleged discussion of
the subject in 1858 by this star debate team was printed in
the *Jonesboro* (Ill.) *Gazette*. Lincoln reportedly said that
Douglas reminded him of a scriptural quotation: "The way of
the wicked is short." Douglas responded, "And you remind
me, Mr. Lincoln, of another passage: 'How long, O Lord,
how long!' "

Lincoln's not-so-natty dress was another conversation
piece. After the nomination he bought some new store clothes,
but some of his Springfield friends became concerned that he
might be "putting on airs" with such Sunday-go-to-meetin'
garb.

The case of the new beard was a favorite newspaper subject in the later stages of the 1860 campaign. Lincoln had received a letter from a Grace Bedell, an eleven-year-old girl in western New York state, who thought he would improve his looks with a beard, "for your face is so thin." Lincoln answered her personally and then got busy growing a beard, an ornament not then fashionable in the United States.

A *San Francisco Herald* item noted that Old Abe was sprucing up for his Washington visit. "He has been growing his whiskers, curling his hair, and waxing his mustache to such an extent daily, that he is now described as looking very handsome. His whiskers are considered as particularly becoming, filling his gaunt cheeks and hiding his long, lank jawbones."

The Washington *Confederation* said it accepted Lincoln's whiskers as an indication he would not thereafter "be so barefaced." In another issue the newspaper became more severe:

The oil that a less wise man would have thrown upon the troubled waters, he reserves for his nascent moustaches.

What better evidence for fitness of Empire, than to grow an Imperial? Who knows but that the pillars of confederation may be held together by a Sampson that refuses to be shorn?

We think we see Mr. Lincoln duly studying before the glass the growing beauties of his comely face! Nero did so, in the intervals of fiddling!

Artists, sculptors, and photographers trekked to Springfield, both before and after the whiskers, to record the Great Man of the West. The young Republicans in Newark exhibited large photographs of Lincoln and Hamlin taken by Mathew B. Brady, who later won fame as a Civil War photographer. A group of New York Young Republicans displayed "Barry's fine crayon portrait of Lincoln."

A few people found it in their hearts to laud Lincoln's looks. An Episcopalian rector of Springfield, Illinois, spoke of Lincoln's fine head and expressive face, the fire lying deep within his eyes, his black hair without a touch of gray, his whole look open and honest. The *Portsmouth* (N. H.) *Journal* said of lithographs of "Honest Old Abe Lincoln": "It does look like a man of good sense and much endurance; but quite unlike a dandy, beau, or bully. Without any such beauty as glitters in the drawing room, there are abundant marks of intelligent thought, quiet humor, and reserve power." An item in the *Sacramento* (Calif.) *Daily Union* asserted that the pretended portraits of Lincoln were caricatures of the vilest description. "He has a strong, manly, cordial, winning look, which attracts everyone. . . . He is handsome after the style of General Jackson, Henry Clay, and other men of that type . . ." In other words, he had a homely type of handsomeness. Another newspaper thought he had a "grizzly affability."

Using this guarded approach, one campaigner found Lincoln pretty good-looking except for a protruding lip. Another admitted Lincoln was not handsome but declared his "voice is truly melodious." The *Weekly Wisconsin Patriot* (Madison) gave Lincoln a left-handed compliment, asserting Abe was not "so mortally ugly" as *Harper's Weekly* engravings showed him. "If he were," the *Patriot* added, "he might set up a hardware store in Springfield with the jacknives presented to him in his travels."

A Massachusetts newspaper announced that a new engraving of Lincoln could be purchased safely even by an expectant mother.

Lincoln sometimes joked good-naturedly about his illtreatment by nature. One time, according to the *Easton* (Pa.) *Times,* he told a crowd that as an infant he was so handsome that ladies borrowed him just to feast their eyes on him. Then someone forgot and left him out all night and the dew warped and destroyed his beauty.

The *Albany Atlas and Argus,* after calling Lincoln the ugliest man in the Union, ungainly as a scarecrow, and with the complexion of an octoroon, related this anecdote:

A rough-looking Western hunter met him on the prairie. . . . The hunter leveled his musket. "Hold there!" cried Lincoln, "you don't mean to shoot me?" "Yes, sir," was the answer; "I pledged myself if I ever saw a worse-looking man than myself, I would shoot him." "Well," replied Lincoln, "if I look worse than you do, fire away."

Lincoln looked "like a monkey taking medicine," said the *Prairie* (Wis.) *du Chien Courier*. But it explained that the facial contortions probably were caused by his swallowing that nauseating dose, Republicanism. One newspaper tickled the opposition with a misprint: "Hurrah for Old Ape!"

A Chicago boy selling woodcuts of Lincoln cried, " 'ere's yer likeness of Abe Lincoln—looks better wen it gets its 'ead shampooed and 'air cut!" The *New Albany* (Ind.) *Daily Ledger* cast aspersions at a picture of Lincoln in the *Vincennes* (Ind.) *Gazette,* declaring it resembled the "before taking" drawings in the advertisement of "McLean's Strengthening Cordial and Blood Purifier." This "before" sketch showed a ghastly, emaciated wretch. A *New York Times* article said no one would vote for Lincoln were he proved a saint if he looked as much like a devil as his picture in the *Milwaukee Sentinel*. He would be able to split rails simply by looking at them, it contended. An *Easton* (Pa.) *Times* item commented that Abe looked like the devil and "we are a little afraid he will run like the devil."

A Connecticut newspaper suggested that if Lincoln looked like his pictures, he could be most useful sitting on a rail near a cornfield. And a *New York Leader* item snorted:

A horrid looking wretch he is! Sooty and scoundrelly in aspect —a cross between the nutmeg-dealer, the horse-swapper, and the nightman—a creature "fit, evidently, for petty treason, small stratagems, and all sorts of 'spoils.' He is a lank-sided, slab-sided Yankee of the uncomeliest visage and dirtiest complexion."

Lincoln looked as though he had been dragged through a

knothole and then beaten with a soot-bag, said one journalist; and to another he "defies and exhausts every effort of the cruel freaks of nature to multilate his looks." The *New Albany* (Ind.) *Daily Ledger* conjectured that Lincoln's education was held back because he was too ugly to get into a respectable school. The *Saint Anthony Weekly Express* (Hennepin County, Minn.) reported a rumor that certain Minnesota businessmen were petitioning the town council to haul down a street-banner portrait of Old Abe because it was scaring customers away. Lincoln's attempts at wit during speeches, said a *Washington Constitution* item, were chiefly remarkable for the contortions of the face, "which he has no right to render uglier than nature forms it." It then swung into verse:

> You ask why Abe diverts you with his jokes,
> Yet, if he writes, is dull as other folks;
> You wonder at it; this, sir, is the case—
> The jest is lost unless he prints his face!

A lengthy poem in the *Constitution* suggested that in the attempt to keep people from thinking about Lincoln's ugliness the Republicans "tell us" about Lincoln's fight with Douglas, his splitting cordwood, his genial humor, his resemblance to Jackson, and his avoidance of whiskey. The concluding verse was:

> Any lie you tell we'll swallow—
> Swallow any kind of mixture;
> But, oh! don't, we beg and pray you—
> Don't, for God's sake, show his picture!

A non-Republican speaker asserted the Republicans had injured Lincoln by printing his portrait and that he would have grounds for libel suits. An article in the *New York Times* elaborated on a "hideous" Lincoln photo "pressed into service" by the *Albany Evening Journal*. "What necessity," the *Times* asked, "existed for disfiguring its clean and well-cut columns with the ungainly engravings of a wood-chopper . . . ?

It is impossible to say what effect the *Journal's* indiscretion may have upon babies and nervous women."

The *Milwaukee News* poked this fun at the *Milwaukee Sentinel:*

> The Sentinel has at last become ashamed of the portrait of Lincoln . . . it was so expressive, so life-like; a countenance beaming so full with intelligence, of patriotism, of high and lofty emotions, of grandeur, of beauty, of sublimity, of sternness, of sobriety, of sincerity, of energy, of fixedness of purpose, of morality, of—of Black Republicanism, that we cannot conceive the motives which led to its displacement. Do put it back again.

The *New York Daily Tribune* struck back at such satire. "They cannot find a charge to make against his integrity, uprightness, purity and honor, but take exception to his ornamental qualities only."

Cartoons as well as photographs figured prominently in the 1860 campaign. The *Washington Constitution* described one of them:

> The large picture in *Vanity Fair* for this week, represents Mr. Abraham Blondin De Lave Lincoln, in tights, undertaking to cross a chasm like that below Niagara Falls, on a *rail,* which is giving way. The performer balances himself with a pole, and carries a carpet bag, with a little frightened nigger in it. An interested spectator on the brink of the chasm looking some like H. G. (Horace Greeley), is exclaiming "Don't drop the carpet bag!"

One issue of the *Cleveland Weekly Plain Dealer* devoted four full columns to cartoons ribbing the Republicans. It was headed "Great Republican Exhibition of the Connecticut Western Reserve, at Cleveland, October 4th, 1860." The drawings caricatured the delegations from Cleveland, Oberlin, "Ashtabuly" and Toledo. A cartoon used in another paper showed "a 'rail' old western gentleman." Rails formed the body, arms and legs, with Lincoln's head on top. Another cartoon showed a Negro and Greeley carrying Lincoln on a rail, representing the Republican platform. Still another depicted "the Republican party going to the right house." Greeley was carrying Lincoln on a rail into a "lunatic asylum." They were followed by a group of would-be social reformers. One caricature showed a Democratic vehicle with a span of horses hitched at each end—one pair driven by Douglas and the other by Breckinridge—and pulling in opposite directions. The wagon stood directly in the path of the onrushing Republican locomotive, with Lincoln in the engine cab.

★★★

CHAPTER EIGHT

THE RAIL-SPLITTERS HARMONIZE

Hear the shout of freedom rising,
O'er our mountains, o'er our dales,
'Tis for Lincoln, brave and stalwart—
He's the boy to split the rails!
Split the rails a nation's wanting
For the fence she's building West;
Guarding, with a wall of freemen,
Slavery from her virgin breast.

Republicans were "relieving their lungs," as the Democrats put it, with songs like that during the campaign of 1860. The opposition insisted the Republicans were determined to make up in song what their nominations lacked in reason, but they would "sing small" in November.

Contributors of Republican songs included such heavy-weight names as James Russell Lowell, John Greenleaf Whittier, William Cullen Bryant, and Horace Greeley. Many songs, especially those written by lesser lights, were emotional, like hymns. In fact, an edition of the *Wide-Awake Vocalist, or Rail-Splitter's Song Book* was a hymnal. The publisher, who also printed Sunday School hymn books, accidentally put the Wide-Awake cover on the hymnal. Political songsters were warbling "We Are Passing Away to the Great Judgement Day," "We Are Going to Sin No More," and "A Home in Glory," before they realized what had happened.

Republican glee clubs were organized, a favorite being "Old Abe's Choir" which provided melody for many rallies. A touring Springfield, Ill., Republican Glee Club journeyed as far as Cass County, Va., with their vocalizations.

One of the campaign songs began, "Brightly smiling on our cause, heavenly hosts rejoice." The opposition acknowledged that the moonstruck rhymesters should be allowed considerable license, but thought all bounds were exceeded when "the angels of heaven are roped wholesale into the support of Lincoln."

This was a typical Republican campaign song:

> *Our leader is one who, with conquerless will,*
> *Has climb'd from the base to the brow of the hill . . .*
> *Right loyal and brave, with no stain on his crest,*
> *Then, hurrah, boys, for Honest "Old Abe of the West!"*
> *And fling out your banner, the old starry banner,*
> *The signal of triumph for "Abe of the West!"*

Another went like this:

> *With ballots for bullets,*
> *Let this be your cry;*
> *With Lincoln and Hamlin*
> *We'll conquer or die.*

In still another the Republicans declared: "We'll rout that traitor Douglas, and all his kit and ken, and fill their places quickly with good and honest men." And another, extolling Lincoln's honesty, noted that that virtue would be a great curiosity in Washington.

Of course rail-splitting was a frequent theme:

> *The Democratic log is laid*
> *For Lincoln's wedge to split it;*
> *See how the op'ning rive was made,*
> *The moment Ab'ram hit it.*

Then drive the wedge, my jolly boys,
We'll split the log "by thunder,"
Let's cheer "Old Abe" with heart and voice,
Till Democrats give under.

Stephen A. Douglas, the Northern Democratic candidate, was heckled in some Republican songs. One of these said:

Dug's career is almost passed;
Heigh-ho, heigh-ho,
Though his mischief long will last;
Heigh-ho, heigh-ho.
His name is now a jest and scoff,
The South—when he was worn enough—
Like an old shoe just kicked him off,
Heigh-ho, heigh-ho.

Then let poor little Duggy go;
Heigh-ho, heigh-ho
But we must clip his wings you know;
Heigh-ho, heigh-ho.

The Little Giant was also featured in a melancholy number called "Poor Little Doug":

Dere was a little man and his name was Stevy Doug,
To de White House he longed for to go—
But he hadn't any votes through de whole of de Souf,
In de place where votes ought to grow.

So it ain't no use for to blow—
Dat little game of brag won't go;
He can't get de vote, 'cause de tail ob his coat
Is hung just a little too low.

The opposition also resorted to verse. This sample was carried in a South Carolina newspaper:

Resolved, once more, as we are "John Jones"
Who'll bring the South upon her bones—

A craven set of Knaves.
From Africa's sons we'll loose their gyves
And give them Yankee girls for wives.
And turn ourselves their slaves.

Resolved, (and thus to air the trick),
That to the Negro we must stick,
Till Lincoln takes the chair;
But after that the cuss may go
To Giddings, Sumner, Hale & Co.,
Or H***—for what we care.

King-sized banners went campaigning, too. At a rally at Palestine, Illinois, reported the *Weekly Illinois State Journal,* a Lincoln-Hamlin banner eighty feet long was displayed. The Sixteenth Ward Republicans of New York City inscribed in bunting on their Eighth Avenue headquarters these words by William Cullen Bryant of the *New York Evening Post:* "It is written in the Book of Fate that Abraham Lincoln will be the next President of the United States."

Suspending a campaign banner often was made the excuse for a celebration. A New Hampshire newspaper described such a festival when a large Lincoln-Hamlin banner was stretched across the village street, with "a large number of the sturdy men of the town" in attendance, together with "a numerous sprinkling of the fair sex, whose ballots, if they were permitted to be cast, would bury sham Democracy deeper than the sound of the resurrection can penetrate."

The legend on one banner played upon the names of President "Buck" Buchanan, a couple of former Presidents, and two aspirants. It read "We Polked them in 1844; we Pierced them in 1852; We Bucked them in 1856; we're Breck-ing now and our grave is Doug"!

Testimonials and similar gimmicks were used. The *Louisville Daily Courier* reported that General Tom Thumb, advertised by Barnum as the smallest man alive, was a member of the Little Giants Club, at Bridgeport, Conn. Out in Wisconsin, the *Appleton Crescent* announced that "the Big Giant who exhibited himself at Appleton the day of the circus, is out for Douglas, the Little Giant."

The Republicans reprinted across the land a testimonial by John Hanks, Lincoln's old rail-splitting partner and a Jackson Democrat, which declared he "never knew a man so honest under all circumstances for his whole life as Lincoln."

The reverse twist also was applied. The *New Hampshire Patriot* declared that a Black Republican desperado had been released from jail in Milwaukee and had gone stumping for "Old Abe." Should Lincoln be elected, the item continued, this criminal probably would be sent on a foreign mission or appointed a U. S. marshal.

The campaign stormed its way into the marketplace. "BIG ABE is on hand at the Cooper Market today for inspection and will be distributed to the customers tomorrow," the *Fond du Lac* (Wis.) *Commonwealth* announced. "He is altogether the biggest ox ever brought into this city. Nine cents per pound for the best cuts." The *Cherry Valley* (N. Y.) *Gazette* reported the arrival at the New York Cattle Market of a thirty-three-year-old yoke of oxen, owned in their juvenile days by Abraham Lincoln.

On the Charles River, a boat was christened the "Honest Abe." Rufus Merrill and Son, Concord, N. H., advertised for agents in "every town" to sell its "Paper and Envelopes, embellished with a picture of Lincoln". The *Bellows Falls* (Vt.) *Argus* reported that Lincoln potatoes were advertised in Syracuse; Douglas roosters in Chemung, New York; Breckinridge setters by a dog-dealer; and Bell metal by a Philadelphia foundry. B. F. Wilson, Boston, announced "choice cigars: the Honest Old Abe, the Little Giant, and the Bell of the Union." If voters found this commercial campaigning too straining, they could go to the corner drug store and buy "Wigwam Tonic" to help pull them through the campaign.

Honoring the Young Republican marching clubs, "Wide-Awake" hats were placed on sale, dealers asserting the owner of one "feels really wide awake and enthusiastic." An ad in the *New York Evening Post* declared "Barnum is fully 'Wide-awake,' and is adding to the attractions of the Museum. The latest arrival is the 'Siamese Twins.' "

A new newspaper in St. Peter, Minnesota, was christened the *Little Giant*. On the Republican side of the fence was the *Rail-Splitter*, printed in Chicago.

Newspaper ads played it safe, usually, for the merchants loved all their cash customers, of whatever party. "The four candidates for the Presidency are each hopeful of success in the coming campaign," one advertisement began. "There is not as much certainty in politics as there is in the fact that Redding's Russia Salve cures cuts, bruises, burns, scalds, corns, etc."

"We notice that none of the candidates," said a *New York Leader* ad, "are so popular and hold up their heads so confidently as those who buy their clothing of F. B. Baldwin, no. 70 and 72 Bowery." In the *Weekly Illinois State Journal* readers could find this gratifying information: "The time is drawing near which will decide the exciting contest for President. It has, however, been long decided that Hammerslough Brothers' is the place to buy the very best of winter clothing. . . ."

Sometimes because of the name, the rose didn't smell as sweet. A large Eastern textile manfacturer had been producing "Lincoln cotton drilling" for years. Some dealers tried unsuccessfully to get him to drop the "Lincoln", which now hurt sales south of Mason and Dixon's line.

An Indiana newspaper announced that "Honest Old Alvah" had a lot of buggies for sale. Later it revealed that Alvah Woodstock hadn't appreciated being called "Honest Old Alvah." "We take it all back, Alvah," the newspaper apologized. "We did not mean to say you was *honest*."

Political flag poles, proportioned to the oversized campaign banners, were erected in many communities. The *New York Tribune* noted that a great many people on Staten Island, including many reformed Democrats, joined in raising poles from which they suspended an immense banner for Lincoln and Hamlin. Far away, on the Pacific coast, the *Daily Alta California* (San Francisco) reported that a 130-foot liberty pole was raised by the Lincoln club. In a letter in the *Tri-Weekly Missouri Republican* (St. Louis) a woman complained that her politically aroused husband chopped down an elegant Lombardy poplar from their front lawn to make a pole, then ripped up her wedding garments for the Lincoln banner.

The Democrats, too, put up some powerful poles, one a 215-foot Douglas pole at Crestline, Ohio.

The politicos poked fun at the pole-raising efforts of the "enemy" camps. A Douglas Democrat described the erection of a Republican pole made from a burr oak fifteen feet long, and spliced with a ten-foot tamarack. On top floated an eight by ten-inch flag. On one side, he asserted, was the name "Lincoln"; on the other "Lincon." He assumed the second was the Vice-Presidential candidate. When the pole was set up, he said, three faint cheers were given for "the two Lincons."

The following notice of a Democratic pole-raising was published in Marion, Ohio, according to the *Painesville* (Ohio) *Telegraph:*

NOTOS,—A great duggless meetin is to cum off on Saterde the 14teenth and a poll is to be razed we want to let um no daoun sowth that mary ann kounty is awl rite and that kent go nigger heer we are skawattur soverings and beleeve in the pepul roolin. . . .

A jolly good sport in 1860 was razing the poles which had been erected by the opposition. After one pole was chopped down, a newspaper termed the guilty party a "miserable, infamous, low-flung, narrow-minded, ungodly, dirt-eating, cut-throat, hemp-deserving, deeply-dyed, double-distilled, concentrated, miscreant of miscreants." The *Detroit Free Press* reported that a Democratic farmer near Metamora, Ohio, had erected a large hickory pole topped by a Douglas flag, and it was cut down by "Black Republican ruffians" while the farmer attended a Douglas meeting. A Republican pole raised in Occoquan, Virginia, created such a rumpus that the few Republicans there asked the Governor for military protection of the pole, and it was provided. But quiet was restored to the community only after the obnoxious Republican symbol was removed.

But it was rails rather than poles that figured most in the campaigning. John Hanks and Richard J. Oglesby probably had little idea what they were starting when they introduced the weathered rails into the Illinois State Convention earlier that year. The prestige of rail-splitting spread beyond Old Abe and the Sucker State to encompass his son, Bob, who was attending school in New England. His classmates crowned him "The Prince of Rails" and asserted he was a "chip off the old rail."

Anti-Republicans ridiculed Lincoln's skill with the maul, suggesting he be patented as a rail-splitting machine. The *Vermont Patriot* (Montpelier) reported that the number of rails split by Lincoln had been estimated as high as 150,000, and to prove the point, *two* of them were exhibited at the Chicago Convention. The *Daily Chicago Herald* declared that Lincoln became interested in this endeavor when he was a "big chunk of a boy" and began to appreciate jokes. He was accustomed, at the point where the laugh came in, to exclaim amidst spasms, "O! I shall split, I shall split." When he was eighteen, the *Herald* continued, he averaged 76,000 rails a day, and then for relaxation, split two or three cords of firewood for his mother in the evening. Another newspaper said some of the rails were "like the Republican party, as crooked as a dog's hind leg."

All the rails alleged to have been split by Old Abe, according to the *New Albany* (Ind.) *Daily Ledger,* would make a ten-rail fence from the North to the South Pole. And this accomplishment by a man who, his supporters claimed, "was never on the fence in his life." The *Indianapolis Sentinel* suggested that anyone who had timber should split it right away. "There will be half a million of 'identical rails' sold this year at high prices," it prophesied. Another Indiana paper asserted that an Eastern Yankee had started a rail factory in Illinois to produce rails "split by Abe Lincoln."

There was a great demand for Lincoln rails. [*Century Magazine* in 1900 quoted Mr. Oglesby.] John Hanks sold the two that he had brought into the Convention. A man from Kentucky gave him five dollars for one. The next day he went out and got a wagon-load, and put them in my barn. He sold them for a dollar apiece, then other people went into the business, and the supply seemed inexhaustible.

It was carried aloft in parades; flaming banners fluttered from it at rallies; glee-clubs sang its praises; campaign clubs proudly called themselves "rail-splitters," "rail-maulers," and "rail-splitter wide-awakes;" lusty men, mounted on huge wagons, split rails as processions moved along; and Lincoln rails (of unquestioned authenticity) adorned hundreds of homes.

Pennsylvania Republicans, according to the *Springfield* (Mass.) *Daily Republican,* sent agents to Macon County, Illinois, to try to buy the whole fence built by Lincoln and Hanks and ship it East.

In a Wide-Awake procession at Binghamton, New York, the marchers executed a "rail-fence" drill which drew applause. At a Connecticut parade a couple of lads followed at a safe distance, carrying a third boy on one of the Republican steeds —a rail. Following their parade, Wide-Awakes in another New England community were given a bountiful entertainment, "prominent in which was a rail fence made of doughnuts."

A craft on the Mississippi River, said the *Weekly Illinois*

State Journal, sported a Lincoln Coat of Arms—a twenty-foot rail topped by crossed axe and maul. An Ohio state senator had a tobacco hogshead made of rails split by Honest Old Abe, as an inscription on each stave attested. Filled with choice Ohio tobacco, it was received at a Baltimore warehouse.

Rails were shipped to many cities to be displayed in Republican Wigwams. Some rails, according to Democratic newspapers, were mailed under the frank of Republican Congressmen. Political orators toted Lincoln rails in stumping the states. Speakers' platforms at rallies sometimes were made of rails. Republicans even planned to shove their rails under the "corrupt administration" in Washington and upset the Democrats who "have been revelling for the last eight years."

With all this attention focused on the Lincoln-ware, the *New York Atlas* declared that "fence rails has riz." A pretended stock-market quotation indicated that "rails were up and very much in demand." A Cincinnatian reportedly paid twenty dollars for one pair of rails. A New Englander charged that all the fence rails around his two-acre lot were pilfered one night and the *Republican Farmer,* (Bridgeport, Conn.) conjectured they would all be used by the "Abolition Republicans" as "the rails that Abe split."

An Eastern man bought Lincoln rails to fashion into canes for sale during the campaign, said the *New-Hampshire Patriot* (Concord), which also surmised, in another item, that Illinois rails would be cut up, like the Hartford Charter Oak, into small bits to ornament breast pins and watches of ardent Republicans. An enterprising young businessman sold Abe Lincoln rail splinters at five cents per dozen, reported the *Jonesboro* (Ill.) *Gazette.* The young speculator claimed he had received them direct from Springfield. And the *Albany Atlas and Argus* snickered about an "Abolition" flagstaff in Connecticut which had been converted into Old Abe's rails— when it was struck by lightning.

So Old Abe, like a locomotive, was running mostly on rails,

as the *Manhattan* (Kan.) *Express* put it. Although some people asserted that Lincoln was more successful as a storyteller sitting on rails than splitting them, the legend of the great splitter of rails grew and grew. The *Fayette and Union Telegraph* (Connersville, Ind.) quipped that "The illustrious rail split by the divinely honest hands of Uncle Abe . . . is as the True Cross to the Christian, or the green turban of the Prophet to the Mahometan." The *Binghamton* (N.Y.) *Standard* admitted rail-splitting didn't necessarily make Lincoln more worthy of the Presidential chair, but noted that his background would inspire enthusiasm which hardly could be matched by a silver-spoon candidate. The Republican campaigners even found a Scriptural endorsement: "A man was famous according as he had lifted up axes upon the thick trees" (Psalms 74:5).

The Democrats responded with appropriate "raillery." The *Delawarean* (Dover) pointed to the "set of Jackasses who go round in the hot sun with rails on their backs." The president of the Cincinnati Board of Trade was chastised for "buying up political rails for the wooden-heads who shout and shriek at mass meetings, with lungs whose capacity is in inverse ratio to their brains."

There were references to the "presidential apprenticeship at rail-splitting," "the Lincoln rail road to the Presidency," and "riding on a rail into the Presidential chair." The *Daily Chicago Herald* thought Lincoln's "early capacity for splitting rails and grocery keeping, as well as his more mature accomplishments of whittling store boxes and telling not over-chaste stories, are regarded as quite ordinary village qualifications."

The *New York Atlas* couldn't recollect that any President had ever been called upon, in the discharge of his exalted duties, to split rails. A Wisconsin resident asked that he be considered a Presidential candidate since he had split rails and worn leather breeches.

The *New-Hampshire Patriot* (Concord) thought it was a good thing Republicans didn't know Brigham Young once lived in Cayuga County, New York, and split rails there. If they had, they would have nominated for President a man from the home of Seward, with the accomplishments of Lincoln, who would start his campaign with 75 wives and 240 children.

Stephen A. Douglas once was a cabinet-maker, and the Northern Democrats were quick to make use of the suggested word play. The *Fort Wayne Sentinel* punned: "The Democrats have better timber. They have one who started in life a cabinet-maker, and who will in 1861 be called by the country to resume the business of Cabinet making." One Democratic speaker asserted that voters would send both Lincoln and Douglas back to their original jobs—Lincoln to making rails and Douglas to Cabinet-making. The *Manhattan* (Kan.) *Express* shot back: "Good! and let the first specimen of his handicraft be a cabinet for curiosities—and the first thing deposited shall be that speaker's brain."

Herschel V. Johnson, Douglas' running mate, asserted he had two hundred Negroes who could beat Old Abe in splitting rails, "and so help me God, I would prefer one of them before Old Abe for President!"

An Illinois paper called attention to a log sawed by Stephen A. Douglas when he tended a sawmill part time while teaching school. Although somewhat decayed, the heart was sound, the item said. The *Bucyrus* (Ohio) *Weekly Journal* declared that "Douglas has been sawing away at a 'log somewhat decayed' all his life. After sawing out a number of rotten planks, he sawed it in two at Charleston . . . They [the Democrats] take to rottenness as naturally as a duck does to water."

The divided Democrats were charged with "railing at splits" instead of splitting rails. And there was an anecdote about Douglas comparing Lincoln to a rail, and Lincoln replying that Douglas was the reverse of a rail—that is, rail spelled backwards. Douglas' imbibing was frequently alluded to, and the *Easton* (Pa.) *Times* declared that Old Abe "will split him up in staves to make whiskey barrels next November."

The Democrats prophesied that as soon as the rails gave out the Republicans would come up with Abe's old boots, coats, pants, vests, shirts, and suspenders to be carried around and receive the adulations of the faithful. The devotees of Republicanism, greedy for office, said the *Washington Constitution,* would consider handling Abe's old boots a less honor only to kissing his toe. The *New York Herald* suggested that Republicans might create tremendous excitement by exhibiting other souvenirs of the interesting period when their candidate was fitting himself for the top office by splitting wood. Among the suggested objects were: the handle of the maul with which Lincoln split his first rail, a chew of tobacco masticated while doing the work, waistband of breeches split during the operation, portrait of the man who stood against the tree watching Old Abe split the rail, and horns of the oxen that hauled the rail.

The doorsill of the Kentucky cabin where Abraham Lincoln was born was exhibited in Cincinnati. The *Washington Constitution* predicted that the man who abased himself most before this newest "object of idolatry" would get a political plum from Lincoln. "Great is Diana of the Ephesians!" it cried. At a Peoria rally a gavel, made from a log of the Lincoln cabin, was presented. "Barnum now advertises that he has the iron pap-spoon with which Abe was fed while teething," said the *New York Leader,* "and that he is in negotiation for the 'bottle' out of which the said Abe imbibed his earliest 'lacteal nutrition.' " Republicans soon were to be supplied with exquisite hankies, scoffed the *Weekly Wisconsin Patriot,* "made from swaddling cloths preserved by Abe's ancient nurse."

☆☆☆

CHAPTER NINE

WIDE-AWAKES, WIGWAMS, AND WHISTLE-STOPS

As much a part of the 1860 campaign as Lincoln rails, and almost as numerous, were the torch-toting Wide-Awakes. Some accounts estimated there were at least 400,000 of these Young Republican tub-thumpers, organized into snappy marching groups.

These Wide-Awakes, reminiscent of the "Log Cabin Boys" of the William Henry Harrison Whig campaign twenty years earlier, wore distinctive garb. The *Newark Daily Advertiser* described the seventy-five cent uniforms there as consisting of a cape of black enameled cloth with white edges and a black glazed cap with a white band. In some communities the words "Wide-Awake" were painted on the uniforms in bold letters. The *Weekly Kentucky Yeoman* (Frankfort) termed the cape the "Cape of Good Hope." These garments, which provided a distinctive symbol, also protected marchers from nasty weather and from dripping oil from the torches. Theoretically, little oil dripped, for the tin containers swung freely in a ring at the top of the torches, like a ship's compass, remaining upright regardless of the tilt at which the Wide-Awake held himself or the handle.

In the Biblical book of Judges the Republicans unearthed a precedent for the Wide-Awakes. The *New York Daily Tribune* reported that Old Gideon, whose three hundred men with lanterns had defeated the enemies of Israel—"the Doug-

137

lasites and Buchananites of that day"—was the first Wide-Awake. The Wide-Awake movement of the 1800's originated in Hartford, Connecticut, according to the *Hartford Courant*. It spread through the Republican realm and even took in a voteless female Wide-Awake club in East Chatham, New York, and a Negro Wide-Awake group in Boston.

The movement was not devised—it just grew, declared the *New York Daily Tribune,* and was "a nation's enthusiasm expressing itself in organization." It was a proclamation, the *Tribune* added, "that righteousness exalteth a nation." The young men often were highly charged with zeal. Wide-Awakes at South Danvers, Massachusetts, said the town's *Wizard,* were "diffused by electric fire. They were as explosive as gun powder." The *New-Hampshire Statesman* (Concord) thus described the Wide-Awake movement:

Who ever saw that glorious procession of variegated lights and banners, dancing above the serried columns of youth, and manly vigor, and, to the strains of martial melody, filing through our streets even at midnight, without being stirred to new hopes, new resolves, new endeavors.

Wide-Awakes were the Republicans' cloud by day and pillar of fire by night.

The Wide-Awakes enlisted "for the war and no furlough," boasted the *Worcester* (Mass.) *Palladium.* The *Palladium* meant the political war of 1860, but *Scribner's,* in 1893, noted that the Wide-Awakes of the Lincoln campaign were preparing themselves for the more serious work ahead, when they would exchange torches for muskets.

The Wide-Awakes made a different impression on the opposition. *The New-Hampshire Patriot* declared them "unmitigated nuisances," and compared them with gangs like the Empires and Knickerbockers of New York and the Plug Uglies, Rip Raps, and Blood Tubs of Baltimore. Opposition jokesters re-named them "Sleep-Walkers" or "Fast-Asleeps."

But their effectiveness was also acknowledged in imitative counter-organizations such as the Democratic "Ever-Readies" of Peoria, Illinois, and Brooklyn's "Chloroform Club"—the latter dedicated to "putting the Black Republican Wide-Awakes to sleep."

The torches elicited some harsh words, too. The *Cleveland Weekly Plain Dealer* reported that "the oil-skin-caped Wide-Awakes were . . . out with their damned old candlesticks." Another paper asserted the election would leave nothing of the Republicans except a strong smell of coal oil.

In the *Hartford Weekly Times* the Wide-Awakes were derided in this rhyme:

> The other night I saw a small procession,
> Which like a row of street lamps broken loose appeared,
> Brilliant at first, but had beyond expression,
> Its nauseous fumes, which only daylight cleared.
> Perhaps, however, we may read the moral,
> Which, if we do, we certainly can joke—
> With Wide-Awakes we'll surely never quarrel,
> If, like their shows, their projects end in smoke.
>
> The Wide-Awakes, whenever they turn out,
> Carry oil-lamps that flame and smoke about,
> Leaving dark smudges over hands and face;
> But we for this a reason well may trace;
> Loving the black man better than all other,
> They black themselves, that they may call him brother.

Wide-Awakes were a semi-military organization which went about at nights with a torch in one hand and a ballot in the other, a Georgia newspaper charged. The *Delawarean* (Dover) ridiculed the Wide-Awakes with this burlesque of their initiation ceremony:

Q. What are the chief objects of the Wide-Awake society?
A. To disturb Democratic meetings, and to furnish conductors for the underground railroad.

Q. What is your opinion on the great questions of the day?
A. I believe Abraham Lincoln was born; that he built a flatboat and split three thousand rails. . . .

Q. If you are admitted a member of this society, do you promise to love the nigger, to cherish him as you would a brother, and cleave unto him through evil as well as good report, and hate the Democrats as long as life lasts and water runs?
A. All this I solemnly promise to perform, so help me—Abraham.

The Candidate is then invested with the cape and cap; somebody gives him a slap on the side of the head and tells him to be "Wide-Awake."

A "curtain lecture by a Wide-Awake wife" was published by the *Old Line Guard* (Indianapolis). The wife said, in part:

Talk of sulphuretted hydrogen, or superannuated eggs! They ain't anywhere. Say, where have you been? Here I've been lying awake for the last five hours waiting for you to come home. . . . Had to carry a torch? That's sweet business for a man who pretends to be the father of a large family.

The Wide-Awakes sometimes were badgered about their youthfulness. The *Wizard* (South Danvers, Mass.) reported a night meeting of the "Juvenile Rail Splitters," who came home at a late hour, but "we suppose their Mothers knew they were out." One newspaper, describing a visit of Derby, Connecticut, Wide-Awakes to the nearby town of Seymour, observed that "the plucky men of Derby marched all the way back to their homes again with undiminished courage." The *Columbian Weekly Register* (New Haven, Conn.) retorted: " 'Plucky men of Derby!' they had to pass a burial-ground, take which way they would—and they did it with 'undiminished courage.' "

A mercenary motive in connection with Wide-Awake activities was suggested by the *New York Journal of Commerce*. A shrewd New York City Democrat was alleged to have contracted to furnish two hundred Wide-Awakes for Republican processions. One consideration was that the marchers keep the caps and capes, which made good bad-weather garb.

But most Wide-Awakes, at least, meant business—and not the mercenary kind. Greeley's *Tribune* admonished them: "On the day of battle, don't be preparing a programme for celebrating the victory, don't be burnishing your banners and filling your lamps. Work at the polls from early dawn to set of sun." And in that robust spirit, the Wide-Awakes marched on, chanting:

> *Old Abe Lincoln came out of the wilderness,*
> *Out of the wilderness,*
> *Out of the wilderness,*
> *Old Abe Lincoln came out of the wilderness,*
> *Down in Illinoy.*

Besides the young Wide-Awakes, there were other Republican groups. The Central Republican Club of New York City claimed 1,600 members. It strategically chose its headquarters across the street from the New York Hotel, a rendezvous of Southerners. A *Washington Constitution* item told of a large Hartford, Connecticut, Republican group that had a president "aided by six vices."

There were even some Republican groups in the South. One of that rare species notified the *New York Daily Tribune* of a new Republican club in Portsmouth, Virginia, organized despite the fact that, four years earlier, the city council had ordered the destruction of a Republican Fremont pole, declaring it a disgrace to the community.

Northern Democrats boasted their "Little Giants," "Little Dougs," and other such clubs. The *Easton* (Pa.) *Times* reported that "the Douglas wing of the split-tail democracy have organized a campaign club and call it the 'Douglas Invincibles.' After the election, its members will be 'Douglas Invisibles.' "

Bell-Everett supporters in New York City formed the "Minute Men of the Union." They featured a new-model cheer which consisted of shouting in chorus the separate letters of the word "Union," then the names of Bell and Everett, ending with a simultaneous "Ha!" In some communities there were also "Bell-Ringers," "Bell Everetters," "Clapperites," or "Everett Guard."

Like the Republicans, the men of various other political clubs plunged into colorful parades, torchlight processions, rallies, and barbecues during the 1860 campaign. Of a political display in Boston, the *New-Hampshire Statesman* (Concord) said:

> The city had the appearance at the South End of one sheet of flame, so numerous were the illuminations, while the living line of light was seen for miles winding about, with columns of fire in every direction shooting up into the sky.

A Wide-Awake demonstration in Troy, New York, was described as unequaled in the state. "The imagination can conceive of nothing more picturesque and beautiful," commented the *New York Daily Tribune*. The *New York Times* declared that torches, Roman candles, and rockets in a Manhattan demonstration eclipsed even "the lofty and gilded orbs on street corners that guide the bacchanal to his subterranean orgies," and made "the gas lights glimmer like farthing rushlights in the sun."

According to one newspaper, such masses attended meetings in the West that they were counted, not as so many thousands, but as so many acres. More than two thousand persons were in an Iowa Republican procession, said the Washington *National Intelligencer,* including more than eighty persons who rode on two wagons. Better than twenty thousand attended a Republican gathering in Fairfield, Iowa, the *Daily Gate City* (Keokuk) reported. About a thousand Wide-Awakes stayed all night; in the morning, with flags unfurled and music blaring, they circled the park several times in their wagons before levelling off for home. At another gathering it was misstated that "the air was rent with the snouts of three thousand people!" Lincoln, Illinois, declared the *Weekly Illinois State Journal,* "could scarcely be seen for the people" attending a rally there.

Some opposition newspapers underplayed the throngs. The *New-Hampshire Patriot* (Concord) declared that by "industrious drumming, they succeeded in getting together about half as many people as usually attend other 'nigger shows.' "

Some Republican gatherings were rather special, as when the Philadelphia Wide-Awakes were feted like visiting firemen in New York City. Also quite special was the congratulatory meeting for Lincoln in Springfield, with fireworks "rendering the heavens at one time a sheet of brilliant flame and again spangling it with all manner of beautifully colored lights." The *Weekly Illinois State Journal* report continued:

> The Lincoln Wide-Awakes, meanwhile, were out in large numbers, parading the streets with banners, transparencies, and torches, and going through their various evolutions. In the line of their march they took the residence of Mr. Lincoln, and, having drawn up in front of his door, made the whole neighborhood resound again and again with their repeated cheers for Mr. Lincoln. ... Mr. Lincoln, surrounded by a large number of personal friends, stood upon the doorsteps and bowed in silent acknowledgement of the cheers. . . . They must excuse Mr. Lincoln for making a speech to them now, Senator Trumbull, who was in the crowd, explained. He was under another engagement to address the people on the fourth of March next from the Eastern portico of the Capitol in Washington.

Republican rallies often were preluded by seemingly endless processions of wagons from daybreak on. At a tri-county rally at Rockbridge, Illinois, the Fidelity procession stretched the entire seven miles from that community to Rockbridge. More than five thousand wagons brought the folks to the rally grounds to hear Owen Lovejoy, brother of the murdered abolitionist editor, Elijah P. Lovejoy. A demonstration at Bridge-port, Connecticut, was reported to be fourteen miles long, while a torchlight procession in Lynn, Massachusetts, followed an eight-mile route, covering as much of East Boston "as seemed worth cultivating," explained the *Boston Herald.*

Political parades frequently included wagons carrying pioneers or rail-splitters. At a rally in Indianapolis, one wagon was drawn by forty-three yoke of oxen, the outfit extending more than four hundred feet. One part featured men splitting rails and distributing them along the route. Parades often carried mottos such as "The Union Will Be Preserved—Old Abe Will Fence It In," "Abe Lincoln, the Rail-Splitter, for President," "Homes for the Homeless," and "No Splitters except Rail-Splitters in the Republican Party." A New York City demonstration featured a pioneer cabin with the inscription "Uncle Sam Is Rich Enough to Give Us All a Farm."

Touches of feminine pulchritude frequently were included in the parades. Usually there were thirty-three comely and attractively attired young ladies representing the thirty-three states, with a rag-clad thirty-fourth symbolizing strife-torn Kansas, then knocking at the door of statehood. A Berlin, Illinois, Republican rally featured a large company of charming young ladies in four beautifully ornamented wagons. The *Weekly Illinois State Journal* commented, "The sight of them must have been a sore temptation to the few Democrats present." The *Journal* then erased suspicions by explaining that "each woman is supposed to be able to control at least one vote."

Political rallies had their less attractive aspects, but these didn't discourage the hardy voters of '60. A *New York Daily Tribune* article noted that five to six thousand persons flocked to a Republican rally in Detroit despite a gully-washer rain. Even though most of them had stood more than two hours, they cried, "Go on! go on!" when the last speaker capitulated. But this was the era when a Minnesotan reportedly walked two hundred miles to attend a Republican convention; and when a St. Louis crowd stood in nearly ankle-deep mud in front of the courthouse and braved a cold, blustering north wind to hear Republican orators.

The road to a man's vote, it was often considered, was by way of his stomach. So rally planner arranged for hungry ones to fill their breadbaskets and thirsty ones to wet their whistles. At New Brunswick, New Jersey, not only were 2,500 box lunches distributed to Wide-Awakes, but they were also fortified with cider from barrels ranged along the sidewalks. A typical but modest climax to a political pow-wow was one in New York City where, after long, long talks and loud, loud singing, "the clam chowder was then taken into consideration and discussed by a large number who attended the meeting."

Out in Lansing, Michigan, reported the *Boston Journal,* Republican farmers made ready for a big get-together by furnishing fat oxen and several acres of potatoes. A Lincoln festival, reported by the *New York Daily Tribune,* was attended by an estimated four thousand on Long Island, and featured an eight-hundred-pound ox, which was "smoking and smelling" over a great oven. The Wide-Awakes "stacked their lanterns and did duty around the ox." Near the "altar of the ox" was a heap of clams. These delicacies were enjoyed not only by the men but also their "wives and sisters—the strength and charm of the rural campaign."

And what did the opposition think of these Republican jollifications? The *Cleveland Weekly Plain Dealer* headlined a gathering there with "Great Republican M-ass Meeting— menagerie coming." Black Republicans, the newspaper noted, were assembling at the county fair to be exhibited along with cheese, churns, chickens, cabbages, and carpets. The Republican exhibit would include "that long-eared species known as Wide-Awakes." The *Plain Dealer* asserted the Republicans "dare not trust their cause with people without coupling it with fairs, circuses, and such like clap traps." At another time this newspaper remarked that a Wide-Awake procession attracted street-walkers but awakened no enthusiasm for the Rail-Splitter.

A few Republican gatherings were held in the not-very-Republican state of Delaware. To emphasize the conservatism of Lincoln, the Republicans had the state's largest slaveholder preside over a meeting in Sussex County. A sizeable crowd showed up, but this was sometimes explained away by pointing out that "many, inheriting Mother Eve's curiosity, went with the view of seeing this monstrosity—a Republican assemblage—and forming their own opinion of the conglomerate."

To the claim that a Washington, D. C., Republican gathering represented a tremendous moral force, the *Constitution* asserted "its moral force did not equal in strength one fair-sized onion." A letter in the *Daily Chicago Herald,* rated a Republican ratification meeting "the flattest fizzle of the season," declaring that from 100 to 150 Republicans, Democrats, boys, women, and children attended. The *Boston Herald,* describing a Wide-Awake demonstration there one rainy night, explained that the dampness had a "lugubrious effect upon the drums and imparted to them a sad, funeral tone." The *Vermont Patriot* (Montpelier) ridiculed Republicans, suggesting they desperately needed a school teacher. At a meeting in Knoxville, Illinois, the *Patriot* said, a tent erected on a wagon bore this inscription: "Oald AbeS.tent.in.The.Black.hock.waR."

A Boston minister, after watching fifteen hundred men march by in a torchlight procession, pulled out his clerical pencil and came up with these conclusions: (1) Time spent in and preparing for the procession totaled 312 days—time that could have been better spent "spreading the gospel"; (2) Many Bibles could have been bought with the money wasted on the many gallons of torch fuel; (3) An estimated $375 damage was done to 1,500 pairs of boots—"more than equivalent to a whole year's salary of some of your most popular preachers in the rural districts"; (4) Processions frequently lead to drunkenness and rioting—"I am told they seldom end in anything else." Perhaps it was this fourth point the *Boston Herald* had in mind when it reported that at a political rally about nine hundred "illuminated" people joined in a parade.

One of the most spectacular Republican demonstrations of the 1860 campaign occurred in New York City, October 3. The *Tribune* had announced that at least a thousand men would attend from little New Hampshire. The *Union Democrat* (Manchester, N. H.) ventured, however, that not ten New Hampshire men would embark upon any "such fool's errand." But a sizeable number turned up from somewhere. The *New York Times* estimated 11,500 torches in the gala procession, while the *Evening Post* said the official report showed that 19,334 Wide-Awakes participated. The *New York Herald*, always able to restrain its enthusiasm over Republicans, asserted that most of the torch-carriers not only would be too young to vote in November but also at several subsequent elections. It added: "A party of cowled monks, bearing lighted tapers returning from a funeral, would have been quite as provocative of any political excitement as these Wide-Awakes who were so called, as a wit happily observed, 'because they had no place to sleep.' "

But the really grand and glorious Republican rally had already been staged at Lincoln's Springfield. The *Weekly Illinois State Journal* declared it opened a new era in political demonstrations. The gathering had never been surpassed in America, it asserted, and "we are firmly convinced that it never will be. There will be no occasion for excelling it."

In another item the *Journal* declared "Old Sangamon, the home of Lincoln, has covered herself all over with glory." The paper pulled out all the stops on its headlines, which included: "A Political Earthquake!" "The Prairies on Fire for Lincoln!" "75,000 Republicans in Council!" "Speaking from Five Stands," and "Magnificent Torchlight Procession at Night!"

At least five hundred delegations were on hand, the Illinois newspaper reported. The *Boston Journal* said five hundred men drove teams a hundred miles from Champaign County, camping out two nights; a Wide-Awake company marched forty miles from Beardstown; Wide-Awakes from slave-holding Hannibal, Missouri, "fought their way" to a ferryboat, then came nearly a hundred miles; and fifty-two railroad cars carried Chicagoans to the meeting, almost two hundred miles away.

These and other folks joined in a three-hour procession. In it was a power loom on which a pair of trousers were made for Lincoln during the parade. Among the other floats were a full-rigged schooner with sailors aboard, a flatboat on wheels, a horse-drawn wagon with rail-splitters at work, and many cars of delectable young ladies. Forty-three horsemen dressed as Indians impersonated the Boston Tea Party.

Mottoes included "Our Candidate, Abra Hamlin Coln," "United We Stand, Divided They Fall," "That 160 Acres We Must Have," and "The Longest Pole Knocks the Persimmon —Long Abe and Short Stephen." The Springfield glee club gave forth with "There's an old plow hoss whose name is 'Dug'/ Du da, du da/ He's short and thick—a regular plug/ Du da, du da, day."

Highlight of the day was the appearance of Lincoln. The *Weekly Illinois State Journal* reported:

It was announced that Mr. Lincoln had arrived upon the Fair Grounds. This was the signal for a display of wild enthusiasm, the like of which was never before witnessed by an Illinois audience. There was a rush from every stand towards his carriage, which was immediately surrounded by his warm admirers, and Mr. Lincoln was forced almost violently from the vehicle, and carried upon the shoulders of the crowd to an impromptu stand where he was called upon for a speech. The huzzahs and cheers which greeted him were continued nearly ten minutes without cessation, the uproar being so great that he could not make himself heard. When order was partially restored, Mr. Lincoln declined making a speech in the following words:

". . . I confess with gratitude, be it understood, that I did not suppose my appearance among you would create a tumult which I now witness. I am profoundly grateful for this manifestation of your feelings. I am grateful, because it is a tribute such as can be paid to no man as a man . . ."

At the conclusion of these remarks, Mr. Lincoln descended from the platform and with difficulty made his way through the vast throng who eagerly pressed around to take him by the hand. By an adroit movement he escaped on horseback, while the crowd were besieging the carriage in which it was expected he would return to the city.

This magnificent celebration was capped with a night procession featuring fireworks and "a seemingly interminable line of flame" of torches, giving the vicinity, thought the *Journal,* a claim to the title of *"tierra del fuego."*

The opposition reported the Springfield rally in less complimentary terms and with pared statistics. One paper declared that peddlers of Douglas and Lincoln medals at the meeting sold at least as many of the former as the latter.

Rally point of many Republican get togethers was the Wigwam. By mid-July Springfield, Illinois, was preparing to erect one "directly west of Cone's livery stable." The Democrats at Springfield even came up with a Wigwam, which the *Weekly Illinois State Journal* conceded looked pretty good, "though it resembled a barn" more than anything else. Republicans in Cass County, Michigan, designed their Wigwam in the shape of a Lincoln flatboat. The *Washington Constitution* observed that undertaking to run a flatboat on dry land was comparable to running Lincoln for President.

In the East, where there were many public halls, Wigwams

were built more out of enthusiasm than necessity. Enthusiastic Kings County (New York) Republicans erected one on Fulton Street in Brooklyn; and a group of New England Republicans built one to "accommodate two thousand persons with seats."

A "social" by Chicago Young Republicans in the most famous Wigwam drew this comment from the *Daily Chicago Herald:* "They have just announced a new dodge—a way to raise the wind and puff out the sides of their depleted pocket books. They have opened hotels, and invite their friends to attend a strawberry festival at the Wigwam, at a given price per head. Their finances are very low, and they appeal piteously for suckers. Politics and speculation! Shade of Webster, pity them! Waiter, a few more strawberries!"

The *Telegraph* (Bradford, Vermont) suggested that the word "Wigwam" was chosen because it characterized Republican campaign warfare—sly, cunning, stealthy, deceitful, skulking, sneaking behind coverts to avoid exposure, having one object only in view: the spoils of war. The relationship of the word "Wigwam" and Old Abe Lincoln's career was speculated on by an item in the *Herald.* The only chance Lincoln ever had had of seeing a live Indian, it surmised, had been in the Black Hawk War, where he had never come within a mile of one. It urged some of the "harlequins and turncoats" of the party to paint themselves up as Indians, to make the Wigwam rendezvous more attractive.

Douglas men, and to some extent, Breckinridge-and-Bell backers, whooped it up for their favorites, too. One of the largest parades of the 1860 campaign was the Union-Democratic procession in New York City, October 23. The *New York Times* said that by 9 P. M. the streets were ablaze with burning torches and the sky overhead bright with rockets, Roman candles, and other fireworks. Some 25,000 marchers paraded.

"Cannons burst with tremendous din along Broadway," the

New York Daily Tribune reported, "and their smoke obscured the vision and offended the nostrils of all spectators. After a discharge, the artillerymen rushed ahead to gain their place in the ranks, and horses backed afrightened into the standing crowd." The *New York Daily News* thus pictured the celebration:

It was a vast outpouring of the strong-handed, stout-hearted, Democracy; an emphatic expression of the popular voice against Republican fanaticism and disunionism . . . The many colored lights, transparencies, emblems, and devices, the firing of rockets, the booming of cannon, the shouts of the countless multitude that thronged the streets and avenues on the line of march, the thousands of windows filled with "heaven's last, best gift," who, with waving handkerchiefs and hearty cheers bade their noble fellows God speed combined to make a scene that can never be erased from the public memory.

In one float, the *Daily News* report went on, a man impersonating Horace Greeley cuddled "a large and good-looking nigger wench . . . with all the affection of a true Republican." Banners bore such legends as "Massa Greeley and Master Sambo," and "Free Love, Free Niggers, and Free Women."

A large flag suspended from Republican headquarters opposite the Southern rendezvous, the New-York Hotel, was the target for many fire-balls. One set the flag afire, but a daring fellow climbed out on the pole and extinguished the blaze.

A Douglas meeting in Lincoln's home town was claimed by the faithful, as the largest political assemblage within "the memory of the oldest inhabitant." However, this gathering which set the town "ablaze with enthusiasm," preceded the colossal Republican rally there. In Detroit, according to the *Detroit Free Press,* more than 4,000 blazing torches were carried in a Democratic rally.

At a Douglas conclave in Cooper Union, New York City, the chairman, perhaps taking a tip from the Chicago Republican convention, urged public speakers in the audience to go address the throng outside that had been unable to squeeze into the hall. When Doug visited Richmond, Virginia, and the band struck up "Hail, the Conquering Hero Comes," the police were barely able to keep the excited crowd from overwhelming the Little Giant, said the *Washington National Intelligencer.*

One Democratic parade included a wagon carrying some thirty barefoot men. "The barefooted democracy are for Douglas and Johnson!" a sign explained. A Keokuk, Iowa, demonstration featured a company of girls with a banner, "A Democrat or No Husband."

The foes of the Northern Democrats discharged verbal explosives. According to a *New York Daily Tribune* item a Democratic procession was composed of a conglomeration of men and boys who stepped at all paces, in order and out of order, and carried libelous mottoes and indecent pictures. Window panes, along the way, were shattered by the explosions of Democratic cannons. In another item it was asserted that some of the Democratic marchers had been hired at two dollars a head and given a red shirt and cap to top off the bargain.

When the Republican journals publicized Douglas activities—they did it in their own inimitable way. As a case in point, a *Tribune* article reported "A meeting of all kinds of Democrats . . . was held last evening at the saloon at the corner of Thirty-second Street and Fourth Avenue." Said a *Weekly Illinois State Journal* writer of a Douglas Democratic meeting in Olney, Illinois: "Of the forty voters in the crowd, I am confident that at least twenty-five were drunk. Finally the band became so disgusted with the party that they then left and refused to play any longer. The crowd then dispersed, most of them making a beeline for the groceries [grogshops] where a great many of them spent the remainder of the night."

In connection with another Douglas rally in Illinois, the *Journal* used the headline, "An Extra Train Not Needed Very Badly," explaining that the Springfield delegation consisted of "six men and an ambitious but rather uncleanly boy." It added that twenty-three persons were on hand when the speaking was turned on, but considerably fewer when it was finally shut off. The *Daily Gate City* (Keokuk, Iowa) reported that a meeting there drew "nearly half a million—less four hundred ninety-nine thousand." It said a Douglas man termed it "a d——d fizzle."

The Douglas Democrats had foes down South as well as up North. To the *New Orleans Daily Delta,* a Douglas demonstration there was "a fizzle! The Douglasites march off to the tune of 'I Wish I Was in Dixie,' to join their great leader in the New Jerusalem of the 'wooly heads.' " It declared the speakers' platform was scarcely less shaky than the miserable party platform the Douglasites tried to foist upon the South at Charleston. This was Breckinridge country, where there were, according to a newspaper, only two Douglas men, "and one of them is in jail." The Breckinridge men argued in their speeches that backing Douglas was merely "leading the country to Abraham's bosom."

Political speeches were likened to gas. The *Cleveland Weekly Plain Dealer* asserted the Republican party contained enough gas, if it would burn, to light the world. The *Fond du Lac* (Wis.) *Commonwealth* philosophized:

> A man is lucky that's got brass—
> A man is lucky that's got gas:
> With brass and gas and backers, too,
> A smart man ought to wiggle through.

Somehow the audiences in those rugged days were able to tolerate, even enjoy, a horrible lot of oratory. Speakers got wound up and were, as Lincoln once said of a longwinded clergyman, "too lazy to stop."

One newspaper declared a procession was "nearly two miles in length, as was also the speech of Mr.—." A Boston reporter sat through twenty-six miles of speech—on a train. At a Bell gathering, an ex-Congressman "poured forth a continuous stream of most manly eloquence for two hours." But he was a mere tenderfoot. The *Woodsfield* (Ohio) *Republican* reported a "powerful speech of nearly four hours length . . . in exposure of the crimes of the pro-slavery Democracy."

Among heavy-weight Republican orators were Senator William H. Seward, of New York, and Governor Salmon P. Chase, of Ohio. Oliver Wendell Holmes, John Greenleaf Whittier, William Cullen Bryant, and James Russell Lowell, supported Lincoln with their pens.

Horace Greeley both wrote and spoke for the Republican cause. His contention that "this is an age of *stern* political virtue," brought the retort that "he probably means that he has long since left political virtue in the rear." His assertion, at another time, that electing Lincoln was the way to save the Union, was considered by the opposition a remedy "about equal to cutting a hole in a leaky ship to let the water out."

Abe's oldest son, Bob, turned orator briefly in New England. He read the Declaration of Independence at a Fourth of July celebration near Exeter, New Hampshire.

One unscheduled platform appearance was that of John Hanks, Lincoln's old partner at the rails. When he was pointed out at an Illinois gathering, Hanks rose and "showed his honest face to the thousands standing on tiptoe to catch a glimpse of it." He was then called to the platform and asked about his work with Lincoln. After he acknowledged the partnership, said the *Alton* (Ill.) *Courier,* "Old John Hanks at once became a favorite, and thousands took his hard and horny hand in theirs."

Republicans were powerful proud of horny-handed Hanks, but they had at least one platform volunteer they didn't relish. He was described by one paper as "a kinky-headed, thick-lipped, flat-nosed Negro." A Republican paper asserted, however, that Democrats had paid this Negro's whiskey bills and persuaded him to go about the country proclaiming himself a Republican.

Campaign speeches had one element in common—they all neglected to point out any good in the opposing parties. In a rather typical speech at Hoboken, New Jersey, a Wide-Awake speaker referred to forces combining against Lincoln as "the asafoetida ticket." He announced "the death of the Democratic party, which died of lingering illness, aggravated by a severe attack of Charleston fever. A post-mortem examination showed an entire absence of heart." In a "refreshingly scathing manner," it was reported, Republicans in New York toasted "the Democratic party, skinned and salted."

Some speakers did not look far for subject matter. The *Worcester* (Mass.) *Palladium* said:

A speech by Eli Thayer, phonographically reported—I, I, I, I, I, I, I, I, I, I, I, I, I, I, I, I, I, I, I, I, I, I, I, I, I, I, I, I, I, I, I, I, I, I, I, I, I, I, I, I, I, I, I, I, I, I, I, Eyes right! Eli is singularly a man of one universal I-dear. The people will put out his I's in November.

With the nation striding toward a crisis on the slavery question, many political speeches bristled with violent threats. One journal referred to the fearful predominance of metaphors drawn from "bayonets" and "hemp." "The amount of stabbings and hangings (by pen and tongue) is horrible to contemplate." For example, the Washington *National Intelligencer* reported that "Parson" William G. Brownlow, fiery Tennessee journalist and clergyman, said at a meeting at Knoxville: "When the Seccessionists go to Washington to dethrone Lincoln, I am for seizing a bayonet and forming an army to resist such an attack, and they shall walk over my dead body on the way." To which William L. Yancey, of Alabama, replied: "If my State resists, I shall go with her, and if I meet this gentleman marshalled with his bayonet to oppose us, I'll plunge my bayonet to the hilt, through and through his heart, and feel no compunctions for the act, and thank my God my country has been freed from such a foe."

Douglas supplied much campaign oratory. At a clambake in Rhode Island, reported the *Binghamton* (N.Y.) *Standard*, "in addition to several bushels of clams served up in the most *recherché* style, the company were treated to a three-hour speech from Mr. Douglas." While going through the Shenandoah Valley at another time, he made speeches at every town.

On the New England excursion, Douglas had platforms ready at every depot. At the beginning of his carefully planned twenty-minute addresses, observed the *Jonesboro* (Ill.) *Gazette*, he invariably expressed surprise at being called upon.

The opposition newspapers showed no esteem for this whistle-stopping. Douglas, declared an item in the *Weekly Illinois State Journal*, was the first Presidential candidate to mount the stump to advocate his own election. The *Journal* charged that Douglas' electioneering harangues exhibited "miserable taste, and utter disregard for the proprieties of his position."

The *Bucyrus* (Ohio) *Weekly Journal* contended that Douglas had cast off earlier disguises and "now he boldly avows his purpose and glories in his shameless disregard of the decencies of the canvass." And the *Jonesboro* (Ill.) *Gazette* trumpeted:

Douglas is going about peddling his opinions as a tin man peddles his wares. The only excuse for him is, that as he is a small man, he has a right to be engaged in small business; and small business it is for a candidate for the Presidency to be strolling around the country begging for votes like a town constable.

To some extent, Breckinridge took to the stump to defend himself from the "wandering orator." Old Abe, on the other hand, stuck close to home. The *Weekly Illinois State Journal* explained he did not consider it necessary to go about "blowing his own horn." His traveling would come at inauguration time.

Following the October state elections in several states, the *Journal* ran a table listing the times and places Democratic Douglas had spoken and the votes the *Republicans* gained in those places. The article was captioned, "behold the fruits of the labors of the great 'Squatter Sovereign.' " The *Weekly Kentucky Yoeman* (Frankfort) asserted that Douglas' "route" was followed by his "rout" and another newspaper suggested that Douglas' visit to Niagara Falls on his stumping tour was to accustom himself to "great falls."

When Douglas announced that he was going to visit his mother, but then followed a devious route and worked in some speeches on the way, he elicited reams of newspaper copy about "Stephen's search for his mother." The *Portsmouth* (N. H.) *Journal* printed a poem about the search, with this explanatory footnote: "It is said that Stephen did not know where or when he passed his mother; but after travelling South as far as North Carolina, he thought it best to take a 'backtrack' and so found his mother down in Maine, past Monday."

The *Weekly Illinois State Journal* explained that Doug had looked for his mother in all the hotels and Democratic committee rooms in Philadelphia, but failing to find her, made a popular-sovereignty speech. He also searched unsuccessfully in New York—but succeeded in making a speech. It then listed about fifteen speeches he made while looking for his darling mother.

Mr. Douglas will not give it up so. He will presently be peering about in every principal town in Illinois, and to enable him to get a wider range, will mount every stump to which he is invited. It is understood that from Illinois he will go South and push his inquiries for his maternal progenitor there. No son was ever so dutiful before.

The *New-Hampshire Statesman* (Concord) confided that Douglas, going to visit his Mother in Western New York, "naturally came to New Haven, Guilford and Hartford on his way, and at the latter place, he was 'betrayed' into a speech. Still bent on his maternal pilgrimage, he goes toward Boston, attracted by a relative of his wife. It was a case of relative attraction. On his way, at Worcester, some Judas 'betrayed' him into a speech. At Boston, betrayed again. . . ."

The *Weekly Illinois State Journal* published "A Plaintive Pome" about Stephen's search:

> Why did I down to Hartford go?
> 'Twas not my squatter self to show;
> I went to hunt, I told you so,
> >My mother.

The "Pome" concluded:

> At length I hope I shall thee find,
> For thou hast been a useful blind,
> That I might often speak my mind,
> >My mother.

The Wide-Awake Glee Club of Oswego, New York, featured a chant about Douglas' maternal search, which set off "bursts of uncontrollable laughter." But not everyone thought the idea so hilarious. A Maine preacher, speaking on home life, made the mistake of choosing as his text a line from II Kings 4:19, "Carry him to his mother." Not a Douglas man entered his church from that day on, a *Washington Evening Star* item declared.

Anti-Douglasites however kept harping on it. Someone at a Douglas speech in Syracuse, after noting Douglas' dark complexion, remarked, "H-ll! I know where his mother is; she is out on the Indian reservation." At a Democratic pow-wow at Monmouth, Illinois, a placard showed a white man hugging a Negro woman. Someone remarked, said the Morristown *Jerseyman*, "Why, la me! Douglas has found his mother." The *Mississippian* (Jackson) noted that the Illinois Democrat had called himself "The Little Sucker" and this explained his anxiety while looking for his mother.

Such baiting of candidates and campaigners occurred mainly in the public print. But sometimes it took physical forms. Usually it was non-violent, such as three rousing cheers for Douglas shouted in the rear of Boston's Faneuil Hall during a big Republican meeting, or the breaking up of a Republican gathering at Mount Vernon, Illinois, by beating tin cans and other reverberant objects.

The Democrats did not enjoy a monopoly in creating disturbances—that is, they did not *have* a monopoly, although they might have enjoyed one. The *Columbian Weekly Register* (New Haven) declared that the Republican Wide-Awakes "added to their other 'freedom' appliances, that of making free with eatables and drinkables, without paying for them." About two hundred of the "glazed cap and cape rowdies," it reported, jammed into a New Haven tavern and not only refused to pay for what they ordered, but also broke open show windows and carried off champagne and other articles, and stripped the shelves of pies, passing them to the crowd outside. The Wide-Awakes were also accused of feeding their bonfires with rails from fences in the center of town.

In Lexington, Missouri, the *Advertiser* placed the names of Lincoln and Hamlin at the head of its editorial columns. A mob gathered, according to the *Troy* (Ohio) *Times,* seized the edition of the paper that was ready for mailing, and chased the editor out of town. In Pennsylvania, Breckinridge men invaded a newspaper office and put out an edition of this Douglas-loving paper under the Breckinridge banner.

Missiles were occasionally hurled. At a meeting in Hannibal, Missouri, a volunteer injected a pro-slavery speech into the Republican program. The reporter termed it "too obscene and blasphemous for publication." When a man started to reply to the speech, he was pelted with rotten eggs. A Republican speaker in Cairo, Illinois, was smashed in the face with an egg, but, reported the *Boston Journal,* both the Democrats and the Bell forces denounced the assault "in terms as strong as the egg." Rotten eggs were hurled at Republican speakers at the Front Street Theater in Baltimore and it required two hundred policemen "to protect the Niggerites" from injury, asserted the *Floridian and Journal* (Tallahassee).

The missiles sometimes were more firm than eggs. A Wide-Awake procession in Baltimore was greeted with hisses and groans and a shower of bricks, according to the *Baltimore Sun.* At a Republican rally at Dover, the going really got rough for some Democrats. Said the *Delawarean:*

These fellows, calling themselves Wide-Awakes . . . continued to wander about the town in groups and finally went in considerable numbers down to Captain Mullins hotel, the headquarters of the Democrats, and fell upon two or three unoffending citizens, and beat and mangled them in a most brutal manner. . . .

The sheriff rounded up a posse of about a hundred men, the *Delawarean* continued, "but the drunken, infuriated mob persisted in their riotous, brutal and disgraceful conduct." The sheriff then ordered the posse to hurry to the arsenal and arm themselves, whereupon the "blackguards and cowards endeavored to form themselves in a line and marched in double-quick time out of town."

At a parade of Troy (New York) Wide-Awakes, stones and bricks were hurled from windows and even roofs, said the *New York Evening Post.* Among the estimated two hundred wounded were two old men, perhaps fatally. Wide-Awake paraders in Wheeling, Virginia, found the streets blocked with drays and other obstructions. A fight ensued and stones, guns, and Wide-Awake torches were used freely, the *Daily Gate City* (Keokuk, Iowa) reported. A gang of "drunken Democrats" interrupted a Republican pole-raising in Detroit and the riled-up Republicans "licked them handsomely and then demolished the grogshop whence the Democratic inspiration had come."

Sulphuric acid was flung upon a New York City woman viewing a Wide-Awake parade on Broome Street, ruining her dress and cape.

Party headquarters were sometimes invaded. Republican offices in Baltimore were ransacked; Wide-Awake caps and capes were destroyed; ink was poured upon the records; and pictures of Lincoln were shredded. When Douglas Democratic headquarters in Chicago were assaulted, the lamp in an illuminated sign was upset, almost causing the building to burn down, according to the *Chicago Times and Herald.*

In Washington, a Republican meeting was attacked by a "gang of ruffians," who, the *New York Tribune* reported, "poured in a volley of stones, mingled with pistol-shots, and then with shouts made a rush upon the meeting. . . . Six-shooters were handled, sticks were grasped, and stone heaps supplied those otherwise weaponless, and had there been a second rush, there would have been blood shed." During the attack, "the Marine Band took to their heels, having secured their pay in advance." In a letter to the editor of the *Washington Evening Star* deploring the prevalence of roughnecks in the Capital, a man reminded residents there was "considerable sentiment in the country to move the capital to a more central location, anyway."

New York City enjoyed its share of disturbances. The *New York Daily Tribune* gave this report of a political meeting on lower Broadway:

A shower of stones came crashing through the windows, and immediately Fatty Welsh & Co. of the Dead Rabbits made threatening demonstrations toward the Chairman. Policemen present drew their clubs, and quiet was again restored. The name of James Lynch was then offered as a candidate for registrar and declared carried, which in reality it was, at least two-thirds having voted in the affirmative. On this, a number of chairs were demolished and the legs thereof brandished. Fatty Welsh fastened the only door, placing the key in his pocket. A general melee was the result, when not a trifle of blood was drawn. A number of officers rushed into the room, breaking down the door, followed by a large crowd of Dead Rabbits, who were waiting outside to hear the result. A new meeting was immediately organized, and the entire Tammany ticket endorsed.

Chicago Wide-Awakes had a jolly time on visiting Joliet, Illinois, if the *Times and Herald* account is accurate:

The Wide-Awakes having become furiously drunk and disorderly, and even more insulting in their behavior, went into the Empire saloon and one of them struck a Democrat who happened to say something in favor of Douglas.

From this commenced a free fight, and although there were but three Democrats engaged in it, the saloon was cleaned of Wide-Awakes in less than five minutes. Most of them, however, were obliged to creep out on their hands and knees, being unable to rise immediately after coming into such close contact with Democratic knuckles. . . .

It was out of the frying pan into the fire with them, for they were no sooner on the sidewalk than they were assailed by about an equal number of men and boys, many of whom had been the subjects of their insults in the earlier part of the evening. . . .

The Wide-Awakes were completely routed and obliged to seek safety in an ignominious flight to the railroad cars, bearing away with them nothing but black eyes, bloody noses and broken heads, and leaving two of their fellow comrades *hors du combat* on the field of battle. These two martyrs in the cause of Lincoln and liberty were afterwards humanely carried to the depot, on a cellar door, by some of our citizens.

And now a Spartan band emerged from the cars, and armed with swords and pistols, marched upon the Empire saloon again, determined, they said, to clean it out this time or perish in the attempt. They had, however, no more than arrived at the scene of the intended attack, than they were set upon again by their enemies, and handled even more roughly than before. In this skirmish, stones, brickbats, and bottles were freely used on both sides, and several Wide-Awakes, including their General, were forced to surrender their swords. Thus routed and defeated, the attacking party . . . again beat a hasty retreat to the cars and hostilities ended for the night.

Sometimes political differences were handled on a more individual basis. Although dueling was about to be laughed out of court, a number of duels still were fought over supercharged political questions. Two men near Natchez, Mississippi, met and fired seventeen shots without wounding each other, but not all duelers, unfortunately, were so inaccurate. A Florida editor and a Georgian met on the field of honor and both were killed. Causes of duels varied, but often were in the nature of one in the District of Columbia, where a Tennesseean had told a rabid Northern Democrat he considered Douglas men no better than Black Republicans.

So the campaign moved on, with rallies and torchlight processions, with speeches and rotten eggs, and even with brickbats and pistols.

CHAPTER TEN

LINCOLN'S OPEN-DOOR AND CLOSED-MOUTH POLICY

As the political campaign rolled on, Abe Lincoln led the simple life in Springfield, a prairie town with unpaved, tree-lined streets and about 10,000 plain people. The Presidential candidate chatted with friends as he walked to and from his office. At home in the evenings he sometimes chopped and carried in wood for the kitchen fire.

But Lincoln's pattern of living could not remain unchanged. His most trivial actions, said the *Republican Farmer* (Bridgeport, Conn.), were made momentous affairs. "If he ventures to whistle, the echo comes back to him from a thousand partisan journals, and his friends forthwith urge in his favor that he is a good whistler."

During the campaign, Lincoln's youngest boy, Tad, became seriously ill with scarlet fever. A newspaper reported that Abe stayed beside the suffering child despite "the whirl of political excitement that is surging around him." Then a New England newspaper sneered: "Mr. Lincoln's admiring friends will be delighted to hear that he eats, sleeps, coughs, sneezes, and obeys the *other calls of nature* regularly, in spite of the 'surging whirl' or the 'whirling surge.' "

Abe's life was also altered by the streams of visitors that converged on the Illinois capital both before and after the election. Henry Villard, correspondent for the *New York Herald,* wrote late in 1860:

Everybody who lives in this vicinity or passes through this place goes to take a look at "Old Abe." Muddy boots and hickory shirts are just as frequent as broadcloth, fine linen, etc. The ladies, however, are usually dressed up in their very best, although they cannot hope to make an impression on old married Lincoln. . . . Churlish fellows will obtrude themselves with their hats on, lighted cigars, and their pantaloons tucked into their boots. Dropping into chairs, they sit puffing away. . . .

A reporter who visited Springfield, and had walked some half-dozen blocks from the railroad depot to the vicinity of the Lincoln home on Eighth Street, asked a lady which was Lincoln's house. She pointed out a modest two-story structure which had, according to the *Cleveland Weekly Plain Dealer,* two broken window panes. She then added, "Won't you walk in? You'll be welcome there!" The welcome mat was always out.

Tall men made the Springfield pilgrimage to measure with Lincoln. Many young bucks from Sangamon County brought their sweethearts and introduced them to Old Abe, who, said the *New York Herald,* sometimes was surrounded by robust beauty. An Indiana farmer for whom Lincoln had split rails thirty years earlier dropped in to visit his former hired hand. An old lady came to remind Abe she had fed him several times when he was riding the legal circuit.

Journalist Henry Villard pointed out that Lincoln tended to receive everybody with uniform kindness, reply to all questions with unvarying readiness, grant willing compliance with all requests, and accept endless suggestions. He added that many visitors abused Lincoln's patience.

Lincoln's open-door policy apparently attracted some rather unattractive specimens. One Illinois newspaper told about a "seedy individual" who encountered Lincoln at the railway station:

Attracted by the mention of Lincoln's name, he rushed frantically through the crowd, and planted himself in no very graceful manner before the president-elect with the inquiry: "Is this Mr. Linkon?" Lincoln bowed and extended his hand. "Might glad t'see ye ole feller," continued seedy, "I'm a rail-splitter too."

At the Lincoln home folks didn't seem to come and go as much as to come and stay. Villard explained that after the curious "defiled" past Lincoln, many would sit down and stare at him with open mouths, some spending hours in that agreeable pastime. The diurnal jam was followed by a nocturnal one and Lincoln was crowded upon in his parlor and had to undergo "another agony of presentations." "The whole lower story of the building was filled all the evening with well-dressed ladies and gentlemen, whose comfort was, however, greatly diminished by the constant influx of an ill-mannered populace."

Some people, ancestors of modern autograph hunters, resorted to ruses. A Kansan and his family on the way east stopped at Springfield. The man went to Lincoln's office. After being presented to the Presidential nominee, the Kansan asked him what kind of a tree was growing below his window. They walked to the window. Then the man confessed he wasn't really interested in the tree. But he pointed out a woman and children sitting out front in a wagon. "Them's mine," the man declared proudly, "and I told them I would fix it so that they could get a sight of you at this window—that's all." Lincoln enjoyed the joke, commented the *Kansas State Record* (Topeka), but at least no more than did the countryman.

Despite impositions upon him, Lincoln liked to greet old friends and new, both the rough and the polished. He was always the common man. An eastern reporter told of being met at the door by a shirt-sleeved Lincoln when he visited Springfield. The newsman said he accompanied Lincoln to his office, "he on a walk, I on a trot."

Some newspapers ridiculed incidents related to press coverage in Springfield. The *New Albany* (Ind.) *Daily Ledger,* for example, noted that a correspondent of the New York area had "spent a night with Mr. Lincoln." "It is not stated," said the *Ledger,* "whether the correspondent is a man or a woman."

An item in the *New London* (Conn.) *Daily Star* gave this version of a Springfield incident:

In a recent speech, ex-Lieutenant Governor Raymond told the audience that when he visited Lincoln, shortly after his nomination, he heard a voice from an upper room crying out, "Abraham! Abraham! Come and put this child to bed!" Whether Mrs. L. meant herself or the baby by the expression "this child," Mr. Raymond didn't know. Nor did he explain whether he told the story to show what a lady-like person Mrs. L. is, or what a good "dry nuss" Old Abe is.

Many papers paid tribute to Lincoln. A *Manhattan* (Kan.) *Express* article said in praise of him:

He is a strictly temperance man, never using wine or strong drink; and stranger still he does not "twist the filthy weed," nor smoke, nor use profane language of any kind. When we consider how common these vices are, particularly in the West, it must be admitted that it exhibits no little strength of character to have refrained from them.

Reporters declared Abe was a stranger to intrigues and dirty party politics, and that he spoke out strongly against venality in high places. Yet he was not a stargazer. An article by the editor of the *Utica* (N. Y.) *Herald,* reprinted in the *New York World,* declared:

I was greatly impressed with the eminently *practical* character of his mind. No man living has less of the visionary. He is eminently a "good hater" of cloud-capped theories . . . He has all the marks of a man that scans closely, canvasses thoroughly, concludes deliberately, and holds to such conclusions unflinchingly. He seems to me to be rarely gifted with the faculty of remaining faithful to his convictions of right in the face of difficulties and discouragements. . . .

Another characteristic that impresses me is his *truthfulness*. I do not believe any earthly power can drive Mr. Lincoln into the commission of a mean action. I am sure that he would far prefer being right to being president.

Springfield was more than a pleasure resort for visitors and an artesian news well for correspondents—it was a mecca for office-seekers. The *New York Herald* put it mildly:

This handsome little prairie town, with its quiet look of a New England village, its half-dozen churches sending their white spires high up into the clear blue sky, and its snug homes half hidden from view in the thick foliage with which they are surrounded, appears to possess at this time a special interest in the eyes of the politicians.

Crowding up to the public feed trough apparently was an obsession with many folk. The *Bangor* (Maine) *Daily Union* declared there were so many Republican candidates for federal office in that city that there was no one left to sign petitions. With tongue-in-cheek, the *Republican Farmer* (Bridgeport, Conn.) called attention to the "disinterested patriotism" of office-seekers and declared such loyalty surely wouldn't be allowed to go unrewarded.

More frankly, the Republican party had never fed at the federal trough and it was rapaciously hungry. According to the *Columbian Weekly Register* (New Haven, Conn.) Wide-Awakes in Troy, New York, carried axes to symbolize that the Republicans had "axes to grind." Behind the great offensive of office-seekers, suggested the *Springfield* (Mass.) *Daily Republican,* was

> The good old rule, the simple plan
> That they should keep, who have the power,
> And they should get who can.

And plenty of persons continued to try to "get," even though Lincoln asserted that "I have promised nothing, high or low, and will not."

Some nimble-tongued men attempted to talk their way into office. These roving orators who served on the stumps found it necessary to return to GHQ at intervals. "What can all these long winded but empty headed orators have to say to Old Abe?" asked the *New York Herald*. It added:

If these gentlemen do not get an opportunity of serving their country for the next four years, in positions where there is little work and much pay, you may depend upon it that it will not be for want of blowing their own trumpets. Nor from any modesty in magnifying their own achievements.

Some office-seekers even announced their own prospective positions, declared one newspaper, and whom they intended to hire and fire.

A satire on these office-seekers was prepared for *Vanity Fair* by staff writer Artemus Ward, pen name for Charles F. Browne, former editor of the *Cleveland Weekly Plain Dealer*:

Two fat office-seekers from Wisconsin, in endevoren to crawl between Old Abe's legs for the purpuss of applyin for the tollgate-ship at Milwauky, upset the President-elect and he would have gone sprawlin into the fire-place if I hadn't caught him in these arms. But I hadn't more than stood him up strate, before anuther cum crashin doun the chimney, his head strickin me vilently agin the inards and prostratin my voloptoous form onto the floor. "Mr. Linkin," shouted the infatooated being, "my papers is signed by every clergyman in our town, and likewise the schoolmaster. I workt hard for the ticket; I toiled night and day! The patrit should be rewarded."

"Virtoo," said I, gittin up, brushin the dust from my eyes, and holdin the infatooated man by the coat collar, "Virtoo, sir, is its own reward. Look at me!" He did look at me, and qualed be 4 my gase. "The fact is," I cintinued, lookin round upon the hungry crowd, "there is scarcely a offise for every ile lamp carrid round

during this campane. What air you here for? Can't you give Abe a
minit's peace? Go home. Stand not upon the order of your goin,
but go to onct. Ef in five minits from this time," sez I, pullin out
my new siexteen dollar huntin casedwatch, and brandishin it before
their eyes, "ef in five minits fum this time a single sole of you remains on these here premises, I will go out to my cage near by,
and let my Boy constructor loose! & if he gits among you, you'll
think Old solferino has cum again and no mistake!" You ought to
have seen them scamper, Mr. Fair. They run orf as tho Satun
hisself was arter them with a red-hot ten-pronged pitchfork. In five
minutes, the premises was clear.

Feathering their nests was not the only motive of office-
seekers. The *Coos Republican* (Lancaster, N. H.) stated that
"the knife will be put to the throats of the miserable band of
traders now filling the Federal offices, and their hides will be
nailed to the wall like wood-chuck skins on a country barn
door in bean time."

Lincoln was deluged with mail as well as with office-seekers and other visitors. One reason, a newspaper suggested,
was that many small-potato politicians wanted letters to carry
around, showing they were in "confidential" communication
with the next President. One item noted that about fifty letters
that day had solicited autographs. According to one of Lincoln's remarks, he "took good care not to answer many of the
letters." However, he did send in a soap testimonial. It said:
"Some specimens of your Soap have been used at our house
and Mrs. L declares it is a superior article. She at the same
time protests that I have never given sufficient attention to the
'soap question' to be a competent judge. Yours very truly, A.
Lincoln."

Lincoln also received some letters from irate partisans who
threatened his life. These warnings became so common he
paid little attention to them. "There is nothing like getting
used to things," he quipped.

Abe received not only letters but also books, pictures,
poems, and even a whistle made of a pig's tail. Josiah Craw-

ford, of Gentryville, Indiana, sent him a stick from a rail Lincoln had split for him in 1825. He suggested Lincoln make it into a cane.

An old woman from New Salem brought Abe some woolen stockings she had knit for him to wear when he became President. After she left he held them up and joked, "The old lady got my latitude and longitude about right, didn't she?" He also received clothing, including several hats which, he told the donors, "do mutually surpass each other." He once remarked to his wife that the new clothes were at least one thing "likely to come out of this scrape anyhow."

From a devout Jew, Abraham Kohn, Chicago city clerk, Lincoln received a picture of the American flag with a Hebrew inscription filling the white stripes. The closing verse was: "Have not I commanded thee? Be strong and of good courage; Be not afraid, neither be thou dismayed: For the Lord thy God is with thee whithersoever thou goest."

Not all gifts were complimentary. Mrs. Lincoln was sent a painting showing Abe with a rope around his neck, chains binding his ankles, and his body tarred and feathered.

Among the nicer gifts was an LL.D. degree conferred by Knox College. A Republican newspaper remarked that Lincoln already had earned the F. R. S. degree—First-rate Rail-Splitter. However, the opposition contended the letters stood for Frightful Rail-Splitter. The LL.D., opposing journals asserted, meant Long-Legged Disunionist or perhaps Licked Like the Devil. They delighted in referring to "Old Doctor Abe." And there were the inevitable poems. One ended:

> Perhaps it suggests retribution—
> Let him quit the Republican cause,
> Heal its wounds on the poor Constitution,
> And *Doctor* its broken-down laws.

Newspapers also gave Mary Todd Lincoln some attention. A *Baltimore Sun* item described her as "on the advantageous side of forty." The Washington *Evening Star* referred to her as a "zealous Presbyterian" who was "intelligent, social, and easy and graceful in manner." And the *New York Daily Tribune* noted that she "is thoroughly *au fait* in all the little amenities of society."

But the opposition newspapers saw her differently. One compared Mrs. Lincoln's "lack of knowledge of social proprieties" to the situation when a certain man unexpectedly was promoted to major in the militia. His children asked if they also would be majors. "No, you fools," indignantly replied the mother, "none but your daddy and me." One writer suggested Lincoln owed his success to his temperamental wife, since he had thrown himself into politics to escape her.

The *Saint Anthony Weekly Express* (Hennepin County, Minn.) attacked the Republicans for publicizing Mrs. Lincoln. It declared: "They are already trying to get Mrs. Lincoln on the platform with her husband, and in view of the awkward, uncouth and ungainly manners and appearances which it is universally admitted Lincoln displays, their efforts in this direction cannot be wondered at."

Lincoln took time to study the press for information on the grave issues that stirred the nation. He found that the press didn't always stick to these issues. Some of them engaged, with gay abandon, in personalities.

For example, if Lincoln happened to pick up the *Jonesboro* (Ill.) *Gazette,* he might have read:

More rotten, corrupt and unprincipled organization than the Black Republicans of the present time, never disgraced earth with its presence. The fag end of all the isms, devoid of common decency and patriotism, admitting their own degradation by acknowledging the Negro their equal, they select their leaders from the lowest haunts of vice and infamy. . . .

A week later the *Gazette* charged that the Republican party was "a party of lions led by an ass."

Political reasoning of that day was illustrated by an 1860

anecdote concerning a debating society. The question was "Which am de mudder of de chicken—de hen wot lay de egg, or de hen wot hatches de chick?" The chairman and most of the group lined up on the latter side. Then someone tossed a monkeywrench into the machine by asking, "Suppose dat you set one dozen duck eggs under a hen, dey hatch, which am de mudder—de duck or de hen?" This jolted the chairman. Then a bright idea flashed. "Gentlemen," he declared triumphantly, "ducks am not before de house, for chickens am de question; derfore I rule de ducks out."

Another anecdote of the day illustrated political obstinancy. Several men on a New England train were discussing the Presidential candidates, when a Millerite entered the conversation. "Before the election of 1860," he declared, "the world will have come to an end, and Jesus Christ will be President of the Universe!" Another man replied: "Sir, I'll b-b-bet you t-t-ten dollars New Hampshire w-won't g-g-g-go for him."

But many serious voters wanted to know the stand of Presidential candidates in order to decide which one to "go for." And the newspapers—at least some—tried to inform them.

Greeley's *New York Daily Tribune* explained the differences in this fashion:

Lincoln and Hamlin represent a principle—that of National Resistance to the diffusion of Slavery. Breckinridge and Lane represent the antagonistic principle—that of National Protection to the diffusion of Slavery. Douglas and Johnson represent a Dodge —namely, National Indifference to the diffusion of Slavery. Bell and Everett represent a Sham—National Blindness to the diffusion of Slavery.

Another version was: "Lincoln and Hamlin—say you shan't!; Breckinridge and Lane—say you shall!; Douglas and Johnson—say, do as you please!; and Bell and Everett—say nothing!"

Still another interpretation, in the *Jerseyman* (Morristown), stated: "The Lincoln party is in favor of voting Slavery *down* in our Free Western Territories; the Breckinridge party is in favor of voting it *up:* the Douglas party don't care whether it is voted up or down; and the Bell-Everett party don't know anything about nothing."

A Douglas speaker "clarified" the Little Giant's popular sovereignty stand by explaining: "Mr. Douglas believes that if Slavery ain't a mind to go where she is a mind to, she may stay where she is if she doesn't want to; subject to the decision of the Supreme Court and the people of the territories, when they be agreed to that p'int."

As fast as the Republicans could explain their conservative stand, the opposition denied it. To some persons the Republicans were incorrigible abolitionists. For example, a *Detroit Free Press* item declared:

Old Abe contributed fifty dollars to the fund for purchasing Sharpe's rifles for Jim Lane and John Brown in Kansas. The sum would buy two rifles. Possibly one of these rifles is the one with which Lane shot poor Jenkins when he came to get a bucket of water from his own well: and the other the one with which old Brown murdered the Doyles—father and son.

The *Boston Post* accused the Republicans of sleeping with Wendell Phillips, abolitionist orator, all through the campaign, but intimated they would kick him out of bed the morning after election.

These two quotes from Abe Lincoln were published repeatedly in the *New London* (Conn.) *Daily Star.*

I believe this government cannot endure permanently half slave and half free.

I have always hated slavery, I think, as much as any Abolitionist.

"Negro is the only string there is to the Republican banjo and they must play upon that or none," a newspaper asserted. However, the abolitionists generally did not claim Lincoln for their camp. Wendell Phillips once commented: "Mr. Lincoln is a willing Constitution hound, ready to hunt slaves so long as the Union, the party, and the white race seem to need it; and he is therefore just the wood out of which Washington Presidents are carved. If any think such characters useful and necessary nowadays, let them. But that is no reason why I should call such persons honest men, any more than I should call geese eagles because a goose once saved Rome."

Lincoln pointedly denounced John Brown's raid at Harper's Ferry, recall of which still sent shivers down many spines. But there were some Brown zealots who were Lincoln supporters. And it was not easy to shake off the curse of Harper's Ferry by disavowing sympathy. Nevertheless, the Republicans did keep reminding voters that theirs was the only platform which condemned Brown's raid.

One Republican newspaper asserted the Republican policies and purposes were understood about as well by Southerners as by Mongolians or Crimeans. Again and again Republican leaders stressed that the party's stand was merely to prevent the *increase* of slavery by extension into the free territories or by the restoration of the African slave trade. Lincoln had no intention of molesting slavery where it was already established.

The *Chattanooga* (Tenn.) *Gazette* carried an item about the visit of a wealthy Mississippi planter to Lincoln. It said: "He (Lincoln) concluded by advising the Mississippian to purchase as many Negroes as he needed; and expressed the opinion that in twelve months, slave property would be worth more than it ever had been."

Even if this had been the viewpoint of Lincoln and the Republican party, a large portion of the South—and some of the North—would have none of it. They pointed to social and economic conditions which they asserted would come in the wake of a Republican victory. They asked pointed questions—and sometimes got pointed answers. For example, an article in the *Jerseyman* (Morristown) said:

"You, sir, at the next election, with your honest face and patriotic heart would march up to the polls and deposit your vote for, say, Stephen A. Douglas, the people's choice. Following you would come a big, greasy, sweating, rank, kinky haired, thick lipped, crooked-shinned negro, filled with the passions and ignorance common to his race, treading on your heels, and jostling you in the crowd. Holding a ballot in his hand, he would deposit it in the box for, say Abraham Lincoln, thus neutralizing your vote, and doing so much to reduce you to the nigger level. What would you say to that, sir?"

"I should say," responded the man interrogated, "that the nigger had a d—d sight the most sense."

Even if the South believed that Lincoln did not plan to upset slavery where it then existed, this assurance was not enough. "Slavery cannot long endure without this right of expansion," asserted the *New Orleans Daily Delta*. "Everyone acknowledges this. To consent to give it up, is to say that we consent to regard this institution, which is 'flesh of our flesh,' as temporary!"

Some segments of the South were convinced their region faced a life-and-death struggle. Sen. Robert Toombs, of Georgia, reportedly threatened that if Lincoln were elected he would raise an army and cross the Potomac River with drawn sword. "This is an issue to be decided at the ballot box," the Senator challenged, "and if decided against you there, I shall invite you to decide it with the cartridge box."

In exploring the position of candidates on this critical issue reporters tossed them some tough questions. In a satire on such questioning a *Washington National Intelligencer* item quipped: "If elected, will you vote for a sufficient appropriation, by the Legislature, to have the artesian well in Charleston bored through to the Celestial Empire, so that South Carolina may *drap* through in the event of Mr. Lincoln's election?"

Another *Intelligencer* article was more serious when it prophesied:

On the ides of November next, when Jupiter hurls his angry lightning along the wires and announces the election of Lincoln, let the Southern Senators and the Southern people declare the fact, for it will then be a fact, that John C. Breckinridge is chosen the first President of the Southern Confederacy. . . .

Let the South hold the North as she holds the rest of mankind— enemies in war—in peace friends.

As Lincoln sat in Springfield and pondered the issue of slavery, he realized that there not only was cleavage between the South and the North but disagreement even within the Republican ranks. Greeley, as one example, asserted in the fall of 1860 that if the cotton states decided "they can do better out of the Union than in it we should let them go in peace." Henry Ward Beecher, dynamic Brooklyn minister, announced he had no objection to the South seceding. Many northern businessmen, hoping to avoid disruption of industry and commerce, favored compromise or even capitulation to the demands of the slaveholders. Lincoln, however, held steadfast to this principle his party had endorsed. "There is no possible compromise upon the extension of slavery. On that point hold firm, as with a chain of steel."

But the Republican aspirant actually did little "declaring" during the '60 campaign. He considered his tongue was tied. The *New York Daily Tribune* acknowledged the great public eagerness to determine Lincoln's intentions, then added: "Mr. Lincoln, however, is the last man to gratify this curiosity until the proper time shall arise. Not the slightest indication of his future movements is yielded to anybody." A cartoon of "The Great Exhibition of 1860" showed Lincoln with padlocked lips.

The *Cleveland Weekly Plain Dealer* carried a letter from

Eldora, Iowa, titled "Why don't the Black Republicans let Lincoln loose?" It answered:

Because they dare not—Lincoln would let the cats all out of the bag, the big black cats, the Thomas cats and little kitten cats. Such a *cat*astrophe never did happen save to General Scott, and such a caterwauling as there would be all around the Republican Wigwam!

"Honest Old Abe, won't you come out tonight . . . and dance by the light of the moon."

The *Baltimore Sun* declared that if Lincoln had clearly proclaimed his conversatism he would hardly have been heard of again during the campaign. The aggressive wing of the abolitionists, the *Sun* contended, would have dropped him for Gerrit Smith, "the regular abolitionist candidate." If Lincoln became President, declared another newspaper, he could no longer be all things to all people.

Even aside from political expediency, Lincoln had a watch-and-wait attitude toward the divisive questions of the day. He liked to tell about the time during his service as a circuit lawyer, when he stopped at an inn in a torrential rain. He and other attorneys were glad to find a Methodist presiding elder there too, for he was familiar with the treacherous Fox River, which lay ahead. When asked about the stream, the clergyman said he had crossed it often and understood it well, "but I have one fixed rule regarding the Fox River: I never cross it till I reach it."

Lincoln argued that his position on critical questions was well known when he was nominated and that he must not do anything that would modify his stand. So he pointed back to earlier speeches and statements to illustrate his position and he adamantly stuck to his guns. "Those who will not read or heed what I have already publicly said would not read or heed a repetition of it."

Some people looked to the *Weekly Illinois State Journal*

for reflections of Lincoln's ideas, for it was edited by E. L. Baker, a cousin by marriage of Mrs. Lincoln. The paper disclaimed any intention of speaking for the Springfield attorney, but many readers nevertheless believed that it was virtually Old Abe's mouthpiece.

For those persons who still were dissatisfied by Lincoln's silence and who did not consider the Springfield newspaper an adequate echo of his thoughts, the Republicans always had an answer: Lincoln would express his views from the east portico of the Capitol in Washington next March fourth.

CHAPTER ELEVEN

THE FOURTH ESTATE HOLDS FORTH

The newspapers manned the front lines in the political battle of 1860, with famous journalists from the larger cities as the heavy artillery. But much of the action was vaporous. As the *Easton* (Pa.) *Times* put it, a good way to light some of the cities and villages with gas would have been to set fire to their editors. In the opinion of the *Columbian Weekly Register* (New Haven):

One of the striking features of this campaign, as conducted by the Republican papers, is absence of sober appeals to the judgement of the electors . . . [There are] columns of childish trash, announcing forays of young Wide-Awakes into the neighboring towns, and the enormous consumption of baked beans, cider and ginger bread attendant thereon. Matters do not rise to the dignity of petty larceny on their mothers' cake baskets! "Heaven help the country in its hour of need!" if this is a fair sample of New England's coming manhood.

But papers had cordial words for those who saw eye-to-eye with them politically. The *Appleton* (Wis.) *Crescent* said of a "spicy paper," the *Madison* (Wis.) *Argus:*

It advocates Congressional Intervention to protect Slavery in the Territories, whether the people will or not; but that is only a slight variation of the undiluted Shanghai (Republican) doctrine of Congressional Intervention to prohibit Slavery where the People want it; and, like the old Deacon, who responded to the Minister's re-

180

mark that God created woman like man with a slight variation, they ought to throw up their hats and shout, "Bless God for the variation," and at once subscribe for the Argus.

Some compliments were left-handed ones. The *Jonesboro* (Ill.) *Gazette* said it admired the typographical improvement of the *Springfield Journal* and would consider it one of the better papers "were it not for its abominally dirty politics." An Indiana journal noted that one of its competitors had revealed that it might switch to Lincoln. The first newspaper commented that the Republican party had managed to live despite the *opposition* of that sheet, but it doubted that it could survive its *support*.

The Washington *Constitution* dispensed with even left-handed compliments when it referred to the *Richmond* (Va.) *Whig* as surpassing the "foul mouthed journals of its own and the Black Republican party." "We are obliged to soil our columns," the *Constitution* then added, by reprinting some of the statements from the Whig:

Among other things it charged that "Old Lane is sputtering tobacco juice and detestable grammar in the faces of the sovereigns of North Carolina" and that "if he were really to get his just deserts while in North Carolina, we should soon hear of his dangling from the tallest pine tree in that noble old state."

Almost daily some newspaper asserted that one or more— usually more—of its competitors were remiss in veracity. For instance, the *Saint Paul* (Minn.) *Pioneer* charged that the *Winona* (Minn.) *Democrat* would change political positions any day for fifty dollars or less. It added that the editor, when sober, controlled one vote.

Statistics concerning the campaign varied widely, depending on the political complexion of the newspaper. The *Weekly Wisconsin Patriot* (Madison) advised those readers scanning the political reports of its competitor, the *Journal,* to halve its Republican figures and double its Democratic estimates to get approximately correct results.

The *New York Daily Tribune* suggested that the feebleness of the Democratic party was demonstrated by its puny lies and liars. Whereas it once featured "great fat black lies that had venom and sting in them—lies that evinced originality, audacity, and even genius," now Democratic lies were "little, contemptible, picayune falsehoods."

Not all newspapers agreed that the fine art of lying had degenerated. The *Burlington* (Vt.) *Sentinel* took a broad swipe at the "howling, yelping Republican journals" and then singled one out by declaring "for shame, Mr. Free Press! Where *did* you learn to lie so dreadfully." Douglas Democratic papers were the target of this broadside from the *Louisville* (Ky.) *Courier,* reprinted in the Washington *Constitution:* "For downright, hard, intense, deliberate and willful lying, the *Cincinnati Enquirer* is only equaled in all the land by Forney's *Philadelphia Press.* It has, of course, numerous feeble imitators but the *Press* is its only formidable rival in mendacity." One editor suggested as the epitaph for his opponent's tombstone: "Here *lies* an editor."

Besides charging prevarication, newspapers frequently accused one another of shoveling offal into their news columns. The *Daily Omaha Nebraskan* declared that in large Eastern cities, men were hired to make the rounds at night removing the contents of the "basement stories of outhouses, called in agricultural parlance 'night soil.' " Some of these men became wealthy, the *Nebraskan* declared, went West, and became Black Republican editors. "But the old habit of pitching night soil clings to them and its sweetness hangs on around them still."

One New York newspaper imputed that someone from the *Rochester* (N. Y.) *Democrat* hurled a rotten egg at a Douglas procession. It concluded, however, that "a more filthy missive would have been one of the *recent editorials* of that paper."

Compared to these journals, a Hartford, Connecticut paper was quite restrained when it said an opposition paper was so abolitionist "charcoal would make a white mark on it."

Sometimes the lambasting was pointedly personal. The *Republican Farmer* (Bridgeport, Conn.) reported:

We are sorry to hear that the Giant-Killer of the Norwalk Gazette had the misfortune to fracture his unmentionable during a recent excruciating effort to lampoon the Republican Farmer. The cause which led to this terrible strain on his breeching, it seems, was our endorsement of the proposition to unite all national men in this State on one ticket against "Old Abe". . . . We did not think the chap of the Gazette would take hold so strongly as to damage the covering to his caudal appendage in the encounter.

The *Weekly Wisconsin Patriot* (Madison) declared it had not intended to rip all the feathers off the "dainty little editor" of the *Whitewater Register* when it aimed a shot at him, but "the rascal flutters so terribly" the shot must have hit a vital part. And the *Fayette and Union Telegraph* (Connersville, Ind.), said there had been a great demand for rails by the Black Republicans and that it was reported the editor of the *Times* "has been sleeping with an old *rail* every since."

Most newspaper encounters were verbal ones, but a few involved physical action. One Indiana Republican editor finagled a copy of a Douglas paper printed on the outside but with the inner pages still blank. He printed the inside on his own press, displaying the names of Lincoln and Hamlin prominently at the head of the columns. In Raleigh, North Carolina, a couple editors tangled, one enthusiastically caning the other, who fired three wild shots before friends interfered.

In July, the *Washington National Intelligencer* contended there had been an unusual absence of partisan rancor and personal vituperation during the campaign. Apparently the *Intelligencer* hadn't been reading the papers.

The level and nature of the assaults may have been indicated by this anecdote concerning a Congressman. The contender for his office told him, "Why, I could button your ears back and swallow you whole." "Well," replied the Congressman, "if you did, you would have more brains in your stomach than you ever had in your head."

The *New Orleans Daily Delta* declared Lincoln and Douglas were in equally bad odor on the slavery question and that when a Lincolnite and a Douglasite bet with each other on the Presidential race, it was scent against scent.

Among the impassioned attackers of the Republicans was the *Boston Herald,* which declared:

Who are these pompous snobs that undertake to dictate to the people? We meet them on the street, at the eating saloons and in all public places, preaching their damnable doctrines and disgusting everybody with their foul abuse of gentlemen every way their superiors. . . . We shall oftentimes find them inhuman monsters, practicing all sorts of rascality, cheating and defrauding their creditors and refusing to pay their honest debts; and yet they are the loudest in proclaiming human freedom and traducing private character . . . All honest people should go to the polls and vote down the imposters, thereby ridding the community of their disgusting presence.

A New York campaign speaker said: "My friends, General Tallmadge says he has some friends among the Republicans. Thank God, I have not one. I hate them, every damned one of them; and if I was God Almighty, the first act of my life would be to send every damned one of them to hell." A man in the audience yelled, "they are all going there now!" Then the speaker added, "I know it, but damn them, I wouldn't let one of them last his natural term out."

A Republican song which featured the refrain "with Lincoln and Hamlin, we'll conquer or die" prompted the *Fayette and Union Telegraph* (Connersville, Ind.) to comment: "While we do not admit that their deaths would be any positive loss to [the] community we would like to see them yield up the Ghost in a better cause."

The *Weekly Wisconsin Patriot* (Madison) noted that some Republican papers complained that Douglas' coattail hung too near *terra firma*. The *Patriot* admitted that Douglas "never feels above common folks" and added that he had one advantage over the Republican nominee—Douglas' brains were located above his coattail. The *Cherry Valley* (N. Y.) *Gazette* also took a poke at Old Abe. It declared that in view of the insignificance of the head of the Republican ticket and the location of the tail—Hamlin was from Maine—the Republican party could be said to be running with its mite and Maine.

The *New York Atlas* told about a baby abandoned on a doorstep. Its Republican finder, the story went on, christened it "Hamlin A(nd) Lincoln," and sent it to the poorhouse. The *Atlas* commented: "First abandoned by its mother, then named after the Republican ticket, and finally sent to the poorhouse. We can think of nothing more that could have been added to that child's misfortune."

Free homesteads were a Republican slogan, and an Indiana anti-Republican paper pointed to Hamlin as the embodiment of the "Free Dirt Party," asserting that he was noted for wearing dirty shirts.

Among the barbs flung at the Democrats, was the *Weekly Illinois State Journal* comment on the Democratic claim that the Republicans must thank Douglas for making Lincoln what he was. "So did George the Third make a Washington," the *Journal* retorted.

That the Democratic party was worn to a frazzle was illustrated by a speaker with this anecdote: A woman bought a pair of silk stockings for her wedding. After that she wore them only on gala occasions. Finally, a hole appeared and the old lady's daughter patched it with cotton. Then more holes, and more cotton patches, until not a trace of silk was left. "But still the old lady called for her *silk* stockings," said the speaker. "The Democracy has been patching its stockings until now every shred of the old Democracy has disappeared. Still, the candidates who go before the people call for the silk stockings, and they are darned old things."

The tired old Democrats wouldn't be around long, according to the *Daily Gate City* (Keokuk, Iowa). It suggested that Republicans contribute to a certain Democratic meeting, for "it will be the same as a funeral, and therefore assist at the obsequies with all charity and becoming solemnity."

The *Sacramento Daily Union* quoted a Douglas paper, as accusing Lincoln of habitually saying "damn!" It added, "Then Lincoln says more than Douglas is worth." To a Democratic editor's charge that a Republican speaker had struck low punches, the *Manhattan* (Kan.) *Express* asserted those were the only kind likely to hit the mark. A real back-hander, reported one newspaper, was delivered by a newspaper vendor at the Chicago post office, who hung a Democrat's picture between two jackasses' heads. The caption read, "When shall we three meet again?"

Often in 1860 newspaper items provoked rebuttals. And frequently a third and fourth newspaper would pick up the previous comments, each adding its own pungent paragraphs. The *Albany Atlas and Argus* printed contradictory comments by the *Boston Courier* and the *New York Daily Tribune* as to the probable outcome of the election, then borrowed from the poet for this punch line:

> Oh! Wad some power the giftie gie us,
> To see ourselves as others see us!

The *Louisville Journal* declared that "nobody denies the patriotism of John Bell." "We deny it," replied the *North Carolina Patriot*. The *Journal* came back with the clincher, "We know you do; we meant *you* when we said that *nobody* denied it."

The *Boston Journal* carried this double-take: "Lincoln is a dead letter in this county," from the *Eastern Argus;* and the retort from the *Groton Mercury,* "Like other 'dead letters,' he will be sent to Washington."

The *Jonesboro* (Ill.) *Gazette* used this item captioned "Hit 'Em Again":

If the Republican party is faulty, come in and help make it better—*New York Tribune.*

His satanic highness might hold out the same inducements to settle on his premises—"if it is too hot, come in and cool it"—*New Haven Register.*

One Republican editor, bragging about the physical attributes of Old Abe, declared he could run faster and jump higher than any man in the country. To which the *Prairie du Chien* (Wis.) *Courier* rejoined, "So can a kangaroo."

Douglas, as well as Lincoln, was a target for pot-shots. This newspaper barrage was printed by the *Floridian and Journal* (Tallahassee):

Democracy survives.—*Press.*

So does the devil.—*Intelligencer.*

And as both are now fairly in the field for the next campaign, "choose ye whom ye will serve."—*Press.*

"Of two evils, choose ye the least." We'll take the devil.—*Intelligencer.*

Opposition editors go to the devil as naturally as a duck takes to water.—*National Democrat.*

The *Fond du Lac Weekly Commonwealth* printed this exchange:

There isn't a buggy load of Democrats in the State who dream of voting for Breckinridge.—*Fond du Lac Press.*

Admit it. The "buggiest" load goes for Douglas.—*Madison Argus.*

Digging to uncover something on which they could trump up charges against Honest Old Abe, his opponents brought up the allegation that Abe, while in Congress in 1847-49, included three pairs of boots, totaling twenty-five dollars, in his stationery allowance. Republicans were quick to claim that the records disproved the accusation, but they couldn't keep the story from getting a good run in anti-Lincoln papers.

"Whether further examination of the stationery bill," said the *Washington Constitution,* "will disclose the fact that the Government supplied Mr. Lincoln with his shirt and 'unmentionables' remains to be seen." A Republican speaker declared the Congressional boot matter was a "small potato" affair and the *Republican Farmer* (Bridgeport, Conn.) agreed, saying, "we think so too—for any Congressman who will filch twenty-five dollars to pay for his boots from the United States Treasury the way Lincoln did is a very 'small potato'—very!"

The *Republican Farmer* (Bridgeport, Conn.) carried this exchange of blows:

There is a town in Middlesex county, Mass., where it has been ascertained that every legal voter in the town is a Lincoln man.—*Hartford Courant.*

Yes, it is called "Skunk's Misery," and there is only one voter in the town. Lincoln has lately sent him a pair of "those boots"—so he can stand on the Chicago Platform.—*New Haven Register.*

Lincoln's Congressional record, combed thoroughly, although not too objectively, also yielded political ammunition relating to the Mexican War. The opposition asserted that Abe voted against providing supplies to American soldiers in Mexico, and that he opposed a bill to give every soldier 160 acres of land. A satiric article on Lincoln's Mexican War record in the *Cleveland Weekly Plain Dealer* was headlined "Oh; isn't he a darling!"

Having explored Lincoln's early political days in Sangamon County, the opposition publicized his sponsorship of the construction of a toll bridge. They asserted that the toll-keeper never collected "the first red cent of toll, for the simple reason that everybody could ford the creek."

And then there was the liquor issue. The high priority of alcohol in some people's scheme of things was indicated by an item in the *Troy* (Ohio) *Times* in which a husband implored a vamoosed wife to return to bed and board.

"Jane, your absence will ruin all. Think of your husband—your parents—your children. Return—all may be well—happy. At any rate, enclose the key to the cupboard where the gin is."

Some Congressmen were rather uninhibited about liquoring up. The *New York Daily Tribune* in 1860 described a speech by Senator Wigfall, of Texas:

It was quite evident that the Senator had been imbibing too freely on old rye. In plain English, the Senator was drunk, which makes him, as he expressed it, "in a happy humor for speaking." He kept the Senate and galleries in a roar of laughter for some three hours till the inspiration of his potations subsided. . . . He had his grog on the desk before him and drank and talked. . . .

A letter from "Bessy Smith" in the *Tri-Weekly Missouri Republican* (St. Louis) gave proof of the political potency of the beverage a hundred years ago. She quoted her father as saying earlier, "No fear of our losing the election. . . . The corn crop is coming in tremendously large all over the country. Corn makes whiskey, whiskey makes . . . votes! It's a sum in simple proportion."

Lincoln was dragged into the barroom topic when the opposition accused him of having been a clerk in a "common dram shop." The facts were, according to the *Springfield* (Mass.) *Daily Republican* that Lincoln once was a store clerk and as was customary then, the merchant, besides keeping the usual supply of notions, calico, groceries, tobacco, and similar items, always had on hand a barrel or two of Monongahela or Old Rye to sell.

The *American Eagle* (Paoli, Ind.) declared that Lincoln

rose to prominence by "retailing red-eye at a picayune a nip." An Iowa newspaper asserted "There is no evidence that he don't now take his whiskey daily"—an announcement likely to start a stampede of Democrats into the Republican camp, another journal commented. The *New Hampshire Patriot* (Concord) contended that Lincoln made poor whiskey and sold it for a good price.

Douglas shared this ridicule on the liquor issue. One newspaper observed that he "began to imbibe the true spirit of New England early in life," and a competitor rejoined, "Well he might, for it cost him only twenty-five cents a gallon." The *Rochester* (N. Y.) *Democrat* noted that Douglas was regarded by another newspaper as a sort of demigod; but, replied the *Elmira* (N. Y.) *Press,* his friends regarded him as a sort of demi-john.

This purported comment by a good Democrat was reprinted in the *Bucyrus* (Ohio) *Weekly Journal:*

> I—hic—I'm a dem—hic—democrat clear through, soaked—hic —in democracy, but it—hic—it's like goo-hic—good whiskey, too mu—hic—much of a goo—good thing is good for noth—hic— nothing.

Another side issue was a depression, or threat of depression. The *New York Herald* urged merchants "imperiled by the prospective success of the Lincoln ticket" to stump the state against him.

However, "the game of panic . . . is so uniformly practiced that everybody expects it just as certainly as they do any other symptom of our four-yearly excitement," said the *New York Daily Tribune.* Later it commented:

> It is the last chance of the rumor-monger, and they are driving things to the most desperate pitch. The merchants are called upon to fail; the suspension of the banks is advertised; the holders of their bills are called upon to run those institutions; a rapid and ruinous decline in the value of all property is predicted; secession

pointed out as inevitable; revolutionary proceedings invoked and bloodshed and war threatened.

While the passionate partisans delighted in scorching their opponents, they always stood ready to convert them to save them from ruin. But proselyting was a tough task. "A Democrat is like an Indian—hard to make anything else of him," insisted the *Weekly Illinois State Journal*. "Nine cases out of ten when you think one [a Democrat] is weaned from the party, and has become a free man, the first thing you know, he is back in the mire again. . . . Many have gone back to the party and all of them are meaner Democrats than ever."

But the Republicans persisted in their evangelism. The *New York Daily Tribune* suggested they meet every amicable overture more than half-way. A Democratic paper that switched to Lincoln won the plaudits of Republican journals across the land. And they reprinted widely the story of the rescued Democrat who declared he would vote for Abe but was warned he would "get cheated." The convert replied, "I voted for Pierce and for Buchanan, and got awfully cheated both times . . . I had as lief be cheated once by the Republicans as all the time by the Democrats." Another voter "saved" by the Republicans explained: "I tinks I leaves de Democrats long time ago, but every year dey pulls de wool over mine eyes, and so I goes mit tem agin; but dis time dey pull it so tam far dat I sees right ober de top! Dat ish vy I votes de Republics ticket."

Other parties claimed their converts, too. The *Ohio Statesman* (Columbus) declared that Ohio Republicans were stampeding to Breckinridge. How was such defection from the Republican cause engineered? The *Cleveland Weekly Plain Dealer* gave this explanation of one conversion, although it was to the Douglas wing.

Entitled "How Jack Became a Democrat," the story explained that a newly married couple was "snugly ensconced in bed" when Jack unwittingly alluded to his favorite subject, the Republican party. His shocked bride asked if he really was a Republican, and he admitted he was a "regular out and outer, double dyed and twisted in the wool." Then "just double and twist yourself out of bed," she commanded. He left the room and each night knocked at the bedroom door, but his knock remained unanswered. Several nights later, about midnight, three loud raps were heard, followed by more and more raps until the door rattled violently. "Who's there?" cried the wife, as if aroused from a deep sleep. "The best Democrat you ever did see!" Jack replied.

So both sides—or rather, all sides—claimed converts galore. The outlook for the election, then, depended somewhat on which paper you read—and believed. According to some journals, Lincoln had about as much chance as a snowball in Hades. The *Union Democrat* (Manchester, N. H.) said if Lincoln lost New York "he is a goner." If he lost Pennsylvania "he is a goner," if he lost Ohio and Rhode Island "he is a goner." It plunged on and on, then concluded, "I consider him 'a goner' any way."

Enthusiasm over Abe Lincoln's nomination, said the *Daily Chicago Herald,* had completely subsided. "The pop bottle burst, effervesced for a moment, and now there is nothing left but the flattest kind of beer." The *New York Evening Post* stated that Republican "rowdy clubs" were breaking up and their members were having to go back to honest work, stealing, or the prize ring for a living.

A Southern Illinois correspondent said there was a stampede away from Lincoln there, and that by election the Lincoln supporters would dwindle to "the little end of none at all." The *Nebraska City News* thought Lincoln's defeat just as certain as any event ordained by God. The Black Republican party was fast breaking up, chimed the *Jonesboro* (Ill.) *Gazette.* And a *Cleveland Weekly Plain Dealer* headline called attention to poor

A⚬Ⅎ L—N⊃OⅠ⪰

SMASHED UP AND DONE FOR

Some Indianapolis picnickers, said an item in the *Fort Wayne Sentinel,* heard the firing of cannons for two Republican VIP's arriving in the state capital. The picnickers asked what the shots were for, and someone suggested that someone had drowned and they were trying to raise the body. The newspaper thought the man had unconsciously pictured the inevitable fate of the Republican party. The *Plain Dealer* headlined the outlook this way:

LINCOLN LAID OUT
THE LAST NAIL IN HIS COFFIN CLINCHED
No Black Republican Can Ever Be President
Of These United States

Election of Lincoln, shouted the *Albany Atlas and Argus,* would be the greatest calamity which could befall the nation. A *Prairie du Chien* (Wis.) *Courier* item suggested that if the Republicans were going to win, the stronger the better. Then with more power they would have more responsibility and "the sooner they would swallow each other." But the Washington *National Intelligencer* conjectured that Lincoln might well retire in disgust after his first year in office, having neither power nor patronage.

Other journals foresaw a kinder fate for the Republicans. The *Troy* (Ohio) *Times* reported that a Michigan editor had predicted a bumper crop of wheat and Republican votes in his area. In some neighborhoods farmers were confident of "thirty bushel to the acre, and not a Democrat within five miles." Democrats were so scarce in one Pennsylvania county, another newspaper item said, that rail-splitters had to maul each other to stir up any excitement.

In state elections in early fall, the Republicans swept Pennsylvania, Indiana, and Ohio, and the outlook for Lincoln grew rosier. His law partner, Herndon, who was making a speech when these results were announced, said the crowd ran yelling out of the hall and he never succeeded in finishing his speech. Republicans agreed with Seward that their party, only six years old, "was no sapling, but a sturdy oak, from the acorn seed of necessity."

The *Exeter* (N. H.) *News-Letter* quoted Seward as explaining that the prevalent political commotion in the 1860's was a result of the country's trying to turn over, having "lain too long on one side." "For forty years it has been lying on its South side; now, it is going to try its North side."

By October the newspapers and magazines were expressing considerable confidence in Lincoln's triumph. A *Weekly Illinois State Journal* headline declared "Lincoln's election unmistakably indicated." The *Atlantic Monthly* said the relative quiet near the wind-up of the campaign arose chiefly from the general belief that Republican success was signed and sealed. The *New York Daily Tribune* thought "the Republican President will be inaugurated, as it were, by universal consent, amid an era of good feeling."

One reason for the favorable Republican outlook was the large number of German immigrants in the Old Northwest who lined up with the Republicans. Influential factors included the party's position on human freedom and homestead legislation, and the devoted services of the German campaigner, Carl Schurz, a Wisconsin member of the Republican National Committee. The *Cleveland Weekly Plain Dealer* called "Squirtz" (Schurz) a "hair-lipped [sic] renegade who left his country for his country's good," but to German-Americans and Republican leaders he was a great politician who packed a powerful punch.

The Republicans also had some backing among the French-born, and there were French Republican Clubs in New York

City, Newark, and other places. The Democrats tended to hold the Irish, who were heavily represented in the United States at this time. The *Portsmouth* (N. H.) *Journal* reported that a marshal in a Douglas Democratic parade yelled out, "Pat, your torch is bustin!—Throw it away!" And instantly a hundred and fifty torches fell to the ground.

Settlers beyond the Mississippi had some interest in these struggles among Lincoln, Douglas, Breckinridge, and Bell forces, too, but these frontiersmen were more often occupied with interests closer to home. For example, the *Grasshopper Fall Gazette* in Kansas Territory was reporting the presence of wild horses in that area. Pioneers out there also were reading about buffalo hunts, new stage routes, wind wagons, rigorous trips to Pike's Peak, Indian affairs, the Great Drought, Moline plows, homesteading, and railroads. Yet the *Kansas State Record* (Topeka) said that "Hurrah for Lincoln and Hamlin!" was a postscript to nearly every letter it had received recently.

In the Far West many residents were more interested in the Pony Express than the political campaign. An 1860 item in the *Manhattan* (Kan.) *Express* said:

Indian warfare is at work on the California side to stop this great enterprise. The scalping knife and the torch are doing their work. Red-skins are combining, murdering families, shooting at riders, burning stations and shooting horses, and will not stop till defeated and overthrown.

But even way out yonder there was considerable interest in political news. The *Oregon Weekly Times* (Portland) explained in one issue that "we are indebted to Wells Fargo, Reynolds and Barrett for a good supply of Eastern and California papers" from which a selection of political items were gleaned. One *Times* article told about a Republican gathering in Oregon at which a Democrat was allowed to speak and that he "utterly demolished" the Republican orator's "sophistical, evasive harangue."

The other side of the story was indicated in a Pony Express news item in the *New York Daily Tribune*. It said "large gains for the Republicans in California were counted upon in case that party carried Pennsylvania and other states voting [in October]."

Douglas—not Lincoln—was about to be seated in the Presidential chair, if some newspapers were to be believed. The *Chicago Times* pointed to a Democratic triumph in November, asserting that "all the guns in the campaign in Illinois thus far speak Democratic thunder." Small lads in some Democratic families proclaimed themselves "Douglas boys," not "Lincolnpoops."

Illinois Democrats sought to have an old log schoolhouse near Winchester, where Douglas had taught thirty years earlier, adopted as a national Democratic emblem. This, it was asserted, would be especially suitable for a party which "believes in the intelligence of the people." It would be in appropriate contrast to the old fence rail which the Republicans were riding as their hobby horse.

"Every vote cast for Stephen A. Douglas," the *Chicago Times and Herald* assured, "is a vote for liberty and self-government. Every vote for Lincoln is to take that right from ten millions of free white Americans and confer it on four millions of barbarous Africans."

Ridiculing a Douglas "carnival and ox roast" a hostile journal rambled on in this vein for several thousand words:

But the early crowd came to see, not Douglas, but dinner, and they expected to see that dinner cooked then and there. They hoped to be delectated with the sight of a large ox cooked whole in their august presence, and served out for their watering mouths in hot and juicy slices—also the calf—also the hog—also the sheep. Alas! for human hopes; the human carnivora were disappointed all. Not only was the ox not cooked in their presence, but there was no fire on the premises. No, not enough to light half an ounce of blasting powder. The ox had apparently been cooked for uncounted days—also the calf—also the hog—also the sheep. But even the cold cooked corpus of the slaughtered ruminant was not observable—the ox in addition to being already cold and cooked, was cut up—also the hog—also the sheep. The calf was as yet intact, having been, indeed, roasted whole, and was now calmly reposing in dignified integrity, on an ashen rail, which impaled him lengthways. Significant spectacle! A Democratic calf split by a Republican rail.

"Never was a party so badgered as the Democratic party," chortled the *New York Daily Tribune,* proving that "there is no peace to the wicked." Some journals labeled the Little Giant the "Big Dwarf." One paper declared that "to an arrogance unprecedented he united a dictatorial temper" and without question was "the most heartless, cold, and designing demagogue" who ever existed.

The story of a Tennessee woman who didn't like corn, cornbread, corncakes, corn puddings, or corn in any form, but when it was made into whiskey "could worry a little down," was related by the *Daily Gate City* (Keokuk, Iowa). Some people didn't like the Democratic party, the paper explained, but when offered as Douglasism, they could "worry a little of it down." The paper moralized that tampering with Douglasism, like drinking too much hooch, could bring on the "delirious thimbles" and that before long "the man with the poker may be after you."

A Democratic lady, according to the editor of another paper, had proposed that he might kiss her and a dozen of her kissable friends if he would support Douglas. He added that if he were to swallow the Little Giant, he could not have the impudence to kiss a lady for six months, for his breath would smell worse than if he had eaten raw onions.

When Republican papers covered Douglas rallies and processions, they were careful to temper their praise. The *Weekly*

Illinois State Journal said Douglas spoke at a Douglas rally and "reflected the highest credit upon—Mr. Douglas!" The procession that night, the *Journal* added, "reminded us of the boy going through a graveyard at night whistling to keep up his courage."

Even as Lincoln's stock rose higher some optimistic Douglasites kept asserting that Doug was doing okay. A farmer near Wooster, Ohio, was positive the Little Giant would win in a landslide. A cherry tree on the farm was loaded with fruit, he explained, and this happened only in Presidential years when a Democratic candidate was destined for victory.

In many areas, however, the cherry trees seem barren, figuratively speaking. One newspaper item said there had been only one "full-blooded Douglas squatter" in a certain Kentucky county and, to the honor of the county, he had scrammed. From the Southwest came the report that "there cannot be found enough Douglas men in Arizona to fire one round over his grave in November."

A New York City Republican speaker suggested setting aside several cages in Central Park for exhibiting rabid Democrats. They were fast disappearing, he explained, and "there would not be an opportunity to catch this singular biped a few months hence."

An item from Syracuse, New York, published in the *New York Tribune,* declared that the Giant Killer of Illinois was going to rout the "Sham Democrats." "We propose to have a good time in splitting rails and fencing in the Democrats where they can ruminate for the next four years for their past unfaithfulness and rascalities." The *Bangor* (Maine) *Daily Union* agreed that Douglas was not a sectional candidate, "because there is no section . . . from which he will receive a solitary vote."

"A short sermon to Douglas worshipers" in the *Weekly Illinois State Journal* was headed by this extract from Scripture: "And devout men carried Stephen to his burial, and made great lamentation over him.—Acts VIII: 2." The article warned of the folly and sinfulness of worshipping man, then concluded:

My dear Douglas brethren, I know it is hard for us to believe that Stephen is snuffed out. . . . We shall never behold his coat-tail dragging on the ground anymore. Its beautiful folds have been wrapped around his wounded seat of honor, and he has been lain at rest. The "irrepressible conflict" has dealt him a smasher on the gob, and his voice will no longer charm us with the beautiful song of popular sovereignty. Therefore cease your blubbering for Stephen.

The Southern Democratic faction also had equally ardent supporters and detractors. When Breckinridge and Lane were selected as the standard bearers, a St. Louis newspaper said that all good men rejoice at this decided repudiation of "Douglas' odious heresy of squatter sovereignty." A Memphis paper proclaimed that "the hilltops are blazing with beacon fires and the welkin is ringing with the shouts of the multitude."

When Breckinridge Democrats hoisted a hickory pole and banner in a Southern Illinois community, their cheers "shook the very hills to their center," trumpeted the *Jonesboro* (Ill.) *Gazette*. The Washington *Constitution* on July 4 pulled all the stops in this fashion:

The earnest and eager enthusiasm manifested on all hands in behalf of the National Constitutional democratic nominees for the Presidency and vice presidency, Messrs. Breckinridge and Lane, as far eclipses the mere brag of the Lincolnites and Douglasites, and their spoils-seeking, mere mercenary demonstrations for their respective candidates, as the light and warmth of the July sun eclipses that of the sky-rocket and Roman candles that are fired on the night of the fourth.

Not all Breckinridge support was confined to the South. Although the North possessed "little that is marketable, except ice and granite," according to a Southern speaker, it did have a few newspapers valued below Mason and Dixon's. These included the *New York Journal of Commerce, New York Day Book, Brooklyn Eagle, Buffalo Post, Schenectady News,* and several other Breckinridge supporters.

Breckinridge's running mate, Lane, drew considerable criticism and occasional abuse because of his limited education. One newspaper alleged that Lane, when he sold cordwood in Indiana, used an "X" mark in signing receipts. But Breckinridge papers bounded back with the rebuttal that this U. S. officer in the Mexican War "has written his name upon his country's history with the sword." Another newspaper vowed that Lane would leave a legible mark on opposing candidates in November and would "Xpel them all from the White House." Lane was greeted with considerable enthusiasm in the South, especially in Raleigh, North Carolina, where his grandfather had owned the estate that became the state-capitol site.

One did not have to look far to find those who pooh-poohed Breckinridge and the claims of his faction. A Bell man who attended a Breckinridge mass meeting asserted there weren't enough Breckinridge men present "to lynch an Abolitionist" or to make a decent funeral procession.

Breckinridge's youthfulness—he was in his late thirties—was focused on by the *Binghamton* (N. Y.) *Standard.* It added, however, that his age was not really important. "Even had he not reached the age required by the Constitution, he would have ample time to remedy that defect before his election."

Some newspapers asserted that Douglasites preferred the election of Lincoln to that of Breckinridge, for voting Lincoln into the White House would be sweet revenge on Southern Democrats. Another journal scorned "men ready to sell the South—to sell their souls for a mess of Federal favor."

One of the most fervent Breckinridge leaders was Alabama's Yancey. While this "Fire-Eater" was a hero in much of the South, he had foes even in that area. The *Spirit of the Age* (Woodstock, Vt.) reported that Yancey was hung in effigy in Okolona, Miss. The *New York Evening Post* quoted the *Louisville* (Ky.) *Journal* as saying "We don't wish Yancey dead, but we are sorry his mother didn't refuse to have his father." Then the *Journal* revised its wishes a bit: "Mr. Yancey never stood upon a platform that we could approve [and] we presume he never will till he is about to be hung."

The Breckinridge group claimed President James Buchanan for their camp. One newspaper alleged that the President had declared every Democrat was free to vote as he wished, but at the same time "Buck" was busy chopping off the heads of Douglasites. This reminded the paper of the French officer who told his company, "you are at liberty to vote as you please; anyone who doesn't vote as I do will be shot."

A New England newspaper half-heartedly supported Lincoln, contending that "a change cannot be for the worse." And a New Jersey journal quipped that Lincoln had always been an honest man, but "he will at last turn out a rascal—about the fourth day of March." The *Portsmouth* (N. H.) *Journal* said that Buchanan, the fifteenth President, had completed his last annual message. "Like the shoemaker, he never will get beyond his last. He has made a cobbling piece of work of his administration."

"I wish old Jackson was in old Buchanan's place," an admirer of the late Andy Jackson was quoted in the *Worcester* (Mass.) *Daily Spy*. "I ain't so particular about that," replied another. "I'd be satisfied if old Buchanan was in old Jackson's place."

Thus, with stabs in the back and pats on the back, went the campaign for the Breckinridge faction.

To a sizeable segment of the voters, the heroes of the campaign were neither Lincoln and Hamlin, Douglas and John-son, nor Breckinridge and Lane. They were Bell and Everett, standard-bearers for the Constitutional Union Party. This group had its own hoopla. One of their mass meetings in Philadelphia was advertised by a six-horse omnibus carrying a band, and a wagon on which a large bell was tolled. By October the *Abingdon Virginian* could herald "the most cheering promises of the success of the Constitutional Union ticket in Virginia. Many men are coming to their senses everywhere."

Not everyone was so optimistic, and they pulled out the puns to say so. For instance, one young man was asked if he thought the people would elect Bell, whether or no. "Elect Bell-Wether?" he remarked. "I should as soon expect them to elect Ewe!"

At a Bell reception in Nashville, there was a banner upon which was inscribed "We Honor John Bell, of the Union." The staff snapped and the banner dropped upon the speaker's head. "May the Gods avert the omen!" he exclaimed.

The chances for election looked mighty slim for some of the four chief candidates, but at least they could be said to be *running* for President. In the case of some minor candidates, you had to look closely to determine if they even were walking. Old Sam Houston of Texas was backed here and there, again and again. A big demonstration for him was held in Union Square in New York City, and the *New York Sun* beat its drums for the old warrior, but not many heard and heeded. Gerrit Smith, abolitionist, occasionally was mentioned as a candidate, too, usually when some barb was being hurled at him.

An interesting development of the 1860 campaign was the Fusion movement in the East, especially in New York, New Jersey, Rhode Island, and Pennsylvania. A New York City newspaper had called attention earlier to the wranglings of

Douglas, Bell, and Breckinridge men, and added: "We have the extraordinary spectacle presented of all these factions devouring each other, while their common enemy is marching by in full procession, as on a holiday excursion, to the White House." Another paper termed the separate State conventions a grindstone upon which the Democrats were sharpening their knives to cut their own throats. "It is either murder or suicide," it declared.

The Democratic party, then, was in a bad way. A Republican newspaper suggested that by uniting, the factions possibly could cure the disease—although they might be unable to withstand the doctors.

The nature of the Fusion movement, which sought to encompass Northern Democrats, Southern Democrats, and Bell-Everett forces, was illustrated by a telegram reprinted in the *Toledo Blade:* "Charley and Julia met . . . yesterday—quarreled and parted forever—met again this morning and parted to meet no more—met again this evening and were married."

In New York, it was maintained, "there seems to be a perfect union upon one electoral ticket." Such fusion was a coalition against—not for. It was a concerted effort to beat Lincoln. "This disposes of Mr. Lincoln's pretensions for the Presidency," the *Nebraska City News* rejoiced. "He is gone up!" But even if Lincoln did win, a Southern newspaper calculated, the Democrats still would have the power in Congress and the Supreme Court. "We trust our Government, under a good Providence, will still live; and that 'the everlasting negro' will be permitted to quit politics, and, unmolested, to cultivate cotton; and his Northern friends mind their own business, and spin their own yarn."

However, most Easterners had refused to swallow Fusion, the *New York Daily Tribune* asserted. Republicans poked fun at Fusion's "succotash" ticket or its "mongrel" ticket. The Presidential candidates from the three Fusion groups sometimes were referred to as "the world, the flesh, and the devil."

A Congressional candidate, observing that his competitor was trying to please both Breckinridge and Douglas, pointed out that this was a great circus equestrian act. It wasn't easy, he explained, to ride upon two Democratic horses that were racing in opposite directions, "and the great question is whether he will split or stretch." Republican Senator Seward quipped, concerning the New York Fusion movement: "The more they unite, the more they won't carry it [New York]."

So there were attempts to fuse and confuse. And there were also many attempts, through straw votes, "to see which way the cat was going to jump" in November. For twenty-five cents, Bostonians received a triple ticket to the Boston Theater, Music Hall, and Tremont Temple where they not only could listen to brass bands and quartets, but also ballot for President. About five thousand votes were cast, with Lincoln, Bell, Breckinridge, and Douglas scoring in that order. A few votes went to Sam Houston and the Prince of Wales! A similar affair was held at McVicker's Theatre, Chicago. Straw votes were also taken on trains and river boats. When one poll was being taken, a fellow remarked, "As against all the candidates in the field, I am for the devil!" The census taker then announced the results: 47 votes for Douglas, 43 for Lincoln, one for Breckinridge, and one for "another candidate." The census taker commented, "It is pretty even with Douglas and Lincoln, but is neck and neck with Breckinridge and the devil."

A Connecticut newspaper attributed the large Lincoln majorities in many polls on trains and steam boats to the "thimble-riggers, gamblers, pickpockets, and pugilists [who] are always traveling about the country." Democrats, who earn their bread honestly, stay home and vote where it counts. Lincoln did not win all the straw polls, however. One man voted for him on a river boat at Natchez, Mississippi, according to the *Daily Gate City* (Keokuk, Iowa), and "the other passengers immediately stripped him, covered him with tar and feathers, and set him afloat in a canoe." A straw vote taken on the steamship *Alabama* gave sixty-four votes to Breckinridge, thirty-one to Bell, ten to Douglas, and one to Lincoln.

Predicting the outcome of the election became a pastime. Many people placed their hard-earned cash on their ability to guess correctly. The *Boston Herald* reported that "the bluster of betting" was heard in hotels, barrooms, political headquarters, business houses, at pleasure resorts, on the streets, and even on church steps. "Companies were organized, and rates established, and gamblers in stocks forsook the 'curb' and stood all day long in the anterooms of the halls of politics, eager for a speculation." On the Presidential race, election bets as high as $5,000, a huge sum in those days, won mention in the newspapers.

Even as the Presidential campaign got underway, newspapers were reporting the pay-off of a local election bet in Chicago—the winner being privileged to kick the loser repeatedly in an appropriate place while they walked from the Tremont House to Springer Street. The winner had been practicing kicking; the loser had become skilled at wearing bricks in the seat of his pants.

The *Painesville* (Ohio) *Telegraph* told of a Republican who bet $100 he could name fifteen states that Lincoln would get, and $500 that he could then name five more that Lincoln would capture. He gladly sacrificed the $100 by listing fifteen slave states and took a sure $400 profit by naming Republican-safe Maine, Vermont, New Hampshire, Massachusetts, and Wisconsin.

The October state elections in some states provided clues on how to bet. The *Daily Gate City* (Keokuk, Iowa) carried an item which declared, "Boys, we've got 'em! Pennsylvania has done it! . . . As the colored gentleman remarked about the expiring quadruped, 'there's no use in doing anything about *that* hoss. His eyes is sot!' " And the *Coos Republican* (Lancaster,

N. H.) announced, "Fusion is stone dead. The Rubicon of the campaign is passed. The enemy's front is broken." The *Easton* (Pa.) *Times* carried drawings depicting the downfall, including one of a funeral procession with the explanation, "Ye demise of Democracy . . . beare ye body away to ye grave . . ." And the *Exeter* (N. H.) *News-Letter* carried a poem, "The Quakers Are Out." Two of the verses were:

> The plot has exploded—we've found out the trick;
> The bribe goes a begging; the fusion won't stick;
> When the Wide-Awake Lanterns are shining about,
> The rogues stay at home, and the true men come out!

> Give the flags to the winds—set the hills all aflame;
> Make way for the man with the patriarch's name!
> Away with misgivings—away with all doubt,
> For Lincoln goes in when the Quakers come out!

A burlesque on the behavior of Republicans when they heard of the victories in Pennsylvania, Indiana, and Ohio was printed in the Chicago *Times and Herald*. Here is an extract:

> Goodly numbers of them went crazy. . . . [They] frothed at the mouth and stood on their heads in a row, kicking their heels wildly in the air, others threw themselves upon the ground and rolled over with the rapidity of a saw-log rolling down hill. . . . Some shouted, some screamed, and some were too drunk to do either. All who were in a capable condition varied the exercises by singing rail-splitting songs.

Then followed a long rail-splitting song, with introductions to the various verses such as this:

> Each rail splitter seizes a rail, mounts it, à la hobby-horse, and canters three times around the bonfire, screaming, "Hurrah for old Abe!"

By the time the campaign came down the home stretch in early November, relatively few serious people seriously believed Breckinridge, Douglas, or Bell could win. The best hope of the opposition was that the election would be tossed into the House of Representatives because of a lack of a majority of electoral votes for any candidate.

The ballot box would tell the tale.

CHAPTER TWELVE

BALLYHOO GIVES WAY TO BALLOTS

As election day, November 6, approached, partisan newspapers made eleventh-hour appeals to the voters, while cautioning party workers to look out for shady tricks by the opposition. The *Weekly Illinois State Journal* suggested that Republican committees be watchdogs to guard against ballot-box stuffing. "Douglasites are preparing to rush illegal votes into the ballot boxes," the *Journal* warned. "A wholesale system of importation of fraudulent voters has been agreed upon." It advised Republicans to post themselves near the polls and challenge every man they were not sure was a legal voter. The *Bucyrus* (Ohio) *Weekly Journal* urged Republicans to counsel their friends against "selling their liberties and the control of the government to a corrupt and slave-extending Administration."

About the same time the *New York Herald* warned hotel keepers that "princely hotels" would be virtually empty if Lincoln won and North-South travel were interrupted. Carpenters, it declared, would lose their jobs, for no more ships for Southern trade would be built. Resorts such as Newport and Saratoga would suffer from the loss of Southern gold. The *Herald* continued through a long list of businesses, alleging that a depression in each would follow a Lincoln victory.

In another article, the *Herald* described the "magnificent panorama of youth, beauty, and fashion" on Broadway the previous sunny day. It added:

What if all this gayety should be suddenly eclipsed by the triumph of the black republicans? What if the child is now born who will see the grass growing on Broadway? Think of these things, matrons and maidens of New York. See that your male relatives vote for the Union and the Constitution.

The Chicago *Times and Herald* spelled out to voters what a Republican victory in 1860 might mean, reminding them that Ohio Negroes had been practically declared white men and 17,000 of them had voted at the recent election; in New York, Negro voters had only to met a trifling property qualification; the Negro already was legally equal to white men in New England; and, in Chicago, a judge had permitted a Negro to testify against a white man.

Then the hour for admonition ended and the people began converging on the polls. In villages, towns, and cities, many men passed out cigars and malarkey, made and took bets, and cautiously marked their ballots.

In Poseyville, Indiana, Joseph Endicott and his seventy-four sons, sons-in-law, and grandsons put down their X's for Douglas and Johnson, according to Joseph. "In a dignified, manly, and frank manner, Millard Fillmore deposited his vote against sectionalism, and for the Union Electoral and State ticket" at Buffalo, said the Washington *National Intelligencer*. In Worcester, Mass., hundred-year-old Ebenezer Mower, who asserted he had voted for George Washington in 1789, went to the polls. A ninety-year-old voter in New England, who also had cast his ballot for the first President, "indicated" said Republican papers, "that he has retained his mental as well as physical facilities" by voting for Old Abe. A hundred-year-old, Ralph Farnham, then said to be the sole survivor of Bunker Hill, walked six miles to cast his vote in Maine.

Lincoln had intended not to vote, feeling it would be improper. However, when it was suggested that he clip off the Presidential electors and vote for the state officers, he acquiesced. The *New York Herald* described the historic vote, during a lull in the balloting about 3 P.M., as follows:

Accompanied by a few of his most immediate associates, he walked leisurely over to deposit his vote at the courthouse. He was not observed by the masses until he reached the courthouse steps; but at that moment he was suddenly saluted with the wildest outburst of enthusiasm ever yielded by a popular assemblage. All party feeling seemed to be forgotten, and even the distributors of opposition tickets joined in the overwhelming demonstrations of greeting. Mr. Lincoln passed through the hall and up the stairs without impediment, but upon reaching the courtroom, the crowd gathered about him with such excess of zeal that it was with some difficulty that he made his way through. Here, as in the street, there was only one sentiment expressed, that of the heartiest and most undivided delight at his appearance. Mr. Lincoln advanced as rapidly as possible to the voting table, and handed in his ticket, upon which, it is hardly necessary to say, all the names were sound Republicans. The only alteration he made was the cutting off of his own name from the top, where it had been printed. As he emerged after voting from the temporary enclosure, the manifestations of enthusiasm were doubled, and Mr. Lincoln, removing his hat, bowed in acknowledgement. Many persons pushed forward to take his hand and exchange cordial words with him; but the crush was too great for comfortable conversation, so he was soon released, and escorted out with all the popular honors that could be lavished upon him. He at once returned to his room in the State House, after an absence of not more than five minutes altogether.

The *Louisville* (Ky.) *Daily Courier* declared that "each man was desirous of having the privilege of handing Lincoln his ballot." One fellow yelled out: "You ought to vote for Douglas, Uncle Abe; he has done all he could for *you*."

The parties all took precautions to avoid voting frauds—at least by the *other* parties. The *Daily Gate City* (Keokuk, Iowa) appealed to voters to "look for the rail mauler—all the genuine Republican tickets printed at our office are headed with a cut of a man with an uplifted maul standing over a 'rail cut.' " Some Northern Democrats warned that a group of Republicans had issued bogus Democratic tickets, inserting names of certain Southern Democrats for the Northern ones.

The possibility of importing voters was widely—and wildly —discussed. The *Hartford Courant* declared there was less chance of illegal voters being brought into Connecticut by the "Sham Democracy" than in recent elections because all the voters would be needed in New York if the Douglas Democrats had the faintest idea of carrying that state.

The *Chicago Times and Herald* and other Illinois Democratic newspapers asserted that Senator Seward and General Nye had gone to Kansas and arranged to import into Illinois several thousand "Black Republicans" to swing the state for Lincoln. Kansas Black Republicans were pouring in by hundreds on every train from the West, the articles asserted, one item declaring "Kansas Depopulated."

The *Times and Herald* warned the Democrats that they "had never a more determined or unscrupulous foe. You will be assailed by falsehood, chicanery, fraud, and perhaps force itself." It urged Democrats to be eagle-eyed while votes were being counted so that no new ballots were slipped into the pile and that any cast legally did not disappear by sleight of hand.

Concerning a Republican proposal that Wide-Awakes guard the polls, the *Times and Herald* bellowed: "Men whose heads are white almost in the cause of Democracy will not suffer themselves to be catechized at the ballot box by beardless boys!" It characterized these Wide-Awakes as mainly "inexperienced, injudicious, hot-headed, foolish young men."

Some politicians dreamed up novel strategy for getting favorable results at the polls. A Wisconsin candidate hired fifty-three Republicans to work in his coal mine near Shullsburg on election day, a newspaper reported. When they were 140 feet below the surface, he had the ladder drawn up for repair and somehow neglected to return it until the polls were closed. He won by a majority of thirty.

Actually, the election was orderly, despite a few free-wheeling skirmishes. The *New York Herald* reported a melee in which ballot boxes were broken up, the pieces being wielded as clubs. Several combatants suffered severe head injuries and one poor fellow was knocked senseless. Another *Herald* item told of an affray in which "there were two or three knock-downs, a good deal of shouting, and interference of police using their clubs 'judiciously.' "

As a Wide-Awake victory parade passed the Astor House about midnight, the men singing a song to the tune of "Dixie," "knives and pistols were drawn and the former used. Clubs and stones were flung in all directions."

Out in Keokuk, Iowa, a champion of the young Democrats got a black eye for "alleged impertinence and insult to a Republican." A man at Fairfax Courthouse, Virginia, who had voted for Lincoln, was carried out of the village and daubed thoroughly with printer's ink, then covered with feathers. Another Lincoln voter in Kentucky got a rough ride on a rail.

As the votes were tallied, it soon became apparent that plenty of other people had voted for the Rail-Splitter. In round figures, Lincoln received 1,800,000 of the popular vote, compared to 1,350,000 for Douglas, 850,000 for Breckinridge, and 600,000 for Bell. In the electoral votes which determined the winner, the score was 180 for Lincoln, 72 for Breckinridge, 39 for Bell, and only 12 for Douglas. Thus Lincoln had 180 to a combined total of 123 for the opposition. His popular vote, though, was almost a million less than the combined votes of his opponents.

Lincoln received all the electoral votes from the Northern states except the fusion state of New Jersey, where three of the seven votes went to Douglas. Abe not only captured the New England states but swept them almost county by county.

On the Pacific coast, however, he won the two states, California and Oregon, only by narrow margins. In his home county, Sangamon, Lincoln lost to Little Doug. In some other

Illinois counties, though, Lincoln strode in by large majorities —eighty-five per cent of the votes in Boone County, for instance.

In ten Southern states Lincoln went voteless. (The Republican Party did not appear on most Southern ballots.) George Washington's home town of Alexandria, Virginia, gave Lincoln fewer than twenty of its more than 1,500 votes.

Lincoln's vote was decidedly sectional, and many persons considered his victory the cue for secession. On the other hand, Breckinridge, sometimes labeled the Disunion Candidate, failed to make a clean sweep of the South, although he did carry the deep South, Arkansas, North Carolina, Maryland, and Delaware.

Bell, who straddled the slavery fence, won Virginia, Kentucky, and Tennessee. He proved strongest in border states and the upper Southern states that were to be the last to secede.

Douglas, although he piled up about two-thirds as many popular votes as Lincoln, won only Missouri's and part of New Jersey's electoral votes. Missouri, incidentally, showed the tightest competition. It was the only state in which each of the four main parties carried one or more counties.

The three anti-Lincoln parties had held slim hopes of winning the election outright. And the decisive vote for Lincoln swept away their last chance—that of throwing the election into the House of Representatives where one of them would have had a possibility of success.

So ended the election of 1860, which the *Baltimore Sun* called "the most important event of the age." Voters had elevated the first Republican to the highest office in the land. He was also the first President born outside the thirteen original states.

Compared to a half-century earlier, news of the election spread rapidly, for this was the age of the marvelous telegraph. An article in the *Newark Daily Advertiser* stated:

Most of the telegraphing in our country is now performed . . .
simply by sound . . . the mysterious agent speaks through the
wires; the pen has given place to the tongue of lightning. . . .

The forty miles of wire between Washington and Baltimore in
1844 have grown into about forty-thousand miles in fifteen years—
an almost miraculous achievement.

The *National Democrat* (Lecompton, Kansas Territory)
pointed out that news of the election of 1856 reached them in
ten days, but in 1860 it "came to hand here, in these ends of
the earth, the day following the election." For sure, it disliked
the nature of the news, the *Democrat* added, but was impressed
that "we live in an age of wonderful advancement."

Not every geographical area enjoyed this miracle a century
ago. Appleton, Wisconsin, for instance, did not even have good
rail connections. Only two days before Lincoln's inauguration
the *Appleton Crescent* announced "the snort of the iron horse,"
and the iron bands connecting the city with East, West, and
South. The day following the election, the *Daily Gate City*
(Keokuk, Iowa) complained that virtually the whole nation
except the Pacific coast knew who was elected President, and
yet Keokuk didn't know how Lee County had gone. "Will we
ever have a telegraph?" the newspaper sighed.

The far-off Pacific coast was just beginning to experience
the awakening effects of improved communication and transportation. The *Oregon Sentinel* (Jacksonville) emphasized
that a message had recently been rushed from Portland to
Washington, D. C., and back in forty-two days through the
cooperation of Tracy & Co., Wells Fargo & Co., the Pony Express, the telegraph, and a steamer. A jubilant demonstration
was held in San Francisco in 1860 to celebrate the receipt of a
transcontinental message by telegraph and Pony Express in
eight and a half days, "thus spanning the North American continent, with lightning and horse flesh, in about the same time
that about forty years ago it took to get the news from New
York to Boston."

The *Daily Alta California* (San Francisco) informed readers it hoped to announce election results within seven days after the November sixth balloting. Maybe the west-to-east flow wasn't so good, for it was not until December 1 that the Washington *National Intelligencer* printed an account from San Francisco, brought by Pony Express and telegraph, that Lincoln "apparently" had carried California and Oregon.

How did the newspapers play the report of this historic election? Almost without exception, they capped it with mere one-column heads, for this was before the age of screaming banner lines. The *Weekly Illinois State Journal,* one of Lincoln's warmest admirers, announced the victory on the day after the election with one-column headlines which modestly began, "Presidential Election." Among the subheads were "The Entire North Probably for Lincoln" and "Mr. Lincoln's Election Confirmed."

In most cases, even in Republican journals, this historic event was relegated to an inside page. On the front pages were advertisements, sentimental stories, and other matters. Abe Lincoln, destined to become a hero for the world and for the ages, generally failed to make page one!

Although the newspapers refrained from multiple-column headlines, some did stack up the heads rather deeply in the single columns. The *Chicago Press and Tribune* used heads and subheads which included: "The Great Victory"; "Republicans Triumphant over Fraud, Fusian, Cotton, Disunion, and Treason"; and "Honest Old Abe Elected, Carried Chicago by 4,500."

The *Bucyrus* (Ohio) *Weekly Journal* exclaimed: "The Thing Is Did! The Most Glorious Triumph Ever Achieved! Lincoln Elected! Disunion Rebuked! Doug. Non Est! Breck. No Where! Bell——— The Country Saved." Not so enthusiastic was the *Cleveland Weekly Plain Dealer,* which announced, "Old Abe elected!—the irrepressible conflict inaugurated."

The news of Lincoln's success triggered his home town of Springfield to go off like a cannon, according to the *Chicago Times and Herald*, which reported that, at a gathering in the State House, some excited men actually flopped down on the carpeted floor and rolled over and over. "Parties ran through the streets singing . . . till they were too hoarse to speak . . . All night there was howling for Lincoln—cheers for 'Old Abe' kept up, and toward morning some of the boys procured a cannon and fired several rounds."

With excitement swirling around him, Lincoln took the news in his usual calm, almost detached way. Toward midnight he and a group went to Watson's confectionery, where Republican women had heaped a long table with food. As Lincoln and his wife entered, several scores of voices rang out with—

Ain't you glad you joined the Republicans?
Joined the Republicans,
Ain't you glad you joined the Republicans,
Down in Illinois?

A dispatch from the Illinois capital reported that Lincoln was being greeted by well-wishers not only from the Republican but also from the *recent* Democratic and Bell-Everett parties.

Springfield gave an official pat-on-the-back to its favorite son about two weeks after the election. Many homes and business buildings were specially illuminated. One establishment featured four hundred lighted Chinese lanterns. The roof of one building was illuminated with Wide-Awake torches. Some stores had huge Lincoln-Hamlin transparencies entwined with colorful decorations. One establishment featured an immense revolving red ball representing the earth. Below it, flanked by German and American flags, was a lighted banner inscribed "Our whole country and the Union."

At a spectacular fireworks display one pyrotechnic feature, said the *Weekly Illinois State Journal*, was " 'Lincoln,' in dazzling letters of fire, as it is impressed on every patriot's heart."

A large procession toured part of the city, halting at Lincoln's home en route. "In all our rejoicing," he told them, "let us neither express, nor cherish, any harsh feelings toward any citizen who, by his vote, has differed with us. Let us at all times remember that all American citizens are brothers of a common country, and should dwell together in the bonds of fraternal feelings."

The *Journal,* in describing the whole Springfield celebration, declared that "the splendor and effect of the grandly brilliant scene is beyond the reach of the pen"—but the writer continued reaching anyway:

The Lincoln battery kept up an unceasing roar at the several corners of the square. With pulsating hearts, the crowds surged to and fro, and shout after shout rose from the triumph of the Republican principles. . . . The strange glare of the bonfires, the flickering torches, the strange and colored hues from the Chinese lanterns gave an inexpressibly attractive character to the celebration of last night . . .

The scene reminded one of those gorgeous Oriental fetes in the country of the Genii, the dazzling garden of Aladdin; and had Solomon's army, with all its unnatural and grand couterie of men and beast, with all the strange creatures of earth, heaven and fiend-land, passed over with rushing wings, it would not have astonished in the least some of our country friends.

More restrained was the demonstration at Harvard College, where a large group of students called on young Bob Lincoln, a student there, and congratulated him on his father's success. But the typical post-election response was "eating to repletion and drinking to excess, in the spirit of great events," as one newspaper put it.

The *Chicago Times and Herald* asserted that Republicans, since the election, were unable to tell whether they walked on their heels or their heads. It added:

Wide-Awakes were out with their torches smelling up the atmosphere. Fireworks streaked the skies and clapped applause in the galleries up aloft. Joyous partisans shouted until they were hoarse and still tried to shout. Impromptu orators spoke to impromptu audiences in a way that "mortal man has never been able to appreciate."

In a Connecticut village, "decorum was turned out of doors" when the news indicated Lincoln was on the victory road. Republicans cheered for fifteen minutes without stopping, reported the *Worcester* (Mass.) *Palladium.* On election night in Portsmouth, New Hampshire, "volunteers" for oratory were plucked from the crowd:

Singling out one whom they thought *ought* to speak, a dive was made for the luckless individual, and strong arms bore him bodily to the Speaker's desk, when after the customary "three cheers," he was introduced and actually compelled to talk. This system of "impressment" was borne with a great good humor by the victims, and elicited some very capital speeches.

At Mount Holyoke Seminary, in Massachusetts, the young ladies celebrated Lincoln's election by marching about the grounds, carrying lighted lamps. Their banner declared, "President—Abraham Lincoln. Behind a homely exterior, we recognize inward beauty." Far out on the Kansas frontier, people in Wabaunsee held a "joyous festival" in a large schoolhouse, the *Kansas State Record* (Topeka) reported. They passed a resolution declaring that Lincoln's election was "an abundant reward for all we have suffered in the defense of liberty against the cohorts of a debased administration that now fills an ignoble grave."

At Liberty and Galion, Ohio, the Republicans "jollified" with speeches, bonfires, and fireworks. And across the whole Republican realm there was a happy feeling that, as the *Boston Daily Atlas and Bee* worded it, "a new era has dawned upon the country; the chapter of official corruption and pro-slavery propaganda is definitely closed."

But joy had vanished in the camps of Douglas, Breckinridge, and Bell. In some areas, however, such camps weren't easy to track down. On the day after election, a *New York Times* reporter commented that he "searched in vain for someone who could tell us the feeling of the defeated. Everyone declared himself a Lincoln man or else said nothing." The editor of the *LaCrosse* (Wis.) *Union,* who had staked his printing office on Douglas' carrying Illinois and Wisconsin, printed this plea: "WANTED—a large Bible with very coarse print. Any person having such a work, with a few consoling passages marked, will get a good bargain. Inquire at the editor's room all day."

Some press comments were accusations. The *St. Clair* (Mich.) *Chief* charged Douglas' defeat to President Buchanan, a supporter of Breckinridge. "We sincerely hope he [Buchanan] will not only be politically but eternally damned," thundered the *Chief.*

Sunk in sadness, the *Baltimore Sun* at first laconically announced Lincoln's election and explained it could not offer congratulations "upon so inauspicious a result." The *Charleston Mercury* was more vocal. "The tea has been thrown overboard—the revolution of 1860 has been initiated!" A *New York Express* correspondent declared:

I am assured by those who know him well, that a more illiterate man it would be difficult to find, even among the self-made lawyers of Illinois. His chief characteristic is an immense "gift of gab," and a wonderful command of language, unaccompanied by a corresponding copiousness of ideas. The election of such a man at such a crisis is undoubtedly the greatest evil that has ever befallen this country. But the mischief is done, and the only relief for the American people is to shorten sail, caulk the hatches, put in the dead-lights, send down the topmast, and prepare for a hurricane.

Action, not merely words, sometimes erupted as the aftermath. In Washington, D. C., a group at Breckinridge headquarters on Pennsylvania Avenue hatched the idea of going to the Republican headquarters to "wreck the shanty." They recruited reinforcements at Brown's Hotel and along the route. The *National Intelligencer* reported:

The united party, 250 or 300 strong, marched in regular order toward the Republican rooms. Having arrived at Berth's corner, on Third Street, they raised rallying cries, and moved across Indiana Avenue in semi-military order, and when in front of the Republican building, they began to fire pistols and throw stones through the windows of the same, which were soon demolished all through the second story.

The commandos then stormed the building and destroyed flags, banners, furniture, type, and other equipment. After the havoc was completed, they reassembled in the street and marched off in military order.

Anger over Lincoln's success surged high in South Carolina. At Charleston, announcements of Lincoln majorities were greeted with cheers—for the Southern Confederacy. A couple of days after the election, huge crowds gathered around the *Mercury* office and applauded whenever the bulletin board revealed that another federal officer in South Carolina had resigned. At Savannah, Georgia, a mass-resistance gathering called upon the South to arm, vowing that Lincoln's election would not be tolerated. Three days after the balloting the *Baltimore Sun* reported:

The election of Lincoln . . . has created a profound sensation all through the South. "Minute men" are forming in several of the slave States. In Charleston they are equipping a "volunteer rifle corps" of one hundred young men, who are being instructed in Hardie's tactics. They will tender their services to the Governor for any emergency.

Meanwhile, jubilant demonstrations continued in many

northern communities. In a speech in New York City celebrating the victory, William Cullen Bryant, of the *New York Evening Post,* said that the youngest in the audience might live until the 1950's and never see another election so pregnant with crucial results. And poet Henry Wadsworth Longfellow observed, "This is a great victory. It is the redemption of the country. Freedom is triumphant."

☆☆☆

CHAPTER THIRTEEN

THE SLAVE ISSUE ENGROSSES THE NATION

The four months between Lincoln's election and inauguration were a time for critical thought, for study, for counsel, by the President-elect. Only six months had passed since the State convention at Decatur was electrified when John Hanks and Richard Oglesby displayed the old rails that became the Republican campaign symbol. But since that first rush to the Lincoln bandwagon, the mood of the Nation had changed. The country had become more serious concerning the critical question which divided it. There was less banter and more bitterness in the journals. To thinking people it was apparent that the nation might rip apart at the seams.

Slavery, like a rail-splitter's wedge, was the main issue that had divided the nation. What was this slavery situation as Lincoln might have viewed it by reading newspapers during late 1860?

One aspect of the problem was the fact that slaves were a form of wealth, which in turn affected power politics. The *Mississippian* (Jackson) pointed out, two days after Lincoln's election, that the Republican party threatened to tamper with the property interests of fifteen states in four million slaves worth over three billion dollars—even though relatively few Southerners owned slaves. Had they "ever read of a people willing to submit to the destruction of so much property" by legislation? the newspaper asked.

But the North, emphasized the *New York Daily Tribune,* rejected the doctrine "that property in men stands on the same foundation with property in horses." The *Atlantic Monthly* of October, 1860, described the slavery issue this way:

> The encroachments of Slavery upon our National policy have been like those of a glacier in a Swiss valley. Inch by inch, the huge dragon with its glittering scales and crests of ice coils itself onward. . . . But it has its limit, the kindlier forces of Nature worked against it, and the silent arrows of the sun are still, as of old, fatal to the frosty Python. Geology tells us that such enormous devastators once covered the face of the earth, but the benignant sunlight of heaven touched them, and they faded silently, leaving no trace but here and there the scratches of their talons and gnawed boulders scattered where they made their lair. We have entire faith in the benignant influence of Truth, the sunlight of the moral world, and believe that Slavery, like other worn-out systems, will melt gradually before it.

The slavery issue was debated on rostrums across the land, but more especially on Capitol Hill. A Negro was looking in the door of the House of Representatives, wrote the *Jonesboro* (Ill.) *Gazette,* when the doorkeeper remarked, "Jim, they are talking about niggers in there." "Yes," Jim answered, "Dat's dere business. Lor, bless you, if it wasn't for de niggers, dere wouldn't be no Congress." The *San Francisco Herald,* adhering to the prevalent practice of punning despite the gravity of the times, noted that the nation was in a crisis because it had become so niggard [niggered].

Pro-slavery journals delighted in items which purported to prove the mental or moral inferiority of the Negro race. In one a Negro asked another the price of a new hat he was wearing. He replied, "I don't know, nigger, I don't know. The store man wasn't dere."

The *New York Daily Tribune* noted that the *New York Weekly Journal of Commerce* clung to the idea of natural superiority and inferiority of races. To survive the greater energy and activity of the superior race, the *Journal* argued, the inferior race must submit to slavery. This, the *Tribune* asserted, was dangerous doctrine. "We shall scarcely stop short with justifying the enslavement of Indians, Negroes, Malays, and Mongolians," the *Tribune* said. "The natural superiority and inferiority of individuals and families, as compared with each other, is no less marked and distinct than that of races."

A reverse twist to the inequality theory was given in a Fourth of July speech by a Massachusetts Negro. He scorned being placed on the same low footing with the white man, the *Jonesboro* (Ill.) *Gazette* reported. He declared the "blood that he boasted was immortalized in song and story, at a time when the Saxon was wearing an iron collar with the name of his master written there."

At any rate, the institution of slavery was a top-priority issue as Lincoln scanned the newspapers and consulted with party and government leaders in late 1860. An advertisement in the *Mississippian* on Nov. 13 said:

I wish to sell my plantation in Holmes county . . . containing 640 acres. . . .

I will also sell sixteen Negroes, four Horses, and six mules; stocks of Hogs, Cattle, and Sheep . . . Among the Negroes is twelve hands and four children, viz: four Negro men, from 22-30 years of age; seven women from 16-25 years of age, and a plow boy.

Often slaves for sale were listed by name. An 1860 item in the *New Orleans Daily Delta* announced:

Sale to Effect Partition . . . Valuable Slaves and Real Estate . . . The following property, to wit—
    1. Harriet, negress, aged about 30 years, and her four children.
    2. Mary, negress, aged about 25 years, and her two children.
    3. Two lots of ground, etc., etc.

Another item in the *Delta* reported that W. Cox & Co. had "just arrived with a choice gang of Carolina and Virginia

Negroes," adding that the firm "will be receiving fresh gangs during the season."

Occasionally the Southern papers reported how the slave market was faring. The *Mississippian* (Jackson) carried a letter from a Richmond trading firm which said:

"No. 1 men sell here from $1600 to $1,650; second class men from $1,400 to $1550. No. 1 grown field girls sell from $1,400 to $1475; one extra sold today at $1,500. Tendency of the market upward."

Seventy-eight slaves were sold in New Orleans one Saturday in 1860, the *Daily Chicago Herald* reported, for $74,720. They averaged forty years of age. Eighty others, ranging from twelve months to fifty-five years, brought an average of $1,250. Highest price paid for field hands was for men between eighteen and twenty-five ($1,600 to $2,000). The *Charleston Mercury* reported that a Negro blacksmith was auctioned off at $2,800. An item in the Christmas Day issue of the *Mississippian* (Jackson) stated that 166 slaves had been sold at Huntsville, Alabama, the previous week for $136,642.

Another December item in the *Mississippian*, however, told of the sale of a forty-year-old field hand for $451 and another for $905. It declared that two months earlier—before Lincoln's election—these Negroes would have brought $2,000. The *Daily Gate City* (Keokuk, Iowa) insisted, on the other hand, that if the value of slaves was reduced by Lincoln's election, the value of white men would be increased proportionately.

Although the African slave trade had been curbed, there still were instances in 1860 of such slaving, which supplemented the natural increase of Southern slaves. The *Mississippian* reported that a "cargo of ebony strangers landed on the coast not two hundred miles from this city on Wednesday morning. Many of them have gone to the interior to study the growth of Cotton, Corn, and Rice." Another item in that newspaper, possibly concerning the same shipload, disclosed that a net profit of $35,000 was made on the cargo of 103. The *Washington Constitution* carried an article about an American slave vessel which, while being chased by a British and a Portuguese ship, was wrecked by the master when he realized escape was impossible. The article related:

As the brig struck and was overwhelmed by the breakers, the poor miserable creatures on board, probably to the number of 500, set up a howl of despair that could be heard even above the roaring of the hungry sea. But it was too dark, by that time, to see much, and beyond human skill or power to aid the drowning wretches, so that they soon must have met their doom; for on the next morning the beaches in sight of the rocks were strewn with the corpses and fragments of the wreck . . . the monsters who manned the vessel are supposed to have escaped in their boat before she struck. . . .

A slaver called the "Wildfire," captured in 1860 near Cuba for violating laws against the slave trade, reported that when it left Africa, fourteen American vessels were waiting for cargoes of Negroes. Two Spanish armed steamers also were lying at the Congo River waiting for 1,500 Negroes each, bound for Cuba. One ship sailed eight days earlier with 750 on board.

After the "Wildfire" was captured, it was taken to Key West, Florida. Newspapers and magazines throughout the country carried stories about it. A reporter for *Harper's Weekly* wrote:

Soon after the bark was anchored we repaired on board, and on passing over the side, saw, on the deck of the vessel, about 450 native Africans, in a state of entire nudity . . . About 50 of them were full grown young men, and about 400 were boys aged from 10 to 16 years. Ninety and upwards died on the voyage. But this is considered a comparatively small loss. Ten more died since their arrival and there are about forty more sick in the hospital. . . . [An item two months later said 200 more had died.]

From the deck we descended into the cabin where we saw 60 or 70 women and young girls in Nature's dress. . . .

We think it would be difficult to find anywhere in our own country four hundred finer and handsomer looking boys and girls than these are.

What should be done with the Negroes? The *Daily Chicago Herald* thought the Government wise in deciding eventually to ship the Africans back from whence "the good niggers come." It suggested that excellent alternatives would be to enslave them in Florida or free them in Boston. Even better, it proposed, would be to allow the "nigger worshippers" a peep at them. "Nothing would be more impressive than to see a couple of thousand of these naked, musky, greasy, cannibals at one of their usual feasts of raw beef and dead Negroes, exhibited at Jackson Hall, and Long John [Chicago editor] lecturing on the Declaration of Independence and equality of the races."

To people opposed to slavery the articles about the slave trade intensified their hatred for the institution. As pro-slavery elements saw their traditional way of life becoming less secure, they tightened the grip on the Negro. In some states, Negroes were not allowed to assemble without an authorized "respectable white person" present. A *New Orleans Daily Delta* item reported that a grocer was arrested for "allowing a slave to remain in his grocery over the time prescribed by law."

Anti-slavery newspapers could find, without too much difficulty, examples of the ill treatment of slaves. These items ranged from the quasi-humorous to the blood-chilling. Among the first was an anecdote about a Negro who, when forced to transfer from a railway passenger car to a freight car, insisted in being weighed as freight. The conductor yielded, said the item, and the Negro paid by the pound.

In another anecdote a Negro visited a zoo and became interested in one of the apes. The ape shook the Negro's hand amiably but remained silent. "You too sharp for 'em, old feller," the Negro declared approvingly. "Keep dark; if you jes speak one word of English, white man have hoe in yer hand in less dan a minit."

Lincoln must have read stories about lynchings of Negroes, for many newspapers carried such items in 1860. The *Mississippian* (Jackson) reported that a vigilance committee hanged a Negro charged with attempting to incite insurrection, "knowing well that the law is too tardy in its course, even if it could be effectual in its process, to obviate the dangers and punish the offenders in trouble of this character." The *Daily Chicago Post* reprinted this account from the *Harrison County* (Ga.) *Enterprise* about the punishment of a Negro believed to have attacked a white woman:

They [a group of men] rushed to the jail, and despite of all remonstrances, with axe, hammer, and crowbar, violently broke through the doors and took the prisoner out, carrying him about two miles from town, where they chained him to a tree and burned him to death . . . We understand that the negro protested his innocense with the last breath. . . .

One newspaper reported the hanging of a North Carolina Negro by a mob which had first "tried to make him confess the crime by roasting him slowly over a fire." Another reprinted a letter which a Tuskegee, Alabama, resident had sent to the *Columbus* (Ga.) *Enquirer*. It said:

The boy belonging to Major Cockey, of this county, was arrested today. A large number of the citizens, perhaps 150, met, tried, and sentenced him, and before the sun set, he was burned to ashes . . . No judge presided, no jury was empaneled. Horrid the punishment, but just.

An item from the *Augusta* (Ga.) *Dispatch* stated that twelve persons took from the sheriff's custody a Negro accused of killing a white man, giving bond for his re-delivery. They tried, sentenced, and executed him, then returned his ashes to the sheriff.

The "code" of the slave states was ridiculed in this declaration which the *Daily Chicago Post* reprinted from *Punch*. It was called "The Slave Owner's Declaration":

We the states whose representatives have subscribed to the following declaration, do hereby assent and affirm—

That all mankind have a perfect and equal right to freedom, if they can keep it.

That their being unable to keep it is the proof that they have no right to it.

That the lawfulness of slavery is clearly and indisputably proved from the Bible, inasmuch as St. Paul, writing to Onesimus, a slave never told him to run away.

That slavery is the most humane institution in the world, for, inasmuch as half of the sorrows of white persons arise from the sorrows of their husbands, wives or children, in forbidding a race to have any husbands, wives or children to call their own, we deprive that race of one half the suffering we undergo. . . .

Some Negroes, failing to see the advantages in slavery, tried to escape. One article headed "Another Northern Outrage" told of a Negro girl who was "spirited away" from her distinguished mistress while they were visiting in New York. The Negro girl was a gift from the mistress' mother.

Operations of the Underground Railroad were referred to in a number of items in 1860. One mentioned a clergyman in Syracuse, New York, to whom fugitives in that area should be directed. It also solicited contributions of money, clothing, or provisions. A Chicago newspaper reported that twenty-five slaves had just passed through Milwaukee on the "railroad" en route to Canada. According to the *Jonesboro* (Ill.) *Gazette* an estimated 24,000 run-away Negroes were in that country.

Southern readers often came across items such as this one from the *New Orleans Daily Delta:*

Fifty Dollars Reward—ran away from the Bel Air Plantation, parish of Plaquemines, the girl named Sally Bell, about five months ago. She is a stout black girl, about 30 years old, 5 feet three or four inches high, and has two of her upper front teeth out.

An item in the *Charleston Mercury* announced a hundred-dollar reward for the apprehension of Henry, a slave who had run away two years before.

Even in serious matters such as this, some editors and speakers could not resist puns. The *Jonesboro* (Ill.) *Gazette* quoted a "neat after-dinner speech" in which the orator declared that "fugitive slaves should be given up, because we should tender unto the seizers things that are the seizers'."

Besides escape, another possible way to gain freedom was through purchase. One newspaper article told about a twelve-year-old boy who passed through Wheeling, Virginia, en route to Columbus, Ohio. His father in Ohio had bought his freedom for $1,000. He was shipped for eleven dollars, "finding his own grub."

The *Worcester* (Mass.) *Daily Spy* reprinted this item from the *Boston Traveller:*

A colored man, named Richard Bruce, died a few months since in this city, leaving by his will about $1,100 for the purchase of one or more of his children from slavery. He was an old man, and having purchased his own freedom, and that of his wife, a few years since, had by industry and economy, laid by this sum.

On the lighter side, the *American Eagle* (Paoli, Indiana) told how an Ohio Negro explained his freedom. He said he impressed upon his missus that he was "berry feeble . . . a mis'able nigger," and that she should get rid of him. She agreed to sell him for $100, and he started earning the money to pay her. "My health has been gettin' better eber since," he remarked. "I 'spects I made 'bout $900 out of dat nigger."

Sometimes the whites came up with suggestions for solving the slave issue. A resolution introduced into the Massachusetts legislature recommended that the Federal government be asked to buy and free all slaves within the U. S. Another suggestion was to transport Negroes to colonies in other lands. Lincoln, at least for a time, advocated such emigration. One movement concerned colonization in Liberia.

An appeal in the *New York Daily Tribune* urged emigration of Negroes to Mexico, Central America, or South America. The *New York Weekly Journal of Commerce* retorted:

This is a capital plan. All Republicans in favor of emigrating to the "fine region" thus indicated will assemble at the *Tribune* office with suitable tools and baggage. Perhaps Mr. Greeley, Mr. Giddings, and a few others of that stripe might be induced to accompany them. Sowing cotton seed is better employment than sowing discord among brethren.

Some Southerners expressed fear or disgust at the inroads Negroes reportedly were making in Northern white society. An item from Washington telling how Republicans raised money to purchase the freedom of a mulatto slave girl caused quite a stir. The fact that four wagons of Negroes and some mounted Negroes acting as marshals had participated in an Ohio parade evoked acrid comments. Some Northern hotels employed free Negroes as servants, and in Washington, handbills listing hotels whose proprietors "are known not to be tainted with Abolitionism" were distributed to Southerners headed north.

Cleveland was termed by the *Cleveland Weekly Plain Dealer* a "Nigger Town." It asserted Black Republican politicians "talked nigger" six days a week and on the seventh day the ministers took up the "doleful theme." The alleged comment of a Cleveland Republican leader created considerable commotion. He declared "I would rather my little girl should sit beside a colored girl [in school] than by a frizzle-headed Irish or bare-heeled Dutch one."

Anti-slavery journals delighted in pointing out the mile that Negroes allegedly would take if given an inch. The *Mississippian* (Jackson) reprinted this item from the *Philadelphia Ledger:* "Wanted, by a respectable colored family, a white boy, fourteen or sixteen years of age, to wait on table and make himself generally useful about the house." The *Portsmouth* (N. H.) *Journal* discussed the tumult in a Virginia community when it was found that a light-complexioned Negro had been living there four years, married a white woman, had two children, and "also deposited his vote at the ballot box time and again."

Fraternization items were plentiful. One described an "amalgamation ball" of black men and white women in New York City. About 1 A.M. festivities were interrupted when the hall was invaded by Broadway gamblers having bags of flour and soot hidden in their clothing. "They commenced by throwing the flour over the black men and the soot over the white women. At this juncture the lights were extinguished, and then commenced the scene which beggars description." A *Delawarean* (Dover) article stated that a Negro reportedly offered $15,000 to $20,000 to a white man who would marry his daughter. A reply from a man eager to accept was also printed. The *Burlington* (Vt.) *Sentinel* told about a white girl, a graduate of Oberlin College in Ohio, who eloped to Detroit with a Toledo Negro. An item in another newspaper insisted that seventy-two white women had married Negroes in Massachusetts the previous year.

What was the *Southern* viewpoint on slavery, as Lincoln might have sized it up by reading the newspapers? There was no single viewpoint that all Southerners accepted, but many endorsed the philosophy expressed in a toast by the Mayor of Savannah in 1860: "The element of Southern prosperity— African muscle directed by Caucasian brains." The *New Orleans Daily Delta* quoted a speaker as emphasizing that since slavery "is ours, to do with as we please, we have neither motive nor interest in discussing its ethics before the nation." If the North-South rift could not be mended, "you still have left manhood's last and highest prerogative, the right of revolution."

There were an estimated 320,000 Southern slaveholders, according to the *Oregon Weekly Times* (Portland), compared with five million non-slaveholders. If slavery were degrading, the *Times* asked, why didn't the non-slaveholders throw it off?

The Republican party had assured the South it did not intend to disturb slavery where it was already established. But, inquired the *Chicago Times,* if the party doesn't mean to "meddle with slavery where it exists, where does it intend to meddle with it?" The South wanted to be left alone, declared the *Jonesboro* (Ill.) *Gazette.* "Leave us alone," it stressed, means "no John Brown and his pikes, no underground-railroad operations, no incendiary documents to inflame the passions." "Mind your own business," it demanded, "and we will mind ours." The *Charleston Mercury* printed a letter from Houston, Texas, that asserted the Southern Negro was less free than a few years earlier "simply because his master has been goaded on to desperation by incendiary acts and speeches."

Pro-slavery newspapers liked to publish articles stressing good treatment of Southern Negroes or ridiculing the North's assertion that slavery was barbaric. Here is part of a long burlesque which purported to be the report of a Northerner who had ventured South:

Those beings who wear the human form, and grow fat upon the blood of the poor down-trodden Negro, put forth their most demoniacal wiles to prevent me penetrating to the strongholds of their ghastly traffic. At Richmond I was tarred, feathered and dragged through Main Street for a half a day, with a shrieking mob of 16,000 people about me. In Charleston, I was twice scalped, confined in the calaboose, whipped in the square, and ridden through Meeting street, on a rail. At Savannah, on the day of my arrival, all business was suspended, and the fiends made a general jubilee. I was gagged, gouged, three times hanged, dragged with a rope about my neck through the principal streets, and finally thrown from the bluff . . .

I have shown this down-trodden race how much better it would be for them to be swelling the ranks of their free brethren of the North, even though they might sometimes want food and shelter, than to be revelling in plenty on their plantations with a white man for a master.

The *Delawarean* (Dover) reprinted from the *Philadelphia Evening Journal* these excerpts from a "political dictionary":

Slaves—Negroes bought from their cruel black captors in Africa, and taken to America by British and New England ships, who thus originated Southern slavery.

Slaveholders—men who have taken the degraded barbarian brought by British and Northern ships from Africa, and have given him a home in a Christian, civilized land.

Slave labor—the fruit of the Negroes' improved habits of industry, for which he receives wages, paid in food, clothing, shelter, and kind treatment, on which he grows fat and thrives.

It was often effective to quote supposed Negro self-characterizations. The *Daily Chicago Herald* lifted these alleged remarks from the *Petersburg* (Va.) *Express:*

"All niggers ought to feel de dignity of bein' niggers, 'cept free niggers what dunno what dignity am. Dis minute I'm wuff about fifteen hundred dollars," and he gave a demonstrative gesture with his left forefinger, "and a heap o' white folks can't say dat for deyselves. Now dar," and he pointed to a gentlemanly vagrant, "is a white man; and he couldn't turn himself into money to save his life. More'n dat, he ain't wuff nuffin, he duno nuffin, and he won't do nuffin. I feels de dignity of de fack, and dat's what makes me say what I do say."

The *Daily Chicago Herald* told of a Chicago ex-mayor who journeyed to Mississippi. While he was at a meeting there a group of Negroes entered, lifted him in their arms and "in good old corn-shucking style, conveyed him around the hotel, singing one of their most familiar corn-shucking songs." The *Constitution* (Washington, D. C.) reprinted an item from the *Norfolk* (Va.) *Herald* which pointed out that Southern whites often paid slaves for corn raised on their land. It insisted the Negroes were "as happy as lords," and that they worked cheerfully in the day and "at nights and during the holidays they sing, dance and smoke, eat sweet potatoes, drink hard cider, sit around the big kitchen fires, laugh and grow fat, regardless of the tom-foolery and nonsense about the 'poor oppressed slave.' "

The *New Orleans Daily Delta* published this report by a Northerner concerning his first visit to the South:

Sunday is the slaves' holiday here, and the swarm of colored population that appears upon the streets on this day is something wonderful. It would seem that the white folks remained at home to take care of things, while the Negroes dressed up and sauntered abroad. The Negroes do an immense amount of church-going and they all appeared to have decent and, some of them elegant suits of Sunday-go-to-meetin' clothes. . . . Of the children that swarm upon the streets, far the greater portion are colored—black or yellow—perhaps one-fourth of them having an infusion of white blood. On weekdays the little darkies are not particularly clean, but on Sundays their faces shine, showing the religious application of soap and water. The slave population of this city, seems, so far as I have been able to observe, comfortably clothed, well fed, and contented.

Even at death, Negroes often received tip-top treatment, some articles asserted. The funeral of a faithful slave named King, attended by an estimated 1,500 to 2,000 persons, was described in the *Selma* (Ala.) *Issue* and reprinted in the *Jonesboro* (Ill.) *Gazette*. It said:

Suppose Old King had perished of hunger, or hard usage, or neglect, in some Northern state. Who would have followed his body to the grave? In the public potter's field where paupers and murderers of every kind are earthed, he would have found his last resting place. Here he found protection while in health, attention and nursing when sick, respect when dead, and his body now sleeps in fellowship with the highest of the land in our cemetery.

If slavery was not preferable to freedom for Negroes, why did some choose to return to slavedom? pro-slavery newspapers argued. One item reported that thirteen fugitive slaves had passed through Cincinnati headed back South from Canada.

Another article said sixty-one Negroes were then returning voluntarily to their masters.

Free Negroes sometimes petitioned for permission to select white persons as their owners. About such a case the *New Orleans Daily Delta* commented: "He had the sagacity to perceive and the courage to avow that with a kind and good master his status as a slave would be preferable to the mockery of freedom, with which those seek to delude him who pretend that he can ever sustain himself as the equal of the white man, when Nature and circumstances have made him his inferior." The *Washington Constitution* reprinted an item from the *Columbia* (Tex.) *Democrat* concerning the petition of Sally, a free Negro, praying for the enslavement of herself and her three children.

Inevitably, there were attempts at the light touch. The *Jonesboro* (Ill.) *Gazette* told of a Negro, then buying his own freedom, who went fishing with a slave friend. A storm came up and the friend drowned. The Negro who was buying his own freedom asked his master for his money back, explaining that "nigger property is too unsartin."

It was not always left to the Negro to choose between slavery and freedom. This item in the *Springfield* (Mass.) *Daily Republican* indicated one such occasion:

> At Petersburg, Virginia, 1,193 free Negroes are advertised for sale for a sufficient time to work out their taxes amounting to some $25 apiece. They generally sell for about 10¢ a day so that it will take them nearly the whole year to pay their taxes, and then they will be sold over again for another year.

Enslavement to pay taxes and fines, practiced in several areas, was not the only road to serfdom. Some states had enacted laws forcing free Negroes to flee from the state within a specified time or be sold into slavery. In most cases free persons who remained could choose their owners if they acted before the auction deadline.

Pro-slavery newspapers frequently pointed to examples of unfair treatment of Negroes in the North—in Lincoln land—attempting to prove that the North was hypocritical. The *Daily Chicago Herald* printed a letter in which a Negro charged that the "Republican party, whose professions of love and sympathy for the blacks are piled up in parchment platforms higher than the Tower of Babel, or than even all the rails split by Abe Lincoln, is one grand humbug." Another newspaper observed that when Negroes became unmanageable on some plantations, their masters threatened to free them and send them North to make their living among the abolitionists. Republicans, said a letter in the Washington *Constitution,* do not love the Negroes, they only *hate* their masters. Put an abolitionist in the South, and he would immediately buy Negroes and work them to death. According to a newspaper item, a New York City minister made $18,000 profit from the sale of his Mississippi plantation and fifty-six slaves.

Jibes about Northerners' lack of generosity toward the Negro were frequently published. One quoted a Negro dining-room servant as complaining that while Southerners usually tipped well, the "Abolishun gemmen" usually said, " 'God bless you, my unfortunate friend, and elevate you in the scale of humanity' or something like dat, but never give us a dollar to elevate us."

The *New York Journal of Commerce* ran a letter which asserted slavery had been only partially abolished in New York, for apprenticeship was still authorized. "The City of New York, and every city and town in the state," declared the *Journal,* "is expressly authorized by law to enslave or place in bondage its paupers, who like Negroes, are incompetent to provide for themselves. I myself have had several slaves from the New York almshouse recently. . . ."

The *Jonesboro* (Ill.) *Gazette* reprinted this item from the *New York Express:*

A Negro is not half a man in New York City! He don't vote. He don't serve on juries. He don't "train." He don't work in the workshops. He don't drive the licensed cart. He don't study in the white school. He don't "run the engine." He don't tend behind the counter. He don't print among the printers in the Post's printing office. Living, he don't worship God in the Post's church; and, dead, he is dumped into Potter's Field, or sold to the doctors in 4th ave. or 13th and 14th street, for a skeleton; or, if not thus sold, kicked off into the black graveyard on top of the dozen black bodies there before him. From the bottom of our hearts, we pity the poor, miserable, New York social slave "nigger."

As the relationship between the North and the South grew more tense in late 1860, the pro-slavery South not only struggled to defend its position but frequently "took care of" anti-slavery persons it found in its midst. A schoolteacher, charged with abolition sentiments and being too familiar with slaves, was almost hanged before the vigilante committee, taking pity on his infirmities, allowed him to leave the South. Mississippians stamped "Negro Tamperer" on the back of the coat of one "Abolitionist" and paid the express company sixteen dollars to ship him as far North as the money would carry him. The *Charleston Mercury* reported the arrest of a man in Alexandria, Virginia, for assuring a slave that Lincoln would be elected and then all Negroes would be free.

The *Washington Constitution* reported that a Massachusetts man was tarred and feathered in Conecuh, Alabama, on suspicion of abolitionism; and a British captain in Savannah, who invited a Negro stevedore to his table, was tarred and cottoned by a mob, according to the Washington *Confederation*. The *Mississippian* (Jackson) reported that a Northern white man, charged with plotting a Negro revolt, was run down by dogs and killed by citizens near Montgomery, Alabama.

It was these conflicting and confusing items, some originating in the North and some in the South, that Lincoln may have read while waiting for the journey to the White House. What was *Abe's* stand on this momentous issue that rent the nation?

An anecdote Lincoln told later indicates part of his philosophy. He said:

We've got to be very cautious how we manage the Negro question. If we're not, we should be like a barber out in Illinois who was shaving a fellow with a hatchet face and lantern jaws like mine. The barber stuck his finger in his customer's mouth to make his cheek stick out but while shaving away, he cut through the fellow's cheek and cut off his own finger! If we are not very careful, we shall do as the barber did.

Although the President-elect advocated such practical caution, he disapproved of slavery. And anti-slavery newspapers printed and reprinted any comments along that line he ever made—or was claimed to have made. For example, they told of his flat-boat trip to New Orleans where, seeing a slave-auction block for the first time, he allegedly exclaimed, "Boys, if I ever get a chance to hit that thing, I'll hit it hard." Again and again, he was quoted as remarking, "I have always hated slavery, I think, as much as any Abolitionist." Lincoln said one of his chief reasons for opposing slavery was that a man was forced to work whether he wished to or not, and he could have no hope of improvement.

Lincoln once argued, according to the *Constitution* (Washington, D. C.) that "he who would *be* no slave, must consent to *have* no slave. Those who deny freedom to others deserve it not for themselves, and under a just God cannot long retain it." He declared in a speech in Illinois, "When the white man governs himself, that is self-government; but when he governs himself and also governs another man, that is more than self-government—that is despotism."

At one time Lincoln expressed himself concerning the danger which resulted when one person claimed to have the right to enslave another. If that right were assumed to be based on color, he argued, then the white person might meet a lighter complexioned person and so be enslaved. Was the enslavement to be based on intelligence? Then the white man would become a slave the first time he met a smarter person. Was it to be a matter of interest? Then if another person could make it his interest, he had the right to enslave the white man.

Despite such arguments against slavery which Lincoln may have made, some contended that in 1860 he was nearer to the Southern than the average abolitionist viewpoint. In the debate with Stephen A. Douglas at Ottawa, Illinois, Lincoln had said, according to the *Weekly Illinois State Journal* (Springfield): "Anything that argues me into his idea of perfect social and political equality of the Negro, is but a specious and fantastic arrangement of words by which a man can prove a horse chestnut to be a chestnut horse . . . I have no purpose to introduce political and social equalities between the white and black races." He added that the Negro "is not my equal in many respects—certainly not in color, perhaps not in moral or intellectual endowments. But in the right to eat the bread, without leave of anybody else, which his own hand earns, he is my equal and the equal of Judge Douglas, and the equal of every living man."

So, while Lincoln believed slavery wrong, he did not intend to disturb it in the deep South. But he was inflexible about restricting its spread. A Lincoln lyric in the *Bucyrus* (Ohio) *Weekly Journal* made that point:

> No more soil, which the brave, who are now in the grave,
> Shed their blood from the grasp of oppression to save,
> Must be turned into "commons" for men of black skin;
> So the rails of "Old Abe" will the darkeys fence in.

During the last weeks of 1860, Lincoln did not waste breath in restating his stand on slavery. "Those who will not read or heed what I have already publicly said would not read nor heed a repetition of it," he declared. He was not in a position to proclaim future policies, because they must be built upon public support. He would wait until he took command before making pronouncements.

Lincoln's silence was "a heartless code of conscience," asserted the Washington *States and Union*. It continued:

As well might the captain of a vessel refuse to stop a leakage which might ultimately swamp the ship and drown the passengers, on a plea and a protest that he would wait until he got into port to tinker up her bottom. He must care little for the vessel and the passengers—not to mention his own character. To say in extenuation that he is in the vessel himself, is nothing; because such language is not that of a hero or a martyr, or even of a mean suicide, but of a wholesale murderer. No one would care what such a "captain" would do with himself; but all are interested in the vessel, the gallant crew, and the human freight in her.

But Lincoln felt compelled to bide his time. He watched helplessly while the Buchanan administration disintegrated, states strode out of the Union and formed the Confederacy, and federal property in the South was seized without resistance.

★★★

CHAPTER FOURTEEN

THE UNION BEGINS TO CRUMBLE

"These are Lincoln times," wailed the *Cleveland Weekly Plain Dealer* in the fall of 1860. "Secession, suspension, banks bursting, money shaving, business stopping, poor men begging, women starving, and babies crying. Hoorah for Lincoln. . . . Bring out the Wide-Awakes! Let us go on with the jubilee!"

This was an exaggerated picture by a newspaper that disliked Abe Lincoln passionately. But at least on the first point —secession—the situation was indeed grave as the President-elect waited for March fourth to arrive.

Bloody skirmishes in Kansas, the Dred Scott decision, and the raid on Harper's Ferry by fanatical John Brown had wedged the North and the South far apart. By 1860, rumors of perilous developments were afloat.

Four years earlier, the South had threatened to secede if the Republican candidate, Fremont, was victorious. Now, with Lincoln ready to slip into the Presidential chair, the threat was being put to the test. His election symbolized for many the loss of the last chance to mend the Mason and Dixon breach. "Coming events cast their shadows before," said one newspaper, "and none casts a longer shadow than Abe."

Northern sentiment ranged widely. Some abolitionists, figuratively marching to the stirring tune of "John Brown's Body," concurred with the speaker who in 1860 warned that "ere

242

many more moons revolve, the slave will be offered succor again."

In a more moderate pro-Union view, an item in the *Daily Chicago Post* noted that secessionists complained some runaway slaves were not returned, yet they would dissolve the Union so that *none* would be returned. "Secessionists pretend they want to carry out the Constitution," commented a political speaker, "but they merely want to carry it out and bury it."

A letter from a man who remembered the "wild joy and delight" at the ratification of the Constitution was printed in the *National Intelligencer* (Washington, D. C.) "Awful and amazing thought!" he wrote, "that in the span of an individual's life he may witness the *fall* as he had the *rise*—the *death,* as it were, as he had the *birth*—of a great nation."

An aged veteran of the War of 1812 committed suicide in Hinds County, Mississippi, because of the secession movement, the *New York Evening Post* reported.

Humorist Artemus Ward used his comic speller in defense of the Union. He wrote:

I'm a Union man. I luv the Union from the bottom of mi hart. I luv every hoop-pole in Maine, and every sheep ranch in Texis. The kow pastures of Nu Hampshire are as deer 2 A. Ward as the rice plantashuns of Mississippy. There is mean taters in both them are States, & thar is likewise good men and troo. It don't look well for a lot of inflamitory individuals, who never lifted their hands in defence ov Ameriky, or did the fust thing towards sekewerin our independence, to git their backs up and sware they'll dissolve the Union. Too much blood was spilt a courtin' and marryin' that highly respectable female, the Goddess of Liberty, 2 git a divorse at this late day. The old gal behaved herself 2 well 2 cast her off now, at the request of a parsul ov addle-braned men Un wimmin, who never did nobody no good, and never will again. I'm sorry the picture of the Goddess never give her no shuse or stockin's, but the band of stars around her head must kontiner to shine briter so long as the earth kontiners 2 revolve on its axeltree.

Some pro-Union sentiment could even be found in the South during the fall and winter of 1860-61. "The movement for secession meets with little favor here," asserted an item from New Orleans in the *Baltimore Sun*. The *Richmond News* evaluated the situation this way:

There is no evil, real or fancied, which cannot be better endured within than cured without the Union. Listen not to the delusive tongue of the siren, when she sings of a Southern Republic. . . . Virginia can have no permanent interest and will be permitted to have no eventual voice in such a confederation. She would soon be as powerless as the fly on a coach wheel, and as much accounted of—a mere captive at the chariot wheels of cotton- and sugar-growing States—while her territory would be the Flanders of the inevitable and irrepressible conflict that would ensue.

A North Carolina newspaper suggested that if a selected five hundred Northern and Southern political leaders could be thrown into dungeons for six weeks, the Union would be saved. It declared that a disunionist merely for disunion's sake was either mad or bad. Such a person, the paper charged, was guilty of the most heinous crime since Cain slew his brother.

A *New York Daily Tribune* dispatch from Washington said many Southern leaders believed that if the North did not fan the flames by interference, conservative masses in the South would sweep the disunionists out of existence. At a meeting at Wilmington, North Carolina, the people rose *en masse* "with shouts and waving of hats and handkerchiefs" at every allusion to the Stars and Stripes, the Union, and the Old North State.

And out in Springfield, Illinois, where Abe Lincoln was studiously observing the political pall which hung over the nation, an enterprising store was advertising: optimism. "The masses of the people South, could no more be induced to give up the Union than those who live here could be persuaded to buy their Clothing elsewhere than at Hammerslough Brothers' Clothing House."

Fragments of hope were clutched at by those who valued the Union. Sometimes, though, it was a matter of hiding the head in the sand—or the water. One speaker told of an antediluvian hero who implored Noah to let him into the Ark. After his last futile plea, with chin just above water, the man shouted, "Well go to thunder with your old ark! I don't believe there is going to be much of a shower."

Some persons, including old Sam Houston, of Texas, were better aware of the flood, yet clung persistently to the slim hope of rescue. The *Daily Gate City* (Keokuk, Iowa) pointed out that there had been no Presidential election during the previous thirty years without accompanying predictions that the Union would collapse.

Ex-President Franklin Pierce wrote a friend:

Can it be that this flag, with all the stars in their places, is no longer to float at home, abroad, and always as an emblem of our *united* power, common freedom, and unchallenged security? Can it be that it is to go down in darkness, if not in blood, before we have completed a single century of our independent, national existence? I agree with you that madness has ruled the hour in pushing forward a line of aggressions upon the South, but I will not despair of returning reason and of a returning sense of constitutional right and duty.

Peace hath its victories, reminded the *Daily Chicago Post,* no less renowned than those of war. And the *National Intelligencer* (Washington, D. C.) sounding as though it spoke for Abe Lincoln, declared in its Christmas issue of 1860: "If there be discord in the land, let us at least keep this Christmas day sacred to the Prince of Peace, and, expelling from our minds the leaven of wrath, malice, and all uncharitableness, we may borrow from its genial festivities a better inspiration for the days to come."

On the other hand, sentiment favoring disunion could be found above as well as below the Mason and Dixon line.

Peace, warned the *National Intelligencer,* might be thwarted by extremists of both sections.

Lincoln was hanged in effigy from a sloop at a New York City wharf. An inscription read: "Abe Lincoln, dead and gone to hell." A crowd which gathered threatened to lynch the crew if the objectionable object were not removed. Then police climbed aboard and ordered the effigy cut down. The skipper balked. "The police thereupon immediately arrested the captain," reported the *New York World,* "but as he refused to walk to court, he was summarily knocked down and thrust into a dirt cart, and thus transferred with a large and miscellaneous crowd following, to the courtroom. . . ." This was the third time, the paper noted, that such effigies had been strung up on vessels in that neighborhood.

In the South, of course, violent feelings against Lincoln and the North were widespread. Long before the balloting, Southern newspapers warned that the election of the Rail-Splitter would mean dissolution of the Union. A Kentucky judge, according to the *Tri-Weekly Missouri Republican* (St. Louis), declared that Lincoln's election might produce a national calamity "equal, perhaps, to the San Domingo tragedy and the French Revolution combined." Nearly all Georgia Democratic papers, said the *New York Herald,* came out for dissolution of the Union in case of Lincoln's election. The *Charleston Mercury* advised that South Carolina should not allow "Black Republican domination" to rest upon it a day—nor an hour. "It is idle to waste more words on a Constitutional Union," the *Mercury* insisted. "Its days have been numbered. The *friendship* of the people of the North is a thing to be dreaded. There is but one means of safety left us, and that is *resistance.*" The South Carolina legislature set aside a day for prayer and preparation, and the *Mercury* observed that "we are, then, upon the eve of great events."

Evidences of the strength of Southern sentiment were many. In New York City medical students from the South met to decide whether they should leave school and return home. At Aiken, South Carolina, residents burned in effigy "the first President of the Northern Confederacy," Abraham Lincoln. Over much of the South, people favoring secession symbolized their sentiment by wearing special cockades. The steamer *Keystone State,* said the *Baltimore Sun,* had to haul down the American flag and run up the Palmetto flag before it was allowed to enter the Charleston port.

Tempers ran high, and one's words could endanger him if misconstrued. An anecdote about a stuttering Northerner in the South was reprinted by the *Daily Gate City* (Keokuk, Iowa). "Gentlemen," the Northerner announced, "I g-g-g-g-go for Li-Li-Li——." Before he could finish, he was grabbed and shoved about. He tried again but got no farther when some helpful soul finished the sentence for him. "You go for Li-li-li-Lincoln, do you!" and he was brusquely escorted out of town and told never to return. As he left, he managed to say, "Y-y-you have been t-t-too hasty. I g-g-gg-go for li-li-limiting the power of C-C-C-C-Congress."

By mid-summer of 1860 Southern "fire-eaters" were applying the torch with inflammatory remarks such as these, quoted in the *Vermont Patriot* (Montpelier):

We shall fire the Southern heart, instruct the Southern mind, give courage to each other, and at the proper moment, by the organized concentration action, we can precipitate the cotton States into a Revolution.—*W. L. Yancey.*

Resistance! Resistance! To death, against the Government is what we want now.—*David Hubbard.*

Break up and dissolve this rotten Yankee Government.—*John D. F. Williams.*

Let the Union rip.—*R. D. Gayle.*

My voice is for war!—*George D. Johnson.*

In one of his speeches Georgia Senator Robert Toombs

pointed out to Southern women that patriots of Revolutionary days were inspired by women who stripped their rings from their fingers and jewelry from their necks to mint into dollars to help whip the Redcoats.

The lines had become tightly drawn. On the day before the Presidential election, Gov. William Henry Gist, of South Carolina, had recommended to his legislature that, in the event of Lincoln's success, a state convention should immediately discuss secession.

In the North, Greeley jarred Republican unanimity by contending that the right to secede existed, even though it was a revolutionary right. "We must ever resist the asserted right of any State to remain in the Union and nullify or defy the laws thereof," counseled Greeley. "We hope never to live in a republic whereof one section is pinned to the residue by bayonet." One writer asserted that New England was going to secede if South Carolina didn't hurry up and do so.

But South Carolina did—on December 20, 1860. Mississippi followed on January 9; Florida, January 10; Alabama, January 11; Georgia, January 19; Louisiana, January 26; and Texas, February 1. In some cases, churches even seceded from their parent body.

"The Union is dissolved," announced a headline in the *Union Democrat* (Manchester, N. H.). "We make this announcement in the spirit of unspeakable sadness. . . . The great crime of all ages is consummated in ours, and the men who did it walk abroad among us; but we weep with the weeping millions, and leave the guilty to the certain and terrible retributions of the future."

South Carolina was unquestionably the extremist in the secession movement. The *San Francisco Herald* reprinted a *Nashville Union* item which declared: "The world in arms cannot subdue them. There is not a man, woman, or child in that state that will not suffer torture on the rack before they will submit to coercion."

But not all sentiment, even in the pro-slavery camp, was in accord with South Carolina. The *New York Weekly Journal of Commerce* declared that South Carolina's rashness in refusing to wait until the North had made a move, "but at once plunging the country into all the perils of Civil War, has alienated the sympathies of many patriotic men who have hitherto remained her steadfast friends." What might have been sympathy, the Washington *National Intelligencer* reported, quoting the *Alexandria* (Va.) *Gazette,* was converted into resistance, if not disgust.

The border states became an uncomfortable middle ground. A New England paper described these states as "plunging about since the secession movement like horses frightened by the running away of other horses."

Some newspapers sought to link the border states inseparably with the South. A *Richmond* (Va.) *Enquirer* article conjectured that a large majority of Virginians would vote to line up with the deep South, and "we would advise the Slave States not to hesitate to strike an early blow from fear that Virginia may hesitate in her duty to the South." At Fredricksburg, Virginia, a large black flag of mourning was suspended across Main Street because of the Old Dominion's delay in "going out." On the other hand, this resolution was adopted at a meeting in Rockbridge County, Virginia:

Resolved, that the allegation that Virginia is so hitched to the Southern States that they can drag her into a common destiny with them, no matter what may be the desire of her people, is a foul calumny and aspersion on this noble old Commonwealth, and a gross insult to her people.

At a convention in Richmond, it was resolved that Virginia should demand additional guarantees under the U. S. Constitution and give the Northern States an ultimatum as to how long Virginia would wait for these assurances. Missouri and other states were holding similar state conventions about this time to consider the critical situation.

The *National Intelligencer* (Washington, D. C.) reprinted this item from "that polished exponent of secession," the *Charleston Mercury,* concerning a proposed mission of "ambassadors" from the border states to confer with South Carolina:

Hear them, if you please; treat them with civility; feed them and drench them in champagne, and let them go! Let us act as if they had never come, as if they had not spoken, as if they did not exist; and let them seek to preserve their Treasury pap through some more supple agency than ours. The time has gone by when the voice of a Virginia politician, though he coo like a dove, should be heard in the land of a patriotic people.

The *Confederation* (Washington, D. C.) said of South Carolina's rejection of the proposed mediation: "Thus it is that madness rules the hour. South Carolina is surely bent on self-destruction. She is foolish—worse than foolish—she is mad, and 'whom the Gods destroy, they first make mad.' "

Foes of secession charged that "muttonheads" had thrown away the South's tremendous power in the Federal government. "They were even more silly than the dog that dropped the bone of meat in his mouth to plunge after its shadow." But, for good or evil, the step had been irrevocably taken. And in February, 1861, a few weeks before Lincoln took office, the Confederate States of America was formed. Jefferson Davis, the "George Washington of the Confederacy," was provisional President and Alexander Stephens, Vice-President.

Writers began to refer to the South as "Secessia." One reporter tagged the North "Uncle Sam" and the South "Cousin Sambo." Some newspapers soon declared the Confederacy had panned out badly. Said the *Evening Star* (Washington, D. C.), it is "a naked despotism upon the necks of the masses. depriving them of every vestige of the liberties they enjoyed under the Government of the United States."

Apparently all was not harmony among the seceded states, especially during the earlier days. The *Daily Chicago Post* quoted the *Richmond* (Va.) *Whig* as asserting:

Nothing but the blast of ridicule which would follow prevents South Carolina from seceding from the Southern Confederacy. It finds itself in the position of the pig, which tried to break out of a field by going through a crooked, hollow log in the fence, both ends of which opened inside the field, and its swinish amazement at finding itself still in confinement.

But as war clouds billowed the Southern states huddled closer together. Even before tall Abe of Illinois had assumed the Presidency, the *New York Weekly Journal of Commerce* reprinted this item from the *Macon* (Ga.) *Telegram:*

We should be recreant to our trust as a public journalist did we fail to proclaim that there is *no peace,* and to exhort the men of the South to prepare for war—war desperate and deadly, as it must necessarily be when a people seek to overthrow and reduce to subjection their brethren of the same kindred and tongue. This must come, or Lincoln proves himself a deceiver and a dastard.

Upon the first unacceptable move by the Lincoln administration, warned a Baton Rouge correspondent for the Washington *Evening Star,* the Confederacy would dispatch a large army northward at once. "The South will never wait to be invaded."

Evidences of strained relationships increased. The *Evening Star* chastised the band leader at the play, *Our American Cousin at Home,* for yielding "to the clamor of a squad of half-weaned boys, who imagined themselves secessionists" and performing "Dixie's Land" before "the Union-loving audience." The people did not object to "Dixie" in moderation, "even with all its discordant barrel-organ, harpist and brass-band horrors," the *Star* assured, but they did detest having it thrust upon them as a disunion air to supplant "Hail Columbia" and the "Star-Spangled Banner." A couple of weeks later, the *Star* pointed out, "the popular Ethiopian melody, 'Dixie's Land,' " which the Southern Confederacy had adopted as a national air, had been composed by a Pennsylvania Yankee, Stephen C. Foster.

At a New Orleans theater, according to the *San Francisco Herald,* the "Marseillaise" was heartily applauded while the Union air, "Hail Columbia," was drowned in hisses.

There were the inevitable poems. One entitled "Secession Consummated" ended:

> *Yankee Doodle on a limb*
> *Like another noodle,*
> *Cut between the tree and him,*
> *And down came Yankee Doodle.*

> *Yankee Doodle broke his neck,*
> *Every bone about him,*
> *And then the Tree of Liberty*
> *Did very well without him.*

At the New Orleans' Mardi Gras in February, Negroes carried an effigy of the Rail-Splitter President on a rail. Mobile, Ala., a newspaper reported, changed the names of several streets to erase Northern stigma—Massachusetts to Charleston, New Hampshire to Augusta, Rhode Island to Savannah, Connecticut to Louisiana, Vermont to Texas, and Pennsylvania to Montgomery. A grand jury in Richmond, Va., took steps to cut off the circulation of the *New York World, New York Daily Tribune,* and *New York Times* in that city.

The grave issues and problems of the day elicited humorous expressions. This item was reprinted from the *Knickerbocker* (New York) by the *Daily Chicago Herald:*

Gentlemen and ladies, you'r talkin' of dissolvin' the Union; You can't do it; if you go to —— you can't do it; . . . thar's that good old toon the ban's a playin' out thar, called Yankee Doodle; How you goin't to divide that, eh? Are ye a-goin' to give the Yankee to the Norf and the Doodle to the Souf? I say boldly the thing can't be did! And thar's that stream of water a-runnin' down thar called the Father o' Waters: How are ye a'goin' to divide that? Are ye a'goin' to dam it up with Mason and Dixon's line? I say you can't do that thing! Wal, you can't . . . And thar's all the handsome wimmen around here. How are ye a'goin' to divide them? Are ye a-goin't to give the old ones to the Norf and the young ones to the Souf? Wal, you don't! If you go to thunder, you can't do it.

Punch carried a parody on the "Star-Spangled Banner," which ended:

If this may not be, if the moment be nigh
When this banner unrent shall no more flout the sky
To make fitting division of beams and of bars
Let the South have the Stripes and the North have the Stars.

Someone mailed a marriage notice with the explanation: "States may go out of the Union, but men and women will go in. The Lord have mercy on both parties." *Vanity Fair* suggested that United States senators who had left "the Senate for the Senate's good" no longer should add the initials "U.S.S." after their names. Instead, they should use "A.S.S." (A Seceding Senator).

Always ready with puns, one newspaper suggested South Carolina didn't have any warrant for her conduct but she had plenty of war-rant; and, when a Southern poem contained the challenge, *"Sternly* meet the advancing foe," it drew the comment of another journal, "perhaps that's as good a way as any to meet the foe, but why not secede like a man, and not like a crab?"

The *Providence* (R. I.) *Journal* implored Kansas, which had just entered the Union, not to "go and secede before we have had a chance to spend a few millions on you."

As the breach between the North and the South widened and deepened, bitter words and violent deeds became more common than humor. An article reprinted in the *Washington*

States and Union declared that Confederate residents who still considered themselves citizens of the United States would do well to keep mum about it. Even before the November election, the *Mississippian* (Jackson) had noted: "We understand that an avowed supporter of Lincoln passed up the railroad by this city on Saturday last. Our people should be on the lookout for these incendiaries, and prepare the halter for them whenever they obtrude themselves upon Southern soil."

In Alabama, a disgruntled legislator declared he would have "preferred to live for four years under Mr. Lincoln's rule" than under some newly-enacted Alabama laws. This brought a hiss from an unappreciative member. The first man shouted: "Mr. speaker, a gentleman hisses. No, sir, not a gentleman, but a goose—gentlemen do not hiss . . . If the individual who hissed will make himself known and put himself within my reach, I will put his mouth in such condition as will render it difficult for him to engage in that pastime for a week to come." The man—or goose—did appear and boldly identify himself, then tried to dodge an ink stand that the first fuming legislator hurled at him. The hurler leaped over the desk and charged the hisser, but the warring statesmen were soon separated.

Near Richmond, a man who chose not to reveal his address or his business to the vigilance committee was ridden on a rail. Later, according to the *Wizard* (South Danvers, Mass.), he coolly informed them that he was from South Carolina, the heartland of Secessia.

A young Massachusetts schoolmaster who went to teach in an Alabama town was chased out of that state after someone denounced him as an abolitionist. The *Portsmouth* (N. H.) *Journal* reported that he was compelled to walk many miles in the hot sun, and was beaten and tossed into a pond.

In Washington, according to the *Evening Star,* a young fellow was stoned by a band of drunks who shouted, "Kill the d—d Republican son of a bitch!" He fired a couple of shots above their heads and then made a dash for the Capitol, darting into the north door and escaping through the south wing. When a Capitol guard stopped the pursuing gang from entering, they pelted the entrance with brickbats and cobblestones.

Two New Jersey men working in South Carolina, reported the *Daily Chicago Post*, were arrested as spies, tried and hanged, all within an hour.

Sometimes the violence was on the other side of the political fence. The *Washington Evening Star* reprinted an item from the *Zanesville* (Ohio) *Courier* telling how a young man had been murdered when he sided with the South in a political argument. Pulling out a pistol, he shouted his willingness to fight for her. An opposition debater grabbed the weapon, poked it into his chest, and shot him. "No arrests were made," the paper noted.

Southern anger often was focused directly on Abe Lincoln, rather than on the more impersonal Union. Governor John Willis Ellis of North Carolina was quoted as saying, "Our fathers resisted George III and we should resist Abraham Lincoln," and a poem of the era expanded on that sentiment. One verse declared:

> *O we rise as we think on*
> *That Scamp, Abram Lincoln,*
> *That beastly, belligerent, bucker!*
> *O we swear all together*
> *To tar and to feather*
> *Provided we catch him, the Sucker.*

The *Weekly Illinois State Journal* (Springfield) borrowed this article from the *New York Evening Post* in December, 1860.

Missives which no decent man could write are abundant. . . . Letters threatening death, in all its forms, as the penalty of his high position are more abundant still. They are, of course, mainly anonymous, though a few bear real names. Some are signed in hieroglyphics, said to be known only to the "Sacred Order" or "Southern Brotherhood," which threatens Mr. Lincoln with a sudden and untimely taking-off. A few are ornamented with sketches of executions by the gibbet, assassination by the stiletto, or death by a lightning stroke; and in nearly all the theology of the writers is indicated by rude caricatures of the Devil, ready with his three-pronged fork to receive and pitch into everlasting fire the body of the unfortunate Lincoln whose offense consists in the belief that human slavery is wrong. He is not, I am glad to say, annoyed by these. . . . He tosses all such aside, as he says, to illustrate at some future day the comical side of his Administration.

The resistance movement in the South was neither spontaneous nor sporadic. In many communities there were organized groups of "Minute Men." The *Portsmouth* (Va.) *Transcript* advocated such an organization in order to "visit summary punishment on interlopers or squatters who may raise the standard of rebellion in our midst." Companies of Minute Men would act as "judges, jurymen, and hangmen if necessity demands." In Virginia, ex-Governor Henry Alexander Wise recommended "Committees of Safety" as in Revolutionary times. These committees would supervise the military groups, the Minute Men.

The Minute Men movement apparently started in South Carolina. There, according to the *Old Line Guard* (Indianapolis), members were required to wear the old Revolutionary emblem, the blue cockade, on the left side of the hat. By late October a visitor to Columbia, South Carolina, said that every other man he met wore on his hat "a small blue rosette, with a Palmetto button in the center." Each member was supposed to get a Colt's revolver, rifle, or some other approved firearm.

Minute Men were organized in Montgomery, Alabama, reported the *Mississippian* (Jackson), to declare "to the world that we will not submit to the control of a Black Republican as President of these United States."

The Minute Men drilled assiduously. A New England girl

teaching in Georgia wrote to the *New-Hampshire Statesman* (Concord) that the "most remarkable part of that performance to a Yankee girl was to see each soldier have a Negro along to carry his gun."

Personal bridges that one might expect would have had a uniting effect on the North and the South, were apparently of frail timber. The *Washington Evening Star* observed that "many of the South Carolinians not only have Yankee arms in their hands when they muster in war-like parade but Yankee arms around their necks in the privacy of their own homes." The *States and Union* (Washington, D.C.) noted that married sisters of Mary Todd Lincoln lived in the South and "they are both strong secessionists, and opposed to the government of their brother-in-law, Abraham Lincoln."

From November through February, the South moved rapidly. In an item in the *Washington National Intelligencer* the day after election, the Governor of South Carolina was quoted as recommending arming all men in the state between eighteen and forty-five with the most efficient weapons. He said citizens were "conscious that we are contending for our firesides." By February, another newspaper pointed out, South Carolina was so busy arming, drilling, digging, and pursuing other military tasks that ordinary work had come almost to a standstill. South Carolina was recruiting in other states, such as Tennessee, offering the same pay as the United States Army, according to a Tennessee newspaper.

Arms filtered, and sometimes flowed, into the South. The *Washington Evening Star* reported that twenty cases of Minie rifles and ten cases of Colt's revolvers had just passed over the Orange and Alexandria Railroad en route to Jackson, Mississippi. Another account, reprinted from the *Norfolk* (Va.) *Transcript,* disclosed that 150 huge bombshells, each ten inches in diameter and weighing eighty-five pounds, whose "explosive force must be tremendous," arrived in Petersburg, Virginia, headed for South Carolina.

The *Daily Chicago Post* said an arsenal and armory specialist was about to establish an arms factory at a central location in the Southern States. At Charleston, a war battery which resembled "the carcass or skeleton of a mastodon" was under construction. Rumors that secessionists were bargaining with New England shipowners to act as privateers for the South in case of war were being circulated.

As the tension mounted the *Charleston Mercury* reported U. S. Congressional proceedings under the heading "Foreign News." In Congress a committee was appointed to investigate whether members from the seceded states had toted away Library of Congress books to form a Confederate library. In Georgia, a man imprisoned for robbing the U. S. mails argued he was entitled to a discharge because of the revised status of the Federal government in the South. New Orleans took over and began operating the Federal mint and custom house, and levied and collected duties on imports. At Pensacola, Florida, Federal property was snatched by a "wild and undisciplined gang of revolutionists." The *Baltimore Sun* reported the surrender of the Federal arsenal, at Little Rock, containing 9,000 small arms, considerable ammunition, and forty cannons, to Arkansas State authorities.

A letter in a Southern newspaper, according to the *New York Weekly Journal of Commerce,* said, "It is supposed by many that the President [Buchanan] has given solemn assurances to the seceding States that he will surrender all the forts in these states before the fourth of March." The *Journal* wisecracked that " 'it is supposed by many' that the moon is made of green cheese, and that the earth rests on the back of a mud turtle."

The seceding states, however, didn't wait to see whether the President would make such a gift. They seized several Federal forts at once. Even in far-off Nebraska Territory, old Fort Kearney was captured by secessionists, although it was soon won back. Secessionists also took over Fort Moultrie in

Charleston Harbor after Major Robert Anderson and his eighty men decided to abandon it and go to nearby Fort Sumter. In January, the Federal Government made a half-hearted attempt to send reinforcements to Major Anderson on the *Star of the West*. Confederate batteries fired upon the steamer and she turned tail. Early in February a Southern newspaper warned that Sumter was going to be reinforced. "Keep a sharp look out!" it cautioned. "There is mischief brewing."

An item in the *New York Evening Post,* February 8, 1861, reported the evacuation of wives and children of Fort Sumter soldiers:

On nearing the fort, the whole garrison were seen mounted on the top of the rampart, and when the ship was passing fired a gun and gave three heart-thrilling cheers as a parting farewell to the dear loved ones on board, whom they possibly would never meet again this side of the grave.

The response was weeping and waving adieus to husbands and fathers, a small band pent-up in an isolated fort and competely surrounded by instruments of death, as five forts could be seen from the steamer's decks with the guns pointing toward Sumter.

CHAPTER FIFTEEN

MR. LINCOLN GOES TO WASHINGTON

Lincoln stuck close to home during the four months between his election and inauguration. In fact, about his only trip of importance was to Chicago where he and Mrs. Lincoln met Hannibal Hamlin, the Vice-President-elect. Lincoln attended St. James Church there on Sunday, and in the afternoon spoke briefly at Dwight L. Moody's Mission Sabbath School.

After the Lincolns returned to Springfield, Bob Lincoln wrote to his mother: "I see by the papers where you have been to Chicago. Ain't you beginning to get a little tired of this constant uproar?"

For several weeks before leaving Springfield for Washington, Abe was preparing his inaugural address. In a small upstairs back room of a store building, he carefully fashioned it, drawing on such sources as Henry Clay's Speech of 1850; Andrew Jackson's Proclamation against Nullification; Webster's Reply to Hayne; and the U. S. Constitution. According to some reports, he also used notes he had jotted down from time to time on scraps of paper or on old envelopes.

During January, in preparation for Washington and her role as First Lady of the Land, Mrs. Lincoln made a shopping trip to New York City. Another paper said she shopped in St. Louis, too. For awhile it was thought she would not go to the nation's capital at the same time as her husband because of the dangerous political climate. However, according to the

Washington States and Union, General Winfield Scott, in charge of safety for the national capital, suggested in February that she accompany Lincoln to "show more confidence in the country." The newspaper snorted that it was preposterous that the wife of the President, and not the President himself, should be expected to create confidence.

Moving away from Springfield was not easy for Lincoln. The *Washington States and Union* reported:

The parting with this scene of his joys and sorrows during the last thirty years, and the large circle of old and faithful friends, apparently saddens him, and directs his thoughts to the cherished past rather than the uncertain future. His interviews with the more intimate of his friends are more frequent and affectionate, and visits of strangers are not encouraged; but, although more than ordinarily moved with tender feelings, he evidently fully realizes the solemnity of the mission on which he is about to enter and is resolved to fulfill it firmly, fearlessly and conscientiously.

One prelude to leaving was a visit to his old stepmother, Sarah Johnston Lincoln, in Coles County, Illinois. There he also met other members of the Johnston and Hanks families and visited the grave of his father, Thomas. As Abe left his stepmother, tears streamed down the old lady's cheeks. She gave him her blessing but expressed fear for his life. Before returning to Springfield, he stayed overnight in Charleston, Illinois, where he attended a get-together of old friends who remembered him "when. . . ."

Five days before the Lincolns left for Washington, a party was held in their home. The guests included seven hundred ladies and gentlemen, "composing the political elite of the state," reported the *Confederation* (Washington, D. C.), and "the beauty and fashion of the vicinity."

A couple of days before their departure, the Lincolns sold their household goods, most of them to the president of the Great Western Railroad, who also leased the Lincoln home.

(The railroad executive later moved to Chicago and many of the furnishings were destroyed in the great Chicago fire of 1871). One last-minute task was having a picture made of the dog belonging to Tad and Willie. The dog was not to accompany the family to Washington.

Abe labelled some trunks "A. Lincoln, White House, Washington, D. C.," and sent them on their way. The family moved to the Chenery Hotel, where they spent their remaining hours in Springfield. Abe made a last visit to his law office, where he suggested that the sign remain as it was until he got back.

The twelve-day trip to the Federal capital was to be in style. The Washington *States and Union* informed its readers:

In the Central Railroad Depot in Buffalo are now three cars to be used by Mr. Lincoln on his route to Washington. One is a sleeping car containing all the comfort that could be imagined for a movable bed chamber. Another is a regular passenger car, very handsomely fitted. The third is fitted with luxurious seats, so fixed that the passengers can sit, recline, or lie on its sumptuous velvet cushions . . . At one end of the car is a large framed engraving of the U. S. Senate of 1850, and a rack immediately underneath is filled with china urns and dishes of various kinds.

Not everyone smiled upon the travellers. The *Washington Constitution* later suggested it would have been better for the country if Lincoln had come to Washington quietly instead of "travelling the country and making the outrageously silly speeches which mark his triumphal march."

It was a somber February eleventh when Lincoln, carrying a worn bag, appeared in Springfield's Great Western depot shortly before 8 A.M. In the waiting room, he shook hands with old home-town friends who filed past. Then he worked his way toward the waiting train, saying final good-byes to those he passed. On the train's rear platform he paused momentarily to control his emotions, then said (according to one version):

Friends: No one who has never been placed in a like position can understand my feeling at this hour, nor the oppressive sadness I feel at this parting.

For more than a quarter of a century I have lived among you, and during all that time I have received nothing but kindness at your hands. Here I have lived from my youth, until now I am an old man. Here the most sacred ties of earth were assumed. Here all my children were born; and here one of them lies buried. To you, dear friends, I owe all that I have, all that I am. All the strange, checkered past seems to crowd now upon my mind.

To-day I leave you. I go to assume a task more difficult than that which devolved upon Washington. Unless the great God who assisted him shall be with me and aid me, I must fail; but if the same omniscient mind and almighty arm that directed and protected him shall guide and support me, I shall not fail—I shall succeed.

Let us all pray that the God of our fathers may not forsake us now. To Him I commend you all. Permit me to ask that, with equal security and faith, you will invoke His wisdom and guidance for me. With these few words I must leave you, for how long I know not. Friends, one and all, I must now bid you an affectionate farewell.

Commented the proud *Weekly Illinois State Journal,* "Lincoln spoke only to his neighbors, in childlike simplicity, little dreaming of the mighty influence of his words upon his own nation and upon the world."

As the train rolled away, Lincoln stood at the door and took his last view of his beloved Springfield. With him was his oldest son, Robert, seventeen. Remaining behind temporarily were Mrs. Lincoln and their two younger boys. They would be reunited the next day—Abe's 52nd birthday—in Indiana.

But the Rail-Splitter of the Sangamon Valley was also leaving behind many tried and true friends whom he knew he would not see again for at least several years. "If I live," he promised his law partner, Herndon, "I am coming back some time, and then we'll go right on practising law, as if nothing had happened." But Abe Lincoln was leaving Springfield never to return alive.

While the train was clipping along, Lincoln was urged to write down his Springfield talk. He made a try, then asked his secretary, John G. Nicolay, to complete the job from dictation.

Even the solemn occasion of Lincoln's departure from Springfield provided excuses for satire. The *Washington Confederation* printed what purported to be a preamble and resolutions offered by the Illinois House of Representatives:

Whereas, when he left Springfield "he tearfully expressed the fear that he might never return to this state . . ." a lock of Lincoln's hair reportedly has been obtained by a member of his party during the trip.

It was then resolved "to place the hairs . . . bereft of the head of our distinguished fellow citizen . . . in the custody of the State Treasurer and his successors in office, for all time to come."

If he should return, "as we sincerely hope and trust he will," the State Treasurer would "restore to the Honorable Mr. Lincoln the venerable hairs of which he was so affectionately bereft . . ."

At one stop Lincoln declared, "I am leaving you on an errand of national importance, attended, as you are aware, with considerable difficulties. Let us believe, as some poet has expressed it: 'Behind the cloud, the sun is shining still.' " The *Daily Chicago Post* commented that a friend of Henry Wadsworth Longfellow thought Lincoln paid the poet a dubious compliment when he referred to "some poet." However, the *Post* assured that Lincoln had meant it in the emphatic but well understood Western sense of *"some poet!"*

As the Presidential train rolled eastward across Illinois and Indiana, every precaution was taken to avoid accidents. According to one account, flagmen stationed at crossroads waved the American flag as a signal that all was well. A representative of the Western Union Telegraph company, one item said, was along with apparatus for making wire connections between stations in case of train trouble.

Despite safety measures, an obstruction was discovered on the Toledo and Western Railroad, apparently placed there to derail the Lincoln train. As the *Newark Daily Advertiser* described it, if the train had hit the obstruction at full speed, "the engine and cars must have been thrown off, and many persons killed."

It was further reported that a carpet bag was later found in the train, containing a live grenade which would have exploded within fifteen minutes "with a force sufficient to have demolished the car and destroyed the lives of all persons in it."

Before leaving Springfield, Lincoln had been warned by an Illinois farmer of the danger of poisons. "Eat nothing except what the old woman cooks for ye," the old man counseled. The *New York Journal of Commerce* asserted that Lincoln had adopted this delicate hint as a rule in political matters, especially in the utterance of speeches along the way to Washington.

Lincoln, although making it a policy to avoid significant pronouncements before the inauguration, did appear during many stops along the route and say a few words to the crowds. At a little town near Indianapolis, he started an anecdote but the train pulled out just before he got to the punch line. At the next stop, several miles away, he was told jokingly that some of the folks from the previous town had raced along on foot beside the train and were panting outside, waiting to hear the climax of the story. Good naturedly, he repeated the anecdote.

At Indianapolis, where Abe and Bob rejoined the rest of the family, Lincoln spoke at more length. "By what rightful principle may a state," he asked, "being not more than one-fiftieth part of the nation in soil and population, break up the nation and then coerce the larger divisions of itself? What mysterious right to play tyrant is conferred on a district of a country with its people by merely calling it a state?" Lincoln said he was not asserting anything, but just asking questions for them to consider.

The nation listened closely for any revealing comments from Lincoln, since silence had been his golden policy. The *New York Day Book* asserted that the Indianapolis speech was "an open declaration of war against the South, and will be so regarded." The *Washington States and Union* declared:

Lincoln says if secession is to be acknowledged then the Union is a kind of "free love" arrangement to be dissolved whenever "passional attraction" requires it. Lincoln is greatly in error. The North has dissolved the marriage contract by committing adultery with Aunty Slavery!

In the evening, Lincoln held a reception at the Bates House and there was a great rush and crush to see and congratulate him. The *Indiana State Guard* (Indianapolis) had satirically suggested that all good Republicans be on deck:

"We publish on our first page a list of all the principal offices at Old Abe's disposal after the 4th of March next. Every torch-bearer during the late campaign has a right to 'put in' his claim for the *fat things,* and should be here on the precise day to take the Great Rail-Splitter by the hand."

Despite such jabs, Lincoln's reception on the journey was good. Cannons were fired, bouquets were bestowed, and elegant receptions, dinners, and luncheons were provided. Flags and banners fluttered and brass bands blared. There was appreciative applause and often real enthusiasm for Lincoln's approximately thirty speeches.

Even in far-away parts of the nation, newspaper subscribers read—although somewhat belatedly—about the triumphal journey. The *San Francisco Herald* commented, two days *after* the inauguration: "The Pony Express arrived yesterday morning at Carson City. The following is the summary of news telegraphed to the Associated Press." The summary included this item: "President Lincoln is prosecuting his journey toward the Capital. Nothing important has occurred on the way."

But it *was* important to the folks who gathered along the

railroad tracks and heard the lanky rail-splitter and perhaps shook his hand. In Decatur County, Indiana, he was greeted by an aged clergyman. "I shake hands with the President of the United States for the last time," remarked the old man. "Tears filled the eyes of Mr. Lincoln and of most men who stood by," said the *New York Daily Tribune,* "while sobs broke forth from the women, as the old patriarch tottered back toward his home."

But there was fun as well as tears. At one town where Lincoln knew the stop would be brief, he promised the crowd he would tell them a story if every person swore solemnly never to repeat it. About that time, the train pulled out without his telling the tale, but the crowd, catching the spirit, shouted to the President-elect that they would never tell.

Some people were incensed by Lincoln's laughter at a time when the country was in peril. But Lincoln appreciated the medicinal power of laughter. Beyond that, he was compelled to touch on insignificant points, for he would not unpack his principal policies until the inaugural.

The route had been well publicized and large crowds waited at every stop. An especially large group gathered at Lawrenceburg in southeastern Indiana. There Lincoln looked wistfully toward his native Kentucky beyond the Ohio River and declared, "I say to you that the power entrusted to me shall be exercised as perfectly to protect the rights of your neighbors across the river as of your own."

The crowd was so great at the Indianapolis and Cincinnati depot in Cincinnati that the locomotive had to pause until troops and policemen could open a way. Lincoln, dressed in black and carrying a tall silk hat, stood up in the carriage which was drawn by six white horses, and bowed to the crowd.

An item in the *Cincinnati Enquirer* termed this "the largest funeral procession" ever held in Cincinnati. But the affair appeared quite different to most persons, especially to victorious Republicans.

On the way to the Burnet House, Lincoln listened to the children at the orphan asylum, who were waiting out in front, sing "Hail Columbia" in his honor as the carriage passed. Farther on, a group of girls sang "The Star-Spangled Banner" and one presented flowers to Lincoln, who reciprocated with a kiss. Lincoln appreciated, he indicated, an illuminated sixty-foot sign on the Gibson House, bearing portraits of Lincoln, Hamlin and Washington; the Great Seal of the United States, and mottoes such as "A Union of Hearts, a Union of Hands," and "The Time Has Come When Demagogues Must Go Under."

The reception committee at the Burnet House included a future President and his wife, Mr. and Mrs. Rutherford B. Hayes. Some newspapers reported that the crowd "almost wrung Lincoln's arms off" when he passed through the lobby. This was probably because, volunteered the *Lynn* (Mass.) *Weekly Reporter,* Lincoln would need only his legs when he got to Washington.

In his Cincinnati talk, as at Lawrenceburg, Lincoln beamed kind words towards the Old Kentucky shore. "We mean to leave you alone, and in no way to interfere with your institution. . . . We mean to recognize and bear in mind, always, that you have as good hearts in your bosoms as other people."

At one Ohio stop, Lincoln remarked that the situation between the North and the South reminded him of his two younger boys. One had a toy the other wanted and demanded it in belligerent terms. After a while he was ordered to let his brother have the toy to quiet him. "No sir!" he retorted. "I need it to quiet myself!"

The *Weekly Illinois State Journal* said no public figure since George Washington had received such a triumphal and spontaneous ovation. This was certainly true of the reception given him at Columbus, Ohio. A state official thus described the hand-shaking in the state capitol rotunda:

The crowd . . . heaved and surged to and fro. For a while the President greeted the people with his right hand only, but as the officers gave way before the irresistible crowd, he shook hands right and left with astonishing rapidity. The physical exertion must have been tremendous. People plunged at his arms with frantic enthusiasm, and all the infinite variety of shakes, from the wild and irrepressible pump-handle movement, to the dead grip, was executed. . . .

Some glanced into his face as they grasped his hand; others invoked the blessings of heaven upon him; others affectionately gave him their last gasping assurance of devotion; others, bewildered and furious, with hats crushed over their eyes seized his hand in a convulsive grasp, and passed on as if they had not the remotest idea who, what, or where they were, or what anything at all was about.

For an hour he was driven from place to place, until he found himself on the stairway leading to the State Senate chamber, reported the *New York World*. There, exhausted by the exercise and heat, he quit shaking hands, merely bowing to the surging crowd as it jostled along.

The *World* then told about a "plucky little state senator" who was shoved against Lincoln several times by the crowd. Finally, one of Lincoln's entourage pushed the senator back, only to receive a wallop in return that sent him reeling. They were promptly separated, the *World* added.

Again Lincoln avoided discussing his policies, and again people protested that he failed to appreciate the seriousness of the situation. His non-revealing talk, suggested the *New Orleans Daily Picayune*, illustrated what Voltaire meant by his epigram that men talk only to conceal their minds.

But Lincoln did make one comment at Columbus that stirred up the opposition. "It is a good thing," he declared confidently, "that there is no more than anxiety, for there is nothing going wrong. It is a consoling circumstance that when we look out there is nothing that really hurts anybody." Some opposition newspapers defied readers to decipher that last sentence. These journals did think it was clear, though, that Lincoln was trying to wish away or ignore the gravity of circumstances.

The *Baltimore Sun,* characterizing Lincoln a "harlequin" or "bar-room phunny-phellow," asserted he was "dealing with the great issues which agitate and agonize the minds of thoughtful and rational men as if they were only the absurdities of a pantomime which would all be 'put to right' by a touch of his magic wand." To the *Washington States and Union* Lincoln's Columbus remarks confirmed that he was correct when he said his abilities had been overestimated.

At the stop in Columbus, on February 13, Lincoln was informed the electoral votes had been officially counted in Washington and he had been declared elected to the Presidency. The *Salem* (Mass.) *Register* quoted a *New York Times* correspondent's report: "When he read it he smiled benignly and looking up, seeing everyone waiting for a word, he quietly put the dispatch in his pocket and said, 'What a beautiful building you have here, Governor Dennison.' "

The peaceful counting of the electoral votes was chalked up as a victory, for trouble had threatened. The *New Orleans Daily Picayune* insisted there had been a plot, had secession not become a substitute, to proclaim Breckinridge the President-elect. Because of fear that the Capitol and other public buildings might be seized, they had been heavily guarded. Each night Capitol police searched the cellars and vaults for bombs. While the votes were counted, the House of Representatives was guarded by a strong police force.

An interesting detail of the electoral count was that forty-seven votes were to be cast, the *New Orleans Daily Picayune* explained, for states that had left the Union without withdrawing or annulling their votes. The majority in Congress had ruled that those seven states were officially still in the Union.

Among the Presidential electors present were three from

far-off Oregon, the *Daily Chicago Post* informed taxpayers. These electors "could not consent to appoint a messenger to Washington as the mileage (over $15,000) was too nice a plum to give away, so they all three came."

But such side features were eclipsed by the significance of the electoral count. The *Weekly Illinois State Journal* exclaimed:

Thus passed into irrevocable judgment the verdict rendered by the American people on the sixth day of November last. Let it stand! God and good men approve it. A civilized world respects it. The unerring pen of history will applaud it. Palsied be the hand that would set it aside or render it null and void.

While Lincoln was still in the Ohio capital where he received the electoral college news and the plaudits of the crowds, another President was en route to a capital for inauguration. Jefferson Davis, too, was a Kentuckian and a veteran of the Black Hawk War. He was chosen President of the Confederate States of America two days before Lincoln left Springfield.

Both of these new Presidents-elect had their supporters. One newspaper item mentioned an old man who had prayed for the success of the President "and to prevent mistakes I just added that I meant Abraham Lincoln and not the *other feller!*"

Davis made some twenty-five speeches on his way to Montgomery. In one talk he declared:

We shall have nothing to fear at home, because at home we have a homogeneity of sentiment. We have nothing to fear from abroad, because if war should come; if we must again baptize with blood the principles for which our fathers bled in the Revolution, we shall show we are not degenerate sons, but will redeem the pledges they gave to preserve sacred the rights transmitted to us, and show that Southern valor still shines as brightly as in seventeen hundred and seventy-six, in eighteen hundred and twelve, and every other conflict.

Arriving in Montgomery, he promised the crowd that those who would interfere with the Confederacy would "smell Southern powder and feel Southern steel."

On February 18, Confederate inauguration day, Montgomery featured "the grandest pageant ever witnessed in the South," said the *New Orleans Daily Picayune*. In his address, Davis asserted that the Confederacy illustrated the American idea of Government resting upon the consent of the governed. He concluded: "Obstacles may retard, but they cannot long prevent the progress of a movement sanctified by its justice and sustained by a virtuous people. Let us therefore invoke the God of our fathers to guide and protect us . . ."

Bets were being made in Washington, the *Washington Evening Star* disclosed, that Davis would be inaugurated again at the Federal Capitol before May.

When Lincoln left Columbus, then officially President-elect of a shrunken United States, he headed toward Pittsburgh. Along the way he continued to meet and greet the people, even the lowliest. At Steubenville, Ohio, a brawny miner struggled to the platform. "God Bless ye, Misther Lincoln!" he exclaimed, according to the *Nebraska Republican* (Omaha, Nebraska Territory). "I didn't vote for ye, sure; but I wish ye luck, and I want to shake yer hand."

In Pittsburgh Lincoln told a crowd he thought it more rare if not more wise for a public figure to keep quiet rather than speak. Therefore, he would merely chat instead of make a speech. Lincoln assured the audience he intended to give the condition of the country careful consideration before he discussed it fully and definitely. "So that when I do speak," Lincoln explained, "I may be as nearly right as possible." He pleaded with folks on both sides of Mason and Dixon's line to hold their tempers. "There is really no crisis except an artificial one. . . . no crisis, excepting such a one as may be gotten up at any time by turbulent men, aided by designing politicians." Just as other clouds have cleared away in due time, so will these, he assured his listeners.

Concerning this Pittsburgh chat, the *States and Union* (Washington, D. C.) declared:

> What a *real* crisis must be, in the opinion of Mr. Lincoln, we should like to know. An artificial crisis, indeed! Six States out of the Union, a Southern Confederacy formed, and a provisional government, with the ablest Southern General and the wisest Southern thinker in the first two positions—this is an artificial crisis!

Newspapers in those days liked to get the facts straight first—then they could do with them as they pleased. But the telegraph did not always cooperate in getting the facts straight. The *Worcester* (Mass.) *Daily Spy* complained that the unpredictable machine began Lincoln's Pittsburgh speech right in the middle. Two days later the *Spy* quoted the *New York Post:* "Had they tried to do their worst, no greater torture could have been inflicted upon a man's words than that to which they subject the public addresses of the President-elect. Important passages are mutilated, words snipped out, meanings perverted and general confusion produced."

Leaving Pittsburgh, Lincoln started north toward Cleveland on Lake Erie. At Wellsville, Ohio, an admirer offered him a couple of apples. A lad amused the crowd by yelling, "Say, Mister Linkin, that man is running for postmaster." At Alliance, Ohio, a sumptuous dinner was given the Lincoln party by the president of the railroad. At that city a thunderous salute was fired, smashing windows, including one near Mrs. Lincoln.

In Cleveland the procession trooped through the principal streets to the Weddell House. There Lincoln complimented the crowd which had marched about two miles through snow, rain, and deep mud. He observed that the large numbers testified to the people's respect for the Union, not for him personally. He also expressed approval of other political groups having joined Republicans in making arrangements. "If all do not join now to save the good old ship of Union this voyage," Lincoln said feelingly, "nobody will have a chance to pilot her on another voyage."

The President-elect pointed out at Cleveland:

There are differences of opinion even here. You did not all vote for the person who now addresses you. And how is it with those who are not here? Have they not all their rights as they ever had? Do they not have their fugitive slaves returned now, as ever? Have they not the same Constitution that they have lived under for seventy-odd years? Have they not a position as citizens of this common country, and have we any power to change that position? What then, is the matter with them? Why all this excitement? Why all these complaints? As I said before, this crisis is artificial. It has no foundation in fact. It was "argued up," as the saying is, and cannot be argued down. Let it alone and it will go down of itself.

Following eastward along the lake, the Lincoln train stopped briefly at Geneva, Ohio. A member of the crowd provided a reverse twist by addressing Lincoln, exhorting him to stand by the Constitution and the cause of liberty.

At Girard, Pennsylvania, the party was surprised by the sudden appearance of Horace Greeley. The *New York World* reported:

He wore that mysteriously durable garment, the white coat, and carried in his hand a yellow bag, labeled with his name and address, in characters which might be read across Lake Erie. . . . At the next stopping place [Erie, Pa.] Greeley suddenly disappeared. His arrival and departure were altogether so unexpected, so mysterious, so comical, that they supplied an amusing topic of conversation during the rest of the journey.

A dinner had been prepared at the Erie station. "As the train drew up, cannon were fired, 'Hail Columbia' experimented upon by a brass band, and the roof of an adjoining shed broken through." The *World* story continued:

The dining room was crowded. There were elderly women, with umbrellas and spectacles, mounted upon chairs; aged gentlemen, with crutches and benedictions; local politicians with fluffy white cravats and tremendous appetites; colored persons of both sexes, one or two infants at the breast, together with all the other varieties which make up Western life.

The *Cleveland Weekly Plain Dealer,* in an item which did not jibe with more reputable accounts of Lincoln's habits, contended that Lincoln was offered wine at Erie, but turned it down with the remark, "If you have got any ale, I don't keer if I take in a tumbler-full or so." The item was headed "What 'ale'd' him."

At a railway station in Pennsylvania, the *Newark* (N. J.) *Daily Advertiser* reported, a flag inscribed "Fort Sumter, the powder keg of the crisis" was carried right up to where Lincoln stood. The President-elect ignored this provocative act.

Some of the most widely printed news stories of the Lincoln tour originated at Westfield, New York. They concerned Abe's follow-up of a letter he had received several months before from an eleven-year-old girl. Lincoln told the crowd, "I have a correspondent in this place, a little girl named Grace Bedell, and I would like to see her." When she came to the platform, he remarked, "You see, I have let these whiskers grow for you, Grace."

The girl had probably written her letter after seeing a lithograph of Thomas Hicks' oil portrait of Lincoln, painted for campaign purposes. The letter said:

> Westfield, Chautauqua County, N. Y.
> October 15, 1860

Hon. A. B. Lincoln

Dear Sir

My father has just home [come] from the fair and brought home your picture and Mr. Hamlin's. I am a little girl eleven years old, but want you should be President of the United States very much so I hope you won't think me very bold to write to such a great man as you are.

Have you any little girls about as large as I am? If so, give them my love and tell her to write me if you cannot answer this letter. I have got four brothers and part of them will vote for you anyway and if you will let your whiskers grow I will try to get the rest of them to vote for you. You would look a great deal better for your face is so thin. All the ladies like whiskers and they would tease their husbands to vote for you and then you would be President. . . .

Although few letters, mainly from friends and important personages, got past Lincoln's secretaries, John G. Nicolay and John M. Hay, this one reached the nominee. And apparently it struck the mark, for he not only answered the letter but also began letting his whiskers grow.

Some journals poked fun at the newly cultivated whiskers. A *Vanity Fair* cartoon depicted an "Agency for the Lincoln Whiskeropherous." The caption was "Mr. Lincoln sets a style." The *New York Herald* used a picture of whiskered Lincoln with a legend which referred to "his new whiskers looking as if not yet naturalized."

All this had been triggered by little Grace, who came meekly to the platform and received a kiss from the President-elect of the United States. The girl, who became Mrs. Grace N. Billings of Delphos, Kansas, still was reminiscing about that big moment when, at eighty-one, she was a guest at the Abraham Lincoln Association banquet in Springfield, and went to Abe's old home and signed the visitors' register.

Some newspapers made hay with the Rail-Splitter's kissing of little Grace in 1861. The *Baltimore Sun* exclaimed with righteous indignation:

People of ordinary dignity and refinement are accustomed to keep their endearments for those who have a right to them, and even to these they are offered only in private. But our new president calls the women he likes up to him and salutes them in public.

. . . What is prohibited even on the Paris stage as too gross to be offered to public women, the successor of Washington commits as he progresses to the capital, of which he is so soon to be the ruler. It is . . . to be hoped there will be no allusions to the important subject of Mr. Lincoln's whiskers in the Inaugural address.

The platform upon which the kiss took place, suggested the *Indiana State Guard,* would become as memorable to Old Abe as the Chicago Republican platform. It raises the question, added the irate *Guard,* as to whether he is more a fanatic or a simpleton.

Leaving his young girl friend, the President-elect moved on up the lake. At Dunkirk, New York, he "grasped the staff of the American flag, under the folds of which he stood, announced his intention to stand by that flag, and asked them to stand by him as long as he should do so." Such a vow seemed quite appropriate in that day since allegiance to the Stars and Stripes could not be taken for granted.

Arriving in Buffalo, Lincoln was greeted by ex-President Millard Fillmore and an estimated 10,000 others. This was the *Washington National Republican's* description of the scene:

He had hardly left his car, and, after heartily shaking hands with M. Fillmore, made a few steps toward the door, when the crowd made a rush, and, overpowering the guard, pressed upon him and party with a perfect furor. A scene of the wildest confusion ensued. To and fro the ruffians swayed, and soon the cries of distress were heard on all sides. The pressure was so great that it is really a wonder that many were not crushed and trampled to death. As it was, Major Hunter, of the President's escort, alone suffered a bodily injury by having his arm dislocated. The President elect was safely got out of the depot only by the desperate efforts of those immediately around him. His party had to struggle with might and main for their lives, and after fighting their way to the open air found some of the carriages already occupied, so that not a few had to make for the hotel afoot as best they could.

The *New York World* declared that an old man "had three ribs broken, and was otherwise badly bruised. When recovered from the press the blood was running from his mouth and nose, and it is believed that he has sustained serious internal injuries."

After experiencing a crowd like that, Lincoln may have been relieved to see the large banner on the Young Men's Christian Union across from the American Hotel. It said, "We will pray for you."

As Lincoln was giving a little speech, a man was sawing wood nearby on a wagon in front of the hotel. He was paying off an election bet, the *Daily Chicago Post* explained.

In Buffalo, Lincoln went to hear John Beeson, who had lived among the Western Indians; and he also attended the Unitarian church with Mr. Fillmore. "Dr. Homer, the pastor," said the *New York World*, "invoked the blessings of heaven upon the incoming administration in a most impressive manner in his opening prayer. Many of the congregation were moved to tears."

The Presidential party crawled from their warm feather beds at 4 A.M. to leave Buffalo at 5 A.M. A reporter swore that "of the weird cluster of men, cloaked and muffled, who gathered gloomily in the dim corridors of the American, not one but thirsted for the blood" of the fellow who made these predawn arrangements.

The train steamed eastward through the falling snow. Near Batavia a heated axle caused a delay. But between Canastota and Oneida—six miles—"some remarkable railroad speed" was made, the *Washington Evening Star* reported. This stretch was covered in five and one-fourth minutes, while the fifty-three miles between Syracuse and Utica were clipped off in seventy minutes. There was another delay at Utica, then, because of an overheated journal.

Lincoln made a number of talks along the New York route, but chose to ignore the platforms which had been erected for him. At Fonda, where he declined to mount one of these structures, he stressed that he wanted it distinctly understood he would never avoid a "platform" on which he properly belonged.

As the train approached Schenectady, an overenthusiastic gunner in touching off the customary salute fired his cannon point-blank at the first car, a *Washington Evening Star* account said. The concussion burst open the door, shattered three windows, and showered several persons with broken glass. No one was injured.

An estimated fifteen thousand persons waited at the new depot at Troy, New York, and a "deafening roar of cheers and shouts" greeted Abe Lincoln's arrival.

At Albany, Lincoln spoke to a throng in Capitol Park, then addressed the New York State Assembly. "It is true," he confided, "that, while I hold myself, without mock modesty, the humblest of all individuals that have ever been elevated to the presidency, I have a more difficult task to perform than any one of them."

As the Washington-bound train rolled through New York State, reporters found occasion to inform readers about the individuals who accompanied the President. One writer described Mrs. Lincoln as "a stout, plump lady, very well-rounded and developed, and her physique as a whole is rather agreeable. She is inclined to be chatty, but is not so smart as has been represented."

The scribe noted that the President-elect "has three or four gentlemen with him—the rest are far from bearing that title rightfully." He said that one—the commander of the Chicago Zouaves—was "the most active and officious, and makes himself particularly offensive by overdoing his part in the play."

The *Washington Evening Star* discussed the elbow-bending propensities of the entourage under the heading, "More Plucking of the Goose":

They remained for less than one day at the Delavan House in Albany, and a bill was rendered to the amount of $1,120. As there were eighteen persons in the party, two of whom, Mr. and Mrs. Lincoln, did not dine in the hotel, the expense for each person, three quarters of a day, was just $70! Included in this bill was a charge of $357 for wine, or about $22 or nine bottles a head. We are not surprised, after such drinking, at a considerable charge for Congress water. Neither is it wonderful that the breakages for stoves, chairs, and so forth, were set down at $150. Fellows with nine bottles of liquor under their belts must have been in a state to break everything about them, even their necks. . . . Mr. Lincoln being a rigid temperance man, the keepers of the Delavan have probably taken their revenge upon him in this manner.

Lincoln and his party enjoyed a special car as the train rolled down the Hudson River Railroad. The *Newark Daily Advertiser* described it as—

lined with royal purple, and the woodwork is of rosewood. Instead of ordinary seats, ottomans and sofas, running lengthwise of the car, have been furnished, while velvet carpet covers the floor. The ceiling is elaborately frescoed with national emblems, including the Star-Spangled Banner, and pendant therefrom are graceful festoons of drapery of commingled red, white and blue, bespangled with glittering stars.

The train with its precious cargo was being pulled in style by a decorated locomotive, the "Union." It was replaced at Poughkeepsie by the "Constitution." A pilot engine, "Young America," served part of the trip in New York.

Church bells pealed, cannons boomed, and people cheered as the train sped through villages and towns. "Bring us the Rail-Splitter!" and "Trot out Old Abe!" the crowds shouted at the scheduled stops. At Poughkeepsie "the hills on the east side of the road were crowded with people, mainly ladies. Every height that could command a sight of the train, and every road winding up the hills, bore crowds of citizens."

Through Ossining and Yonkers rolled the train, and then on into the heart of New York City.

From the Hudson River Railroad's new Thirtieth Street depot, opened only the day before, the Presidential party climbed into eleven carriages and started for the Astor House. Lincoln rode in a barouche pulled by six black horses.

An estimated quarter million people cheered the procession. Boys hurrahed from the top of a statue of Washington. Ladies in a large bay window of Lord & Taylor's, on tiers of seats, "rose *en masse* and waved their cambric welcome." Wide-Awakes in uniform "tested the soundness of their lungs."

On one building hung a huge sign, "Fear not, Abraham! I am thy shield, and thy exceeding great reward." Newspaper offices along the route, except the *New York Day Book,* displayed large American flags.

Arriving at the Astor House, Lincoln endured another hand-shaking marathon. Excited admirers greeted him with "God bless you!" "May heaven reward you!" and "You are the man for the hour, sir!" "The policemen seized every opportunity for having their share of presidential shaking," said the *New York World.* "And Old Abe indulged them all freely. He even called upon those who were backward, and told them to crowd around and take turns."

Police urged other handshakers to use the gentle touch. Earlier, William Cullen Bryant's *New York Evening Post* stressed that Lincoln's having once split rails "by no means justifies the unceremonious mauling of his hands, which have for long years been accustomed to a gentler exercise."

A correspondent of the *New Orleans Daily Picayune* gave his version of Lincoln, the handshaker:

When receiving visitors in great numbers, one at a time, he plants one foot firmly forward, gives them about three firm shakes (or pulls) of the hand, and then allows them to pass on. His pull, if given full scope, would, I'd doubt not, wrench one's arm from the socket, and if manual strength alone was necessary to raise the pillars of the temples that have fallen, "Old Abe" would be just the man for the emergency.

At a reception of Republican clubs at the Astor House, Lincoln, standing where Webster and Clay once had stood, spoke on the subject of not speaking. The *New York Journal of Commerce* quoted him:

I have not kept silence since the Presidential election for any party wantonness, or from any indifference to the anxiety which pervades the minds of men in regard to the threatening aspect of the political affairs of the country. I have kept silence for the reason that I supposed it was peculiarly proper that I should do so, until the time arrived when, according to the custom of the country, I should speak officially.

Large crowds gathered outside the hotel during the Lincoln stay. Many persons overworked their ingenuity in attempting to gain admittance, but generally were unsuccessful.

One evening Lincoln attended the opera at the Academy of Music. The first act was under way when he arrived. When the act ended, said the *New York Evening Post:*

The curtain rose again, displaying the entire operatic company, who sang the national anthem, "Star-Spangled Banner". . . . A large American flag with thirty-three stars was lowered from the proscenium, and the entire audience stood up and the anthem concluded amid the waving of handkerchiefs, and cheers for Lincoln, for the Union and the Constitution.

Mrs. Lincoln took Willie to Barnum's Museum one afternoon. (Tad didn't want to go.) Among P. T.'s displays was a mammoth turkey which had been presented to Lincoln for his inaugural dinner.

The First Lady-elect gave a reception while in Manhattan. Her dress was "of steel-colored silk, made high in the neck, with a trimming of box-plaited satin ribbon, a small lace collar, fastened with a small diamond brooch, diamond eardrops to match, and black chenille and gold head-dress." She carried a small ivory fan "with which she occasionally fanned some of the gentlemen who paid their respects to her, playfully telling them not to get 'too warm in the cause.'"

At one time, while in New York, Lincoln appeared on the hotel balcony and, according to the *Daily Chicago Post,* declared: "I come merely to see you, and allow you to see me, and I have to say to you . . . that, in the sight, I have the best of the bargain." With sarcasm the *Democratic Republican* (Haverhill, N. H.) retorted: "Such a burst of eloquence ought to be printed in letters of sunbeams and hung out from the stars, that all the world may read it."

Lincoln delivered another talk in City Hall. Soon afterward the doors were opened and the common folks gushed in. The *Daily Chicago Post* related:

Men were pulled in by main force out of the crowd by the police, utterly unable to help themselves, with coats torn and hats demolished and lost.

In the heat of the excitement a female made her appearance, and was dragged through the doorway, with hoops and bonnet materially damaged. When introduced to Mr. Lincoln, she told him she was from Illinois, and though she had experienced a rough voyage, she would go through a tighter squeeze to see him.

The crowd was a motley one with rags and broadcloth being indiscriminately mixed, and filing into the room side by side to shake the Presidential hand . . .

Immediately after the ex-Mayor came one of the seediest, unwashed citizens of New York, and thus the crowd continued to pour in until one o'clock, when the audience closed, and Mr. Lincoln returned to his apartments at the Astor House, leaving a large number of the "sovereign people" of the city with hands still unshaken.

By the time Lincoln was ready to leave sophisticated New York, the journals were busy appraising his qualities from close range. In general, they managed to find whatever they looked for—true or untrue. A *Vanity Fair* writer, looking for the worst, wrote:

Abe is becoming more grave. He don't construct as many jokes as he did. He fears that he will get things mixed up if he don't look out, and sincerely as I regard myself competent to fill the consulship at Liverpool I fear he will.

A pleasing incident occurred at Hudson. Several young ladies came into the cars, and the President elect folded them rapturously to his throbbing bosom. They said "don't" which induced the President to believe that they liked it.

It is popularly believed that Mr. Lincoln is not classically educated, which belief had somewhat obtained strength in our party; but at the dinner at the Astor, where the bills of fare are printed in French, Mr. Lincoln unhesitatingly called for a *sine qua non* of beans and an *ipse dixit* of pork, thus showing his thorough familiarity with deceased languages.

A journalist who looked through kindlier eyes wrote in the *New York World:*

A bride who goes to the altar to be wedded to a soldier, not knowing whether in one short month he will fall in battle or be promoted for gallantry, awakens less human interest than does the future chief magistrate of this nation on his way to the federal capital, amid widespread apprehensions that the Union may be finally dissolved. Abraham Lincoln has won all our hearts by the manly simplicity of his character; he has convinced us that the warm interest in his success, felt by all good men, is not thrown away upon a hard, hackneyed, truckling politician, but is bestowed on a man full of fresh human sympathies and native honesty of purpose.

A gaily decorated ferry boat, waiting at the foot of Cortlandt Street, took Lincoln past Bedloe's Island and on to Jersey. Dodworth's band played patriotic airs on the way.

Thirty-four guns were fired from the Cunard Atlantic Steamship Company's wharf. This salute, reported the *New York World,* "alerted New Yorkers to what was going on—or rather, who was going off." The next three ferries to New Jersey were jam-packed with passengers.

The New Jersey railroad depot at Jersey City, which the *New York World* said held 12,000 people, was filled. "Quite a crowd who could not get into the building," it added, "worked their way to the top of the depot and contented themselves with a bird's eye view through the skylights."

One fellow got much closer. He climbed upon the platform and shook Lincoln's hand "with more than ordinary Celtic enthusiasm," the *World* noted. "A policeman made free with the dwarfish son of Erin, and with his club punched him off the platform, to the great delectation of the crowd."

At Newark the procession formed in almost blinding snow, but this weather gave way to a "genial sun and a bland, spring-like atmosphere, emblematic, it is hoped, of the future administration." There was no evidence of disrespect, even though "villainous posters" attacking Abe had been displayed the previous day.

Busy in the crowd at the parade, perhaps, were some visitors from Boston. The *New York Evening Post* said New York police had been tipped-off earlier that Boston pickpockets were headquartered on Centre Street in Manhattan. It was found that "the birds had flown" to Newark to await the President's arrival.

From Newark the train barrelled on through heavy snow squalls to Rahway. The weather, the *New York World* explained, "interfered with the comfort of the ladies who flocked in shoals to see the 'homely President.'"

But Abe could joke about it. A thin, weasel-faced Jerseyite, said the *Daily Chicago Post,* remarked to Lincoln that he had been told "I look like you." Abe agreed and added, "The fact is settled, that you are a handsome man."

In Trenton another huge crowd had gathered. Peddlers of Lincoln badges, medals, and photographs palmed off their wares on the populace who had come to town "from the unexplored counties," the *New York World* declared. Bartenders and pickpockets did a big business.

At dinner time, there was a delay in opening the dining-room where Lincoln was being entertained. He was conducted in state through the kitchen. Men in paper caps "and smelling of burnt pie" saluted him with ladles.

The President-elect addressed the legislators in Trenton, declaring, according to the *Newark Daily Advertiser:* "I shall do all that may be in my power to promote a peaceful settlement of all our difficulties. The man does not live who is more devoted to peace than I am. None who would do more to preserve it; but it may be necessary to put the foot down firmly."

The scene at the Trenton House, where the Rail-Splitter was guest of the politicians, was described by the *World:*

The legislature respectfully refrained from paying too much homage to the Republican victor, they being mostly Democrats. . . .

So they respectfully bid farewell to "Ould Abe," without emotion, or indeed leaving the festive dining hall. The guests departed first, as the "Star-Spangled Banner" was being sung in jubilant chorus for the twenty-fifth time, and the harmony had begun to need repair. There were no symptoms of a loss of spirits among the members, although there were among the bottles.

Leaving Trenton, the Presidential train crossed the Delaware to Philadelphia, the City of Brotherly Love. But even though the citizens treated him royally, the most significant message revealed to Honest Old Abe there was one of hate, not love.

CHAPTER SIXTEEN

A FLIGHT THROUGH THE NIGHT

From the Philadelphia railway station, the Lincoln party rode to the Continental Hotel as an estimated 100,000 persons watched and waved. Four white horses sporting gay plumage on their heads pulled Lincoln's carriage. The driver performed his prominent role from a special seat at the front of the vehicle, a typical arrangement in those days.

At one point, recounted *McClure's Magazine* in November, 1894, some spectators saw a man slip mysteriously through the police lines and hand a note to Norman B. Judd in the President's barouche. The incident was soon generally forgotten—but not by Judd.

Early next day—Washington's Birthday—Independence Square was thronged. A thirty-four-star flag was hoisted aloft by Lincoln from a platform in front of Independence Hall.

At this flag-raising ceremony, Lincoln spoke briefly. He may have thought of the mysterious-note incident, which was followed by a secret meeting at his hotel, when he remarked: "If this country cannot be saved without giving up that principle [expressed in the Declaration of Independence], I was about to say I would rather be assassinated on this spot than surrender it."

The note had directed Judd to seek out a J. H. Hutchinson at the St. Louis Hotel. Hutchinson turned out to be the famous detective Allan Pinkerton, who became the founder of the

Army's secret-service bureau. These two men talked with S. M. Felton, president of the Philadelphia, Wilmington & Baltimore Railroad. Then, at the Continental Hotel, they conferred with Lincoln, to whom they unraveled the "Baltimore plot."

Lincoln's well-advertised route was from Philadelphia to Harrisburg, then to Washington by way of Baltimore. However, the men in the conclave, stressing that Abe's life was threatened, pressed him to go directly and at once to Washington from Philadelphia. Lincoln balked at the proposal, and the party boarded the train for Harrisburg.

As the group rode on toward the Keystone capital, there was time for further analyzing the Baltimore plot and the climate in which it had been hatched.

As *Harper's Monthly* recalled in 1868, Lincoln's election was immediately seized upon by reckless conspirators plotting to overthrow the Union:

Through the press, by popular meetings, public speeches, and in social intercourse, and in every possible way, they painted the alleged wrongs of the South, the outrages past and anticipated of the North, to inflame and excite the inflammable Southern temperament until the slaveholding States became a seething volcano. Especial efforts were made to render Mr. Lincoln personally odious and contemptible. No falsehood was too gross, no lie too infamous, no statement too exaggerated to be used for the purpose.

There were rumors of imminent plots to seize Washington, which was surrounded by, and was largely itself, a part of the slaveholding South. Other rumors were of plots to derail Lincoln's train or to murder him in Baltimore. An item in the *Nebraska Republican* (Omaha, Nebraska Territory) said: "The idea was, if possible, to throw the train from the road at some point where they could push it down the steep embankment and destroy in a moment all on board. In case of the failure of this project, the plan was to surround the carriage on the way from depot to depot in Baltimore, and assassinate him with dagger or pistol. . . ." Another rumor was that the steam ferry on the Susquehanna River at Havre de Grace, Maryland, a vital link between Philadelphia and Baltimore, would be destroyed. By such a blow or blows, the conspirators might prevent the inauguration of a Yankee President while also hindering the concentration of Northern troops in the District of Columbia.

Although rumors of such plots may not have filtered down to the average man in the street, they were picked up by a few influential and concerned persons, such as Felton, the railway executive. So the famous Chicago detective Pinkerton and his staff were hired. The *New York World* described him as "a gentleman of Vidocquean repute in the way of thief-taking— a very Napoleon in the respect of laying his hands upon the right man—a person who has populated the penal institutions of the West with elaborate scoundrels, whose villainy eluded all save the Pinkertonean investigators."

One of the countermeasures against the plots was the recruiting of a special force of two hundred men, secretly armed, organized, and drilled. To camouflage their purpose, which was to guard strategic points along the railway, they were put to whitewashing railway bridges—even six or seven times. This abundantly applied covering made the bridges almost fireproof, although that was not the main intent.

Pinkerton centered his probing in Baltimore, where he opened a business under an assumed name. He and other detectives did not cater only to customers, though—*cherchez la femme* was not neglected. Said *Harper's Monthly* in 1868: "Many Baltimore belles are living who might innocently blush at the disclosures of the daily reports of one whom, in February, 1861, they called 'the fascinating Howard of New Orleans.' "

Some of the detectives were initiated into secret orders in Baltimore, having learned the signs, grips, and oaths. In such associations, some reports allege, they gleaned details of the

Baltimore plot. One story was that as soon as the President-elect left the train to transfer at Baltimore, roughnecks would start a fight a few hundred yards away, giving the police an excuse for leaving the Lincoln party. Then the crowd would close around Lincoln and his aides, pushing and jostling them. In the confusion a conspirator would strike the deadly blow or fire the fatal shot.

Pinkerton's information reportedly disclosed that a Baltimore gang had balloted to determine who should murder the new President as he passed through the city. Said *McClure's* magazine in 1894:

It was agreed that the task should be entrusted to that one of the number who should draw a red ballot. Whoever was thus chosen was pledged not to disclose the fact, even to his fellow-conspirators. To make it absolutely sure that the plot would not be defeated at the last moment by accident or cowardice, eight red ballots instead of one were placed in the box from which they drew, unknown to the conspirators themselves, and eight determined men regarded themselves as thus chosen, by high destiny, to rid the country of "an infamous tyrant."

To the frightening information about a plot which Pinkerton claimed to have uncovered were added warnings rushed to the Presidential party by Senator William H. Seward and General Winfield Scott, based on other evidence.

Such was the menacing background as Abe and his worried aides pulled into Harrisburg.

In his talk in the Pennsylvania capital, Lincoln commented on the display of military force there. He emphasized, "I do most sincerely hope that we shall have no use for them, that it will never become their duty to shed blood, and most especially never to shed fraternal blood."

It was that evening, while Lincoln was a dinner guest of Governor Curtin, that the Presidential party and other top leaders discussed in dead earnest the alleged Baltimore plot and how best to cope with it. The group decided that Lincoln should slip out of Harrisburg that night, return to Philadelphia, and then hasten on to Washington.

Lincoln disapproved of the premature take-off, Colonel A. K. McClure, founder of the *Philadelphia Times* and a Lincoln campaigner, reminisced in *McClure's* magazine in 1895. Some details of the *McClure's* articles have been questioned, but this point seems certain. McClure recalled Lincoln's remark, "What would the nation think of its President stealing into the Capital like a thief in the night?"

The *McClure's* article indicated, however, that the President-elect may not have been nearly as opposed to the precautions as these statements might indicate. At any rate, the leaders soon were perfecting plans to, as someone expressed it, "smuggle the President through the lines as if he were a piece of contraband goods."

Telegraph wires leading out of Harrisburg were cut so that no conspirator who might discover Lincoln leaving the city could notify a fellow plotter. A Harrisburg reporter, according to the *Washington States and Union,* "was forcibly locked up in a room and kept there for two hours" to prevent a news leakage.

A crowd was gathered in front of the hotel when Lincoln left. The President-elect, Governor Curtin and Ward H. Lamon, a law partner of Lincoln, climbed into a closed coach, and told the coachman to take them to the Executive Mansion in Harrisburg—a natural place for them to be going. When they neared the mansion, the coach took off for the railway depot by a winding route.

According to one widely-circulated report, Lincoln went incognito, wearing a Scotch cap and a long military cloak. A contemporary caricature, captioned "The Passage Through Baltimore," pictured lanky Abe in such bizarre garb, peering timorously through a freight-car door. Lincoln did put on an old overcoat and exchange his familiar high hat for a soft felt one, but the other costume details were the embellishments of an imaginative reporter.

Lamon was to be Lincoln's bodyguard on the trip, according to *McClure's*. "In addition to a pair of heavy revolvers," the magazine said, "he had a sling-shot and brass knuckles, and a huge knife under his vest."

The getaway from the Pennsylvania capital was unobserved and the Presidential party was soon rolling through the night toward Philadelphia. Mrs. Lincoln and the members of the party who stayed behind in Harrisburg spent a restless night.

Allan Pinkerton and a famous woman detective, Kate Warn, had been arranging for the hurried trip from Philadelphia to Washington. For this last leg of the journey, Colonel McClure's article explained, reservations for the rear portion of the train were made for an "invalid," and permission was secured to leave the rear door open for his convenience.

"It had been arranged," McClure wrote, "that the eleven o'clock train from Philadelphia to Washington should be held until Lincoln arrived, on the pretext of delivering an important package to the conductor." Another article revealed that this package, which the conductor was told had to be in Washington by morning, actually turned out to be a bundle of old newspapers.

The ruse worked. The "important parcel" was delivered, the tall "invalid" was ensconced in the rear car, and the train steamed southward toward the Nation's Capital. Not even the conductor saw Lincoln, McClure declared. Pinkerton gave the President-elect's ticket to the conductor, explaining that his invalid friend must not be disturbed.

Pinkerton reported later that Lincoln, being unable to sleep, cracked jokes and told stories throughout the night.

The situation, however, was not exactly a merry one as the train raced across slaveholding Maryland. Danger lurked around each curve, for to the South Abe Lincoln symbolized the foe who meant to strangle it. A song being sung in the state pointed at Lincoln in the words: "My Maryland, my Maryland, the despot's heel is on thy soil."

Pinkerton rode on the rear platform of the train a good deal of the time, watching for the signals flashed by armed guards along the way. But all went well, even on the Susquehanna ferry at Havre de Grace, considered a prime danger spot. Telegraph lines near Harrisburg had been repaired and, according to some stories, Mary Todd Lincoln and other members of the Presidential party soon rejoiced over receiving this coded message, "Plums delivered nuts safely." Old Abe had foiled the Baltimore plot and was in the District of Columbia.

Original plans were for Lincoln to arrive at 4 P.M. February 23, and go to a temporary residence on Franklin Row. Washington was really thrown off-balance when he arrived about daybreak at the Baltimore and Ohio depot and was taken to Willard's Hotel. He was greeted by Senator William H. Seward. Few Washingtonians knew he had arrived.

The newspaper and magazine response to the secret run was varied, but voluminous. *Harper's Weekly* printed cartoons about the journey, one showing Lincoln in a Scotch cap and long military cloak. With swinging arms and giant strides he was dashing for a waiting train—and safety. A *Vanity Fair* cartoon, captioned "The MacLincoln Harrisburg Highland Fling" showed Lincoln in exaggerated Scottish costume performing a high-stepping dance at the Harrisburg railway station.

The Commissioner of Patents, said a satirical item in the *Washington Confederation,* was asked to enlarge the glass case containing the sacred regimental suit of General Washington to admit the new historic relics—the long military cloak and Scotch cap—of "Uncle Abe Lincoln in his flight from Harrisburg to Washington City." Thousands would rush to this Republican shrine, the item wagered, to worship these sacred garments "which so miraculously preserved the life of Abraham." Another item on the Scotch garb prophesied: "Trust our word for it, the novelists of 1900 will thank him for this."

On the other hand, some correspondents claimed that Lincoln did not disguise himself at all for the flight through the night. The *Washington States and Union* commented about one "sensation reporter" who had previously embellished his accounts of the Prince of Wales' visit to the United States:

But that, as a whopper, was as nothing to the assassination, cloak and cap story of Uncle Abe. Let Howard alone for getting up a good one. Give him a hook and he will hang more yarn upon it than any man not closely related to Baron Munchausen. Abraham ought to make him his chief biographer and historiographer of his Administration—he fibs so easily.

Harvard Monthly in 1885 insisted that "with the exception of putting on a soft felt hat, in place of his ordinary beaver, Mr. Lincoln made no change whatever in his usual appearance."

Since Lincoln reportedly was ready for bed when the Baltimore plot was first revealed to him in Pennsylvania, the *Albany Atlas and Argus* termed it the "Shirt Tail Plot." The *New York Weekly Journal of Commerce* complained that some clergymen had discussed Lincoln's "Flight of the Imagination" in their sermons, thus disturbing "the sanctity of religious worship."

In mock attempts to justify the flight of "our great stump speaker," the *Daily Chicago Post* pointed out that "Demosthenes, the great Athenian stump orator; Cicero, who adorned the stump in the days of Rome's republican glory, and Sancho Panza . . . who was great on talking and very very trite on philosophy" all took to their heels on the approach of danger.

An iron safe for Lincoln's personal use "when assassins are supposed to be about" was being ordered by the White House, ribbed the *Washington Confederation*. "It is believed it will be safer to transport him from place to place in it, than in a Scotch cap and military cloak!"

A letter from New York in the *Washington States and Union* said:

They tell me that my esteemed old friend Lincoln has got to Washington. He slipped through in the dark they say, completely outwitting those bloody savages and diabolical assassins of Baltimore. Ah, as Fag says in the play, Abe is sly—devilish sly! Do you think he was going to be butchered by the ruffians and stewed into Lincoln soup, his skull set upon a pole, like a death's head, and his bones—gnawed and raw, strung along the lamp posts? Of course he wasn't. He's raw enough, and scrawny enough—lank, lorn, and lantern-jawed enough already, without any further scarification. At all events, he has proven himself a master of the art of "slip, slide—coupee!"

Another item was headlined "Lo, the conquering hero comes!" It said Lincoln arrived like a quiet citizen and decent Christian, crawled into a featherbed at Willard's, and had been sleeping soundly ever since. *"Requiescat in pace."*

And there were the inevitable poems about the dramatic flight. One Southern parody said:

> *Abe Lincoln tore through Baltimore,*
> *In a baggage-car with fastened door;*
> * Fight away, fight away, fight away for Dixie's Land.*
> *And left his wife, Alas! Alack!*
> *To perish on the railroad track!*
> * Fight away, fight away, fight away for Dixie's Land.*

Another poem claimed that "the funniest flight—of the dreariest bore—was Abraham's flight through Baltimore!" It ended:

> *Ah, very noble it seems to be*
> *This modern standard of chivalry!*
> *And very noble and very grand*
> *Is the chiefest magnate in the land,*

Abraham Lincoln, stalwart and tall,
Who ran away quacking from nothing at all!
The "Honest Uncle" in '61,
Who skulked in the night to Washington.

Not all accounts scoffed at Lincoln's secret journey. He undoubtedly would have been killed had he gone to Baltimore on the publicized schedule, said the *Newark Daily Advertiser.*

The *Baltimore American,* in an item reprinted in the *Washington National Intelligencer,* asserted there was no plot to assault or even insult the President-elect. But it admitted the Baltimore Republican Committee, in escorting Lincoln to his quarters, probably "would have been assailed and pelted with eggs, if not otherwise maltreated. This would have involved Lincoln in the disturbance. . . ."

However, the Baltimore police marshal, in an indignant public letter, acknowledged there had been rumors of "an offensive Republican display" at the railroad station, but asserted there was no plot to harm or embarrass the President-elect. "These slanders upon the good name of the city of Baltimore, now one of the quietest and most orderly in the country, deserve to be rebuked wherever uttered."

According to one correspondent, the men who advised Lincoln to take the "moonlit ride" did not really believe he would be endangered by following the regular schedule, else "they would not have exposed Mrs. Lincoln and Mr. Lincoln Junior to these fearful dangers."

There were other explanations of the hurried trip. One was that no official invitation for a Lincoln visit had been received from Baltimore. The *Worcester* (Mass.) *Daily Spy* suggested that he went early to become more familiar with the real condition of the country than he could possibly be "at so distant and retired a place as Springfield, Illinois." Another journal explained that Lincoln hastened to Washington "to consult friends . . . and escape bores." The *New York Weekly Journal of Commerce* conjectured that the President-elect "took the occasion to get rid, for a short season, at least, of the horde of hungry office-seekers who have dodged his footsteps" along the way to Washington.

And it was true that, as Inaugural Day drew near, office-seekers were virtually trampling one another underfoot in Washington.

CHAPTER SEVENTEEN

THE PATRIOTS DESCEND ON D. C.

When the day train pulled into Baltimore from Harrisburg, an estimated 15,000 persons were crowded around Calvert Street Station. To their chagrin, Lincoln was not aboard—only Mrs. Lincoln and her sons and other members of the party. The appearance on the platform of the Baltimore Republican Committee was greeted with groans and boos. A rush was made toward them, but police were able to save them from inconvenience other than having their hats knocked over their eyes.

Leaving the disappointed and disgusted crowd, the train continued on southward toward Washington. While speeding across Maryland, said the *New York World,* "the party became quite jolly, singing the 'Star-Spangled Banner,' with Young Lincoln as leader."

Lincoln's arrival on the morning train not being universally believed, a throng was at the station in Washington awaiting the 4 P.M. train. Despite a heavy rain there was a large crowd in which a *Washington Evening Star* reporter detected an occasional "hungry office-seeker, whose wistful glances at the cake-stand bore unmistakable evidence of a lean purse as well as an empty 'yearning apparatus.'" The crowd "indulged in one or two jokes, a little whistling, and considerable swearing." When the train arrived, an hour late, Mrs. Lincoln and party—but no Abe—appeared. Immediately the group boarded carriages and drove off "while the crowd plunged after through rain and mud, as if determined to escort a Presidential party anyhow."

At Willard's Hotel, Lincoln had been taking things fairly easy. He had slept a few hours, being fagged when he arrived. His day also included visiting the Presidential Mansion and General Scott. The hotel, meanwhile, was crowded with office-seekers "on the anxious benches." They were button-holing everyone from the proprietor to the servants to find out when Old Abe would be ready to greet his interested friends.

In the evening Lincoln received many Senators and Representatives. He was also visited in a body by members of the Peace Conference then meeting in Washington. Planned and promoted by the legislature of Virginia, this ill-fated conference was attended by delegates from fourteen free and seven slave states. For Southerners who still wanted to preserve the Union, it was a final major effort to find a peaceful solution to the slavery problem.

The *New York World* added this description of Lincoln's first evening at Willard's:

Mr. Lincoln passed through the long parlor hall, thronged with the *élite* and fashion of the National Metropolis, shaking hands as fast as he could on his right and left, with ladies and gentlemen, so intently interested that he forgot even to take his hat off; which was excused by a looker-on, who remarked that it was new, and outshined the crowd.

For a while after the Lincoln family, a nurse and a servant arrived, a crowd collected outside Parlor No. 6, on the second floor. Later, according to the Washington *Evening Star,* there was a sign on the main floor: "Positively no persons admitted to the halls above, other than guests of the house."

Willard's was already a popular hotel, but it had hardly started accumulating its historic claims when the Lincolns arrived. Here, that same year, Julia Ward Howe wrote "Mine eyes have seen the glory . . ." and this song, "Battle Hymn of the Republic," became a Civil War favorite. Here President Ulysses S. Grant would stop frequently, as would many other Presidents down through the years. Here the headquarters of the Republican National Committee would be located for many decades.

Some journals pictured the Lincoln days at Willard's as exceedingly jolly ones, despite the critical condition of the Nation. *Harper's Weekly* ran a cartoon entitled "Our Presidential Merry Man." The caption said, "The Presidential party was engaged in a lively exchange of wit and humor. The President-elect was the merriest among the merry, and kept those around him in a continual uproar."

Some Washingtonians had pleasant things to say about Lincoln, as had William Cullen Bryant in the *New York Evening Post* a few days earlier. He chastized a New York attorney for asserting that the sharp face of Lincoln was an entering wedge of disunion. Bryant retorted that the "pleasant, intellectual face of the new President [is] a complete refutation of those persistent slanders."

However, an item in the *Daily Chicago Post* was not as sympathetic as the one by Bryant. It declared:

Mr. Lincoln's real character is beginning to be better understood. People generally seem to have a sort of contempt for him, calling him "Old Abe," not affectionately as they called Gen. Taylor "Old Zack," but rather as they dub the town loafer, "Old Bill." Mr. Lincoln's manners encouraged this feeling. Last night, for instance, he introduced himself and Mrs. Lincoln to a crowd of people as "the long and the short of the Presidency." It is time he should sink the backwoodsman and put on the President. . . .

Mr. Lincoln is naturally shy as a fox and cunning as a weasel. Sharpened by legal practice in Western life, having been always a politician, and posted up in regard to this Washington gang, he humbugs all and is humbugged by none. No danger that he will share the fate of Harrison and Taylor, and, like Actaeon, be eaten up by his own dogs. Western people like to see others' hands before playing their own. But when Mr. Lincoln plays out he will "skin the crowd," as he expresses it. . . .

Although Lincoln was the stellar attraction at Willard's, other associates won attention. The *Daily Chicago Post* reported that Horace Greeley last night "attitudinized at Willard's for a long time, standing motionless, like the statue he expects some day, and the 'observed of all observers.'" Apparently he was not always statuesque, for the *Washington Evening Star* observed that "Horace, the redoubtable, is flying about like a shot out of a hot shovel."

Frequently seen among the ladies at Willard's was Judge David Davis, of Illinois, "a live representative of Western law and literature, with his chapeau in full bloom—in other words, never off his head." The *Daily Chicago Post* continued: "All the other Westerners conform to the etiquette of the city and not one of them has yet been seen with his heels above his head. None of them chew tobacco and expectorate in anything but the privileged spit-boxes; and, in a word, the entire suite are all tip-top specimens of Western bon ton."

And then there was Lincoln's man Friday, Norman B. Judd:

At Willard's one hears nothing but Judd. "Have you seen Judd?" "Where's Judd?" "There's Judd!" "Better see Judd." "Judd knows." "I'll tell Judd." "Judd says so." "Judd's very busy." "Saw Judd just now." "Judd won't do it!" "Judd'll see to *that*."

Bob Lincoln was also spotlighted. The *Washington Evening Star* reported him enjoying a cigar in the smoking-room when a group of "disunionists induced a couple well-known harpists who were performing there to play 'Dixie'," the "adopted National air of Secessia," for the benefit of young Lincoln. However, the item added, the harpists finally realized they were being used by the disunionists, so they evened things up with "Hail Columbia."

The *Worcester* (Mass.)*Daily Spy* indicated that Bob was quite a ladies' man:

Robert Lincoln was an object of much attention to many of the ladies. He promenaded the hall with some of the younger ones, and it was amusing to hear the remarks of others who would have liked to join the promenade. One young miss said quite audibly to her companion as he passed near them, "I am bound to set my cap for that young Bob Lincoln."

Mary Todd Lincoln kept quite busy giving receptions. Concerning one of these, an item attributed to the *New York Times* pointed out that everyone was delighted with the ease, dignity, and good nature with which Mrs. Lincoln "sustained the infliction." She was assisted by her sister, Mrs. Edwards, Mrs. Baker, wife of a Springfield editor, and others.

Harriet Lane, niece of bachelor President James Buchanan and acting First Lady, was reported by the *National Republican* to have invited Mrs. Lincoln to "accept the hospitalities of the White House" as soon as she came to Washington in order to become familiar with arrangements there.

In Washington, as in Springfield, the Lincolns received gifts. One was a $1,500 full-dress coach with maroon hammercloth and crimson brocatelle lining. It had an elaborately carved standard for the footman. The concealed steps descended when the doors were opened. It was also provided with a speaking tube. The carriage was taken to the Union stables on G Street near Thirteenth. A span of carriage horses presented to Lincoln made a practical supplement to the coach gift.

From Cincinnati, Lincoln received a new broom with a handle four inches in diameter and straw a yard long. This gift, suggested the *Washington National Republican,* was a hint to sweep the public offices clean. "It may serve better than many men would wish," the newspaper added. One "gift" was a stuffed figure representing an African.

People as well as gifts poured in upon the President-elect.

Among the more illustrious visitors were Stephen A. Douglas, Lincoln's recent competitor for the Presidency; General Winfield Scott, Commander-in-Chief of the U. S. Armies; Montgomery Blair, who soon would become Postmaster General; ex-President John Tyler; and President Buchanan.

But guests were not limited to luminaries. Lincoln, according to the *Daily Chicago Post*, advised his friends he would be glad to see all comers. He was public property now, he reasoned. And did they come! The *Washington Evening Star* told of Lincoln's being "backed up in a corner, and . . . buttonholed by successive squads of eager individuals" at Willard's. One visitor was the Virginian who had voted for Old Abe and been daubed all over with printer's ink and rolled in feathers.

Many visitors to Washington had coat pockets bulging with petitions for office. Getting these signed must have been an engrossing pastime in 1861. A resourceful upstate New Yorker, according to the Washington *Evening Star,* offered to furnish signatures at a dollar a hundred. "That chap," the *Star* added, "is wanted in Washington City. Let him come on posthaste."

One Bostonian assured Lincoln he didn't come looking for an office, but to *see* him. "Then, sir," Lincoln was quoted as remarking, "you are a rare man."

Someone observed that the Washington crowd was almost the identical one that collected in Chicago in May for the National Republican Convention. The *Daily Chicago Post* commented that the President-elect must have been astonished by a vast number of "old friends" who had flocked to the capital to lend him a helping hand. He probably didn't realize he had practiced law with so many lawyers, or served in the legislature with so many legislators, or split rails with so many rail-splitters.

Commenting about the many office-seekers from Illinois at a time when the Union was in danger of disintegration, Lincoln observed it was not pleasant to know so many of his friends were "applying for rooms in one end of the building while the other end was on fire." So Abe's natural "come one—come all" tendencies had to be tempered. Thus, said the Washington *Evening Star,* it was hardly a "walk-right-in" situation at Willard's, and many men hoping for plush positions spent days in the District of Columbia without being permitted to "bask in the sunshine" of Lincoln's presence.

Some newspapers and public speakers made caustic comments about the office-seekers. These Republican job-hunters were saying, observed the Washington *Confederation,* "Father Abraham, have mercy upon us, for lo, these many years have we been waiting to be comforted, but were not." A clergyman chose as his topic, "Where the body is, there will the eagles be gathered together." And the *Lynn* (Mass.) *Weekly Reporter* declared office-seekers were swarming in Washington "like flies around a molasses hogshead."

"Office-seekers were a powerful rugged set, and as hungry as wolves," was the Washington *States and Union* comment. " 'They smelleth the prey afar off, and prance to the door of the tabernacle.' If they ask for bread, will he give them a stone?" The Washington *Confederation* announced:

Long, lank, hungry-looking Republican office-seekers from the North are already here, prowling around the Departments, smelling out the fat places, seeing which will suit them best. . . . It is said these creatures will, social-like, dwell in communities and live on bran-bread, saw-dust, soup, and cheap tea.

These office-seekers, cracked the *Baltimore American,* were eager to serve their country by grabbing a share of the loaves and fishes. Some optimists even designated what office they intended to have. The Washington *National Intelligencer,* referring to the rush for the spoils by a "hungry set of cormorants," saw only one problem for them: deciding among the important posts which one would require the least work and the most salary.

Well, smirked one Eastern newspaper, these rail-splitting Westerners carrying axes to grind would at least become civilized while in cultured Washington.

Soon after the inauguration, the *Daily Illinois State Journal* announced that about three thousand applications for office which Lincoln had received while still in Springfield had been filed with various departments. The scene in the departments was sketched by the *Washington States and Union:*

> Every avenue, passage, corridor, and room, to which there is the least chance of access, is crowded and jammed with every species of manhood and halfmanhood that can be described among the conglomerated mass of office-seekers which infest our city at the present time.
>
> The green'uns, the sharpers, the tricksters, the business men, the anti-business men, the loafers, the gamblers, the long-limbed, lank, slab-sided, whittling Yankee, the puffy merchant, the squatty Dutchman, the finely proportioned dandy, and the poor and wretched deformity; the man who voted for Lincoln and the man who would have voted for him if circumstances hadn't prevented; the man without whose efforts 'Old Abe' could never have been elected. . . .

Lincoln reiterated he had made promises to no one. However, the *Weekly Illinois State Journal* indicated that the Wide-Awakes "who passed the torch and raised the cheer" would not be forgotten. They certainly would have preference over the "drones and leeches." Lincoln, the item continued, did not suspect campaign supporters of mercenary motives as a group, and he was eager "to reciprocate substantially to the best of his ability their timely and patriotic efforts."

Actually, Lincoln probably was not completely free in choosing officials for some top positions. His convention manager, David Davis, had made certain commitments for the cabinet, apparently without Lincoln's approval. At any rate, cabinet-making was a top-priority task. Here is the way the Republican market looked to the *Washington States and Union:*

Chase has an upward tendency; Blair firm, but at a fair valuation; Cameron, steady, but quiet; Seward firm, but active; Bates steady; Weed in good request; Etheridge unsaleable; Washburne, movements light; Clemens, slow; Davis, dull; Bilmer, below par; Sherman, won't go off; Greeley, buoyant; Lincoln, much sought after; and Judd, fluctuating.

Final winners in the cabinet contest included William H. Seward, New York, Secretary of State; Salmon P. Chase, Ohio, Secretary of the Treasury; Simon Cameron, Pennsylvania, Secretary of War; Edward P. Bates, Missouri, Attorney General; Gideon Welles, Connecticut, Secretary of Navy; Caleb Smith, Indiana, Secretary of Interior, and Montgomery Blair, Maryland, Postmaster General. The first four had competed with Lincoln for the Presidential nomination at Chicago.

Horace Greeley, according to one newspaper, also captured a cabinet appointment. Greeley, who was in Washington in the "capacity of mischief maker, was made Secretary of the Exterior."

Lincoln's time between his arrival February 23 and his inauguration on March 4 was not all taken up by office-seekers. He visited the Capitol, where he was "heartily greeted" in the House of Representatives, the *National Intelligencer* reported, although several Southern members remained seated. On Sunday, the day after he arrived, Lincoln walked with Senator Seward to St. John's Episcopal Church near the White House. "After the services were concluded," said the *Washington National Republican,* "Mr. Lincoln, accompanied by Mr. Seward and several lady friends, proceeded to the residence of Mr. Seward, and spent a couple of hours."

On one occasion Lincoln, dining out, entertained his fellow guests with excellent anecdotes, and the *New York Evening*

Post reported, as "proof that his Unionism continues un-abated, it is said that he told thirty-three of them, ending with a special one for Kansas."

One evening Lincoln was serenaded by Republicans who marched from the Wigwam to Willard's, preceded by Francis Scala's Marine Band. After repeated calls from the crowd, said the *Washington Evening Star,* Lincoln appeared at a window of his apartment. Having no balcony to stand on, the *Star* said, the President-elect climbed upon the window sill, holding on to the window shade as he spoke. The band then wound up with "Yankee Doodle" and the serenade was over.

Lincoln also exhibited some interest in the discussions of the Peace Conference at Willard's Hotel. Here representatives of twenty-one states were seeking to compromise the differences between the North and South. Most, if not all, of the proposal included a surrender of some free-soil principles—a concession Lincoln would not consider.

But while Lincoln stood his guns on that issue, he stressed that he harbored no ill will toward the South. In his reply to the Mayor of the District of Columbia, who visited him at the hotel, Lincoln pointed out that it was the first time in recent years that he had had occasion to speak in a region where slavery existed. He stated: "I think very much of the ill feeling that has existed, and still exists, between the people in the sections from whence I came and the people here, is dependent upon a misunderstanding of one another. . . . I have not now, and never have had, any other than as kindly feelings towards you as the people of my own section. I have not now, and never have had, any disposition to treat you in any respect otherwise than as my own neighbors."

But peace proved elusive. The *Washington National Intelligencer* quoted the *Richmond* (Va.) *Enquirer:*

As soon as the state of Virginia shall take active measures of resistance to Black Republican rule, her authorities cannot and will not brook the presence of a federal army of coercion at Washington. If the army shall remain there it must be driven out and the city captured, even if an assailing force of 100,000 men shall be required, and if successful assault shall first require a cannonade which will level every roof with the pavement of the street.

A more immediate danger was the blowing up of the Capitol, an event that some persons considered quite probable. Every night, reported the *Washington Evening Star,* police examined the Capitol thoroughly.

Also, authorities uncapped a plot to assassinate Lincoln during the inaugural. An organized band of five hundred men, according to an article in the *Daily Chicago Post,* had sworn that Abe would never sleep in the White House. The plan, the item explained, was for this large group to crowd as close to Lincoln as possible, and for one of the number to shoot the President-elect. The gang of accomplices would so hide the assassin as to prevent his detection.

Another *Post* item pointed out that a large body of men from Virginia and Maryland, including some of the notorious Baltimore gang—the Plug-Uglies, had descended on the capital. On the other hand, five hundred special police, among them detectives from Baltimore, Philadelphia, New York, and Boston, had been detailed. Several hundred federal troops, in addition to the Marines regularly stationed at the Navy Yard, were in Washington to keep order. But even with these reinforcements, the situation was not exactly rosy. On the day before inauguration, Lincoln reportedly advised that "it is best for our women to remain indoors on that day, as the bullets may be flying."

A correspondent of the *Philadelphia Press* said, in an item reprinted in the *Daily Chicago Post:* "The night from the third to the fourth of March, 1861, will be one of the ever-memorable epochs in the history of this country. Never since the Revolution was the nation in such danger; never were its difficulties of such a fearful character. . . ."

CHAPTER EIGHTEEN

THEY HAVE A CAPITAL TIME

Tidying up the city for the inaugural day soon to come, was a matter much discussed by civic-minded citizens. And how the city needed it! The streets were ankle deep in mud on wet days, in dust on dry. And so the newspaper announcement of a meeting "at 7½ o'clock" to plan for scraping and watering Pennsylvania Avenue was greeted with enthusiasm. The *Washington Confederation* described the problem these dust-removers faced:

The dust in some places is two or three inches thick, and so fine that the slightest agitation causes it to rise, filling stores and dwellings, much to the annoyance of their inmates. The fact is, Pennsylvania Avenue at this time is more like an unpaved country road than the principal thoroughfare of a large city. The street is never cleaned except by the wind or rain.

One hundred men, divided into small groups, went to work. In two nights they gave Pennsylvania Avenue a good going over. But that didn't mean that Washington had become spic-and-span. Someone commented that the best way to "maul the rail-splitter" would be "by putting him in the Mall near Four-and-a-half street and the canal; and the miasma of that delightful neighborhood will soon finish him."

Before Inauguration Day, and even before Washingtonians began swabbing down Pennsylvania Avenue, visitors were surging into the capital. The *Newark Daily Advertiser* announced that one of the longest trains ever to leave Jersey City, drawn by two locomotives, was headed for Washington. On the eve of the inauguration, said the *New York Commercial Advertiser,* every two or three hours, the whistle of a locomotive announced the arrival of another train. Soon hundreds of newcomers streamed onto Pennsylvania Avenue, most of them carrying carpetbags and all of them in quest of rooms. Their only chance, the *Advertiser* added, was to find a private home where "the hospitalities of the city would be obtained at rates far more exorbitant than the exorbitant charges at the hotels."

To accommodate a portion of the overflow, the Washington *Evening Star* reported, Willard's distributed 475 mattresses to various parts of the hotel, including 114 to the Concert Hall.

The overcrowding at Willard's was cartooned for *Harper's Weekly* by Thomas Nast, who was to originate the Republican elephant and the Democratic donkey. The magazine used this commentary with the cartoon:

Behold a bedroom at Willard's and the population thereof: four bearded and otherwise long-haired individuals of the masculine gender are deposited on a bed which is hardly big enough to hold Tom Thumb and his wife. These individuals are fast asleep, and evidently snoring; four lads are placed in the middle of the bed, and they lie in pairs, poll to poll, their well-breached legs resting sublimely over the bed supports at each end thereof. One happy soul is oblivious on top of the chest of drawers; another sits . . . looking at his turned-up toes; another poor devil is ensconced on the window sill, and looks daggers at the two pairs of happy snorers in the bed beneath him. And on the left lie two more fat gentlemen, dead asleep on their backs with their knees up, and their noses pointing thankfully to the ceiling, in the direction of the far-off heavens. . . .

Getting meals was no simple matter. The *New York Commercial Advertiser* reported that those with hotel accommodations could, "with desperate exertions and a fee to the waiter," obtain meager repasts at the hotels. A group of Baltimoreans brought their own "snack," the principal component being in a bottle.

Surrounding communities were resorted to. Alexandria, Virginia, for example, reported the presence of many Yankees, unable to find rooms in Washington.

Some people, according to *Harper's Weekly,* actually slept in the streets or in the Capitol. "Hundreds have lodged at night upon market stalls and lumber piles," the *Washington Evening Star* reported, "and in the morning have assembled at the public fountains to perform their toilets, dispensing with the luxury of soap for the time being, and using pocket handkerchiefs of dubious purity in lieu of towels." Some "dusty-looking chaps" strolled the streets all night, then caught a nap in a secluded spot in the daytime or wandered forlornly about the town looking for lodging.

Barkeepers lamented that these Westerners were a "cold-water army." Hack drivers and porters complained that they were mainly of the carpetbag order, usually relying on "shank's mare" for locomotion, and they exhibited "mental throes of the deepest on being called on to disburse a quarter dollar." The influx of strangers made it necessary for the Washington post office to advertise in the *Star* a list of undelivered letters. It noted that "because of similarity of names, it should not be thought strange if the letters of some of the old citizens were advertised!"

Not everyone was a stranger to everyone else. "Bearded Californians," said the *New York Commercial Advertiser,* "clasped the hands of those whom they had known in boyhood on the Atlantic slopes." A sizeable portion of the Washington crowd was Republicans who had "labored in the cause." Lincoln had expressed himself definitely opposed, the *New York Journal of Commerce* declared, to having Republican clubs muster or parade at the capital. "As the Republicans are all on their good behavior till they get office," the *Journal* added, "of course his wish will be respected."

The influx included a goodly crop of eccentrics. One of

these, the *Washington Evening Star* reported, paced to and fro in some secluded place speaking loudly and gesticulating violently. "Today," the *Star* noted on March 4, "he was remarkably 'eloquent,' and pitched into things generally."

Concerning one odd character, the *Star* commented:

Among the representatives of crazy-dom on the average day, we notice a well-clad, not ill-looking man of dark complexion, with hair and whiskers slightly gray, who marches along with solemn tread, singing in a low tone an air of most doleful minor strains. At times he elevates his arms to heaven as if invoking aid from above and anon throws out his clenched fist with a jerk, straight "from the shoulder," as if the embodiment of all he hated or feared were palpably before him.

The *Washington States and Union* had its candidate for the bats-in-the-belfry prize:

He was a very comical looking young man—very. He came lumbering along the Avenue, with a carpet-bag and a blue cotton umbrella, a swallow-tailed coat, and a stand-up collar. He had flaxen hair, and no whiskers, and small gray eyes.

"I say, stranger," says he to a gentleman on Brown's corner, "kin you tell me where 'bouts Mister Linkin is a stoppin' at? I'm a drivin' after him—some!"

"The President, eh?"

"Sartinly, the President—Ole Abe."

"Well, he's at Willard's."

"Willud's! Willud's! I wonder if he's a-kin to our Dan'l Willud? I'll just call an see. 'Sides, I promised to git as close to Mr. Linkin as possible, if not closer. I'm a carryin' a letter to him. There's a lady 'oman out with us, that knows him well; she give me a letter. I'm a-goin' fust to see the 'nogeration, then I 'spec' to try my luck after a office. Well, good day, stranger, I'm obleeged to you. Think I'll git 'long to'rds Willud's, its growin' rather late, an' I 'specks to see Linkin afore bed time."

The women, too, had their representatives among the oddities. The *States and Union* remarked about the many ladies at

Willard's, pretty and ugly ones, "but mostly ugly—may the Lord help them." One of these little old women waddled in with the query, "Have you seen anything of Bob?" "What Bob?" she was asked. "Why, Bob Lincoln, to be sure, who else? I want to see Bob! They say he looks like my Billy. Tell me, somebody, where I'll find the chile?"

Eccentrics apparently entertained themselves, but the horde of more normal persons found these ways to while away the time while waiting for inauguration afternoon with its parade and address. Some improved their looks with better clothing. The gentlemen, if they had barrels to wear in the interim, could have their old suits dyed. A Pennsylvania Avenue concern announced: "Gentlemen, if you want a dyeing man to live, have your coats, pants and vests nicely cleaned or re-colored at W. H. Wheatley's." On another occasion before the inauguration, Wheatley's advertised: "Wants to dye in the Union—I shall be pleased to dye in the capital of this Union all colors on all kinds of ladies' and gentlemen's apparel."

Another possible pastime was washing away some of the dust at Shaefer's on E Street near Seventh. "The luxury of COLD OR WARM BATHS" could be had for twenty-five cents each or five baths for a dollar.

Dining out was a favorite recreation for those with the wherewithal. A restaurant west of Willard's informed visitors that a good meal could be had for twenty-five cents, although the customer *could* pay as much as ten dollars. Gautier's Restaurant on Pennsylvania Avenue was "prepared to accommodate . . . any number of gentlemen who desire to take their meals away from where they lodge."

Some visitors whiled away some time in the Japanese bazaar under Willard's Hotel, or at Woodley's on Pennsylvania Avenue, where they could see "the rapid progress of the Daguerrean art." Some looked for novelties or other souvenirs such as French and Richstein's lithographs of Uncle Abe, featuring the new crop of whiskers. Many visitors strolled over to the Mall to see the partly finished Washington Monument, which had been started in 1848—but was not to reach its full 555-foot height until 1884—twenty-three years later.

The sight-seeing for some included two unusual cattle from Fauquier County, Va., exhibited on the Avenue near the Capitol. One measured sixteen feet, four inches, from tip to tip and stood six feet high, the *Washington Evening Star* reported.

Another stopping point for some folks was at Madam Goddard's, the astrologer, on Graham's Alley.

At the National Theatre visitors could see the exciting exhibitions by the famous John S. Rarey, horse-tamer extraordinary, whose ads promised some of the "most vicious and unmanageable" horses and the smallest Shetland ponies in the world. Playgoers could see performances by the popular comedienne, Miss Joey Gougenheim, in the drama, "The Heart of Midlothian," and Duprez and Green's Original New Orleans and Metropolitan Double Minstrel Troupe, in their "unapproachable and unrivaled Ethiopian entertainments."

Those who suffered upsets could try "Lincoln Stomach Bitters"; Doctor McLean's Strengthening Cordial and Blood Purifier, "the greatest remedy in the world"; Professor Reed's Sore Throat Powder; or Simpson's Extra Old Family Rye Whiskey.

However, to make sure of ready cash for either the entertainment or the means of getting over it, one had to guard one's wallet. Washington was said to be bulging with thugs and pickpockets. On Inauguration Day the *Star* commented that Baltimore had contributed her full quota of roughs and plugs the day before. "Their identity was soon demonstrated," the *Star* explained, "for with their first drinks on reaching the city, they began to belch out their—cries, notoriously Baltimorean." Taking another poke at neighbors to the north, the *Star* added that the Baltimore and Philadelphia detectives brought to Washington to spot rogues "seem to have confined their labors chiefly to sampling liquors at our drinking shops."

Nevertheless, some rowdies were arrested. A "red-shirted jack" suspected of stealing a watch at the Wigwam was immediately committed to jail for further examination the following Tuesday, "so as to keep him tight till after the Inauguration." A pickpocket picked up on King Street in Alexandria likewise was jailed "until March 4th, for further hearing."

But there was more than pickpockets to guard against. For a Yankee President was being inaugurated in the slaveholding District of Columbia, which was surrounded by the slave states of Maryland and Virginia. In such a climate nearly everything Lincoln represented aroused hostility.

On Inauguration Day, some Government workers wore secession badges. Some men were caught posting recruiting signs for the South Carolina army. The capital, it was asserted, was "honeycombed with treason."

Stationed along Pennsylvania Avenue, as the time for the procession approached, were many detectives and secret-service men. Peering down from roofs of buildings along the line of march were sharpshooters, members of the Washington Rifles. They were ordered to fire at anyone seen aiming a weapon at Lincoln.

CHAPTER NINETEEN

"I DO SOLEMNLY SWEAR . . ."

All nations, and every citizen of this Union, were watching the fourth day of March, 1861, with world-wide interest, because a ruler of sovereign people, elected President by a section of his own country, and confronted and opposed by another section in revolt, was about to assume office, and thereby indubitably instigate a Civil War that could not fail to become the greatest conflict in the world's long history.

In these words *Frank Leslie's Popular Monthly* in 1897 characterized "the Great Lincoln Inauguration."

Inauguration Day dawned rather inauspiciously with leaden skies and tornadoes of dust, leveled somewhat by a sprinkle of rain.

The stirring notes of reveille resounded from the temporary barracks of the U. S. troops who had been summoned to Washington. Soon the sound of fife and drums and the peal of bells at the fire-engine houses were heard across the Federal City.

Never before had the city seen such a display of the Stars and Stripes, according to the *New York Commercial Advertiser*. On Pennsylvania Avenue alone, between the Treasury and the Capitol gate, there were more than a hundred large flags, "not robbed of a stripe and with every star in the constellation in its place."

By noon the weather had become bright and pleasant. Im-

patient throngs jostled about on the Avenue, waiting for Buchanan and Lincoln who were due momentarily. However,
Buchanan had been detained in his room in the Capitol, signing bills. But before long, according to the *Washington Evening Star:*

> The word was passed along the line of infantry on the avenue,
> and the cavalry on Fourteenth Street, to present arms. This was
> handsomely done, when the President and President-elect emerged
> from the lower (Fourteenth Street) door to the hotel. They were
> warmly applauded. . . .
> Mr. Buchanan's private carriage was first drawn up to the en-
> trance, but from what we could learn of the movements going on
> we judge that the President-elect preferred to make his appearance
> in an open carriage, where all could see him, as one was substituted
> for Mr. Buchanan's closed carriage. . . .
> It moved out to its position in the line, being preceded by the
> company of Sappers and Miners, and flanked on the right by the
> Georgetown Mounted Guard and on the left by the President's
> Mounted Guard. There was some grumbling at this arrangement,
> as it was almost impossible to get a view of the President-elect.

This was the first inaugural procession in which the guard
was for protection and not for show.

So President James Buchanan, now a stooped and heavy
old man with sparse gray hair, and President-elect Abraham
Lincoln, a tall man with a new crop of whiskers on a melancholy face, began the historic ride. Six horses pulled the
barouche.

The crowd along the avenue that Monday was greater than
at any previous inauguration. Public and private schools in
the District of Columbia closed for the day and contributed to
the crowds. The *Star* reported:

> From the Treasury to the Capitol, on both sides of the Avenue,
> from the building line to the curb-stone, myriads were packed in
> solid mass, in incalculable numbers. Every window and balcony

and housetop near the Avenue, and on it, was full of human forms
and faces, till no room remained to stand or sit.

Sometimes the throng coagulated around the Presidential
carriage until it bogged down. Then the procession pushed
forward again "along the broad avenue, the *Via Sacra* of our
republic," as the *New York Commercial Advertiser* put it,
"leading to the Capitoline Hill."

The parade had its colorful aspects. The marshals and
retinues wore scarves and rosettes in combinations of orange,
white, blue and pink. They were dressed in black, with white
or yellow buckskin gloves. Eye-catching banners and adorn-
ments were included in the parade, although "no offensive
emblems or devices" were permitted. The *Washington States
and Union* said of the procession:

> The train of military, mounted and foot, the cavalcade of car-
> riages, the concourse of citizens, waving of banners and plumes,
> flashing of burnished arms, glistening of trappings and uniforms,
> sparkling of colors, almost dazzle the sight in the now golden flood
> of sunshine. . . . From windows and overhanging balconies and
> roofs spectators crowded with waving flags and handkerchiefs. . . .
> The roll of the drums, the pouring strains of the bands, the shouts
> of the people, gave to the scene a grandeur peculiarly graphical
> to the sight and inspiring to the sense. It was the *grande fête*.

A large float furnished by the Republican Association of
Washington, was drawn by white horses bearing a cloth im-
printed with the word "Union." On the float itself, which was
aflutter with small flags and bunting, were thirty-four little girls
representing the States. Ten Wide-Awakes in caps and capes
escorted the car.

Prominent in the procession, as it moved majestically
toward the Capitol, were the Mayors of Washington and
Georgetown.

Five hundred marching delegates from the Empire State

formed one unit. But attracting more attention—from police, at least—was a large group of New Englanders. The *Star* explained:

> As a civic portion of the procession passed up the avenue, there was noticed a singular sound, not easily describable—a sharp, cracking, rasping sort of detonation, at regular intervals of perhaps three seconds. The police on the alert for air guns and other implements of assassination walked up and down the line completely puzzled. The locale of the peculiar noise soon became narrowed down to the New England delegation, and pretty soon the facts of the case came out, creating no little amusement all round.
>
> It seems that the New England folks wear "pegged" heavy soles on account of the deep snows. Coming South, the unusual heat and dryness of the atmosphere here has shrunk the peg-timber in their foot-gear excessively, occasioning a general squeaking with every movement, swelling in the aggregate, when the delegation was keeping step in line, to a volume perceptible in the pauses of the Marine Band for several blocks. "Treasons" and "stratagems" cannot be chargeable to men with so much music in their soles.

One group of a hundred and twenty had assembled at City Hall on inauguration morning, but it was decided they were generally too old and unsteady to march. They were veterans of the War of 1812.

Even without that contingent there were plenty of people in the procession—*Frank Leslie's Popular Monthly* in 1895 estimated 10,000.

When Buchanan and Lincoln, followed by this throng, arrived north of the Capitol, they found a rough, wooden barricade or tunnel, well guarded at the entrance, through which they would walk some two hundred feet to the Senate chamber. Erecting this barricade was only one of the many precautions taken in connection with this unusual inauguration.

Not everyone thought such safety measures advisable. Some asserted they might merely stir up trouble. But the authorities could not forget that some newspaper editorials had advocated the invasion of Washington to prevent the installation of Lincoln as President.

On the other hand, an Illinois newspaper had divulged earlier that there was a movement afoot to call a Republican convention of 100,000 men at Cincinnati in early March. The plan was for these men to be armed and ready to be deployed to Washington or elsewhere if necessary. The president of Rochester University, reported the *Worcester* (Mass.) *Daily Spy,* told his student body that if there was an attempt to prevent the inauguration he would arm them and lead them to the defense of the capital.

General Winfield Scott, Commander-in-Chief of the U. S. Army, and hero of the War with Mexico, made it clear he did not welcome groups of armed uniformed volunteers in Washington. And "Old Fuss and Feathers" meant business.

The Wide-Awakes, the *New York Weekly Journal of Commerce* asserted, had been drilling for several months "for the purpose of marching up and down Pennsylvania Avenue in full regimentals." It continued: "To go to Washington in mere citizen's clothes, and act the undistinguished part of spectators, is not at all agreeable to them, after so long a period of patient drilling. . . . It is really a pity that so much juvenile ardor should be thrown away."

General Scott, a seventy-four-year-old giant—he was almost six and a half feet tall and weighed over 250 pounds—felt that he had the capital and its new First Citizen as well protected as possible. Squads of riflemen were posted in the Capitol wings and underneath the platform from which Lincoln was to speak, newspapers reported. He and General John Ellis Wool had light-artillery batteries stationed a short distance from the Capitol, their caissons filled with grape and canister.

The tunnel through which Lincoln and Buchanan began their walk to the Senate, then, was only a part of the total defense plan.

The scene in the Senate, while awaiting the arrival of the Presidential party, reminded one reporter of the "lying down of the lamb and the lion together." The Senators were in fine fettle and were hobnobbing with others of opposite views. Perhaps they were celebrating their survival of the dull ending of the Thirty-Sixth Congress in which "Senator Bright killed in the most approved manner a certain gas bill, to wit, 'by talking it to death.' "

On the Senate floor, when Lincoln and Buchanan appeared, were Senators, diplomats, and other dignitaries. Persons seated in the overflowing gentlemen's gallery, said the *Daily Chicago Post*, were furnished "intense amusement" by listening to late-comers argue that they had journeyed all the way from Indiana, Vermont, or some other distant place and should merit special consideration. This gallery, said the *Post*, "seemed one black mass of surging, heaving masculines, pushing, struggling, and almost clambering over each other's backs, in order to get a good look at the proceedings." In the ladies' gallery, where the many gay dresses made a flower-garden scene, things were much quieter.

After a brief stay in the Senate chamber, the dignitaries began the procession to the east front of the Capitol, led by the marshal of the District of Columbia and the black-robed justices of the Supreme Court.

By this time a crowd estimated as high as 100,000 had congregated around the platform built over the Capitol steps. Horses and carriages had been banned from the Capitol square, so there was plenty of room for the people. Rubbish which had accumulated in the construction of the unfinished Capitol dome had been cleared away for their convenience. Some of the people chatted about the huge crane which rose above the structure. With war clouds on the horizon, some predicted that the dome would never be completed.

As the crowd milled about before the ceremony, police kept a close watch. They prevented any suspicious-looking individuals from assembling, explained the *Washington Evening Star*, by passing among them "ever and anon."

One eccentric with red whiskers entertained the crowd by

climbing a tree to deliver his own inaugural address. He declared he had been commissioned by the Almighty to be President, and he alone could rescue the nation from the vices of the times. A policeman, said the *Washington States and Union,* invited him to come down but he declined. The determined patrolman scrambled up after him, but a limb snapped, the arm of the law tumbled back to earth, and Red Whiskers resumed his inaugural address. It took a contingent of troops to dethrone the self-elected President.

Now appeared the procession from the Senate with Abraham Lincoln in a shiny silk hat and holding a rosewood, gold-headed cane which had been sent him from the Far West. He was introduced by his friend, Senator Baker, of Oregon.

Abe, so the legend goes, had trouble locating a suitable place to put his new high hat when he rose to deliver his address. Who should come to his rescue but Stephen A. Douglas, for so many years and in so many ways his rival! "If I can't be President," Douglas is supposed to have said, "at least I can hold his hat."

When Lincoln was introduced, he received generous applause. *Frank Leslie's Popular Monthly* in 1897 thus described this moment:

> The frantic peals of voices again rise in a chorus that must pierce the hills of Arlington and the plains of Georgetown miles away, and almost intermingle with the yet lingering echoes at Harper's Ferry far away of the voices of hapless John Brown and his rash but patriotic followers.

"Fellow Citizens of the *United* States . . ." Lincoln began. Those words must have sounded a bit ironic to the speaker, a sizeable portion of the nation having just split off. The President from whom he was receiving the reins, a friend of the slave-holding South, had looked the other way as Confederate states took over forts and federal offices. Many federal and military officers had resigned.

But Lincoln continued his speech in a clear, loud voice, scarcely glancing at his manuscript. "In compliance with a custom as old as the government itself, I appear before you to address you briefly . . ." he said.

Among those who listened were four men who someday would stand in his place—Hayes, Garfield, Arthur, and Harrison. Also present was America's most famous journalist, Horace Greeley, his face "as plump and fat as the body of a picked reed bird in the height of the shooting season." Greeley, according to one report, looked as tickled "as if he had a nail in his foot."

As Lincoln spoke, a New York photographer who had erected a stand about a hundred yards from the gaily decorated platform, took pictures with a large camera. This was the first time a President had been photographed during an inaugural address, according to one report.

Abe, the focal point of the camera and the crowd, appeared a bit unnatural as he stood there, dressed in a new suit with satin vest. But his words were old, common ones that wear well, and carried a big cargo of meaning. They were the plain, homespun words of a man used to chatting with the neighbors out in Springfield or New Salem.

Lincoln's "dull and sleepy cast of face" gave way to a spirited countenance flushed with excitement, said the *Washington States and Union*. He commented later, according to the *Daily Chicago Post*, that he had experienced much greater fear in talking to a dozen Illinois men about temperance than in addressing the inaugural multitude.

Lincoln spoke with fervor, for his was an extraordinary inaugural address. With the nation on the brink of civil war, this paper was an important state document. The message was gentle and conciliatory, yet firm. It emphasized that preservation of the Union came first.

Lincoln reiterated that he did not intend to interfere with slavery where it already existed. He insisted, on the other hand, that no state of its own volition could walk out of the Union. He emphasized that forts and customhouses must be held by the Federal Government, but promised he would refrain, wherever possible, from sending Northerners to fill Government posts in the South. He added: "In your hands, my dissatisfied fellow countrymen, and not in mine, is the momentous issue of civil war. The government will not assail you. You can have no conflict, without being yourselves the aggressors. You have no oath registered in Heaven to destroy the government, while I shall have the most solemn one to 'preserve, protect, and defend' it. . . ."

Lincoln then told the great crowd, "We must not be enemies. Though passion may have strained, it must not break, our bonds of affection." He concluded: "The mystic cords of memory, stretching from every battlefield and patriot grave to every living heart and hearthstone all over this broad land, will yet swell the chorus of the Union, when again touched, as surely they will be, by the better angels of their nature."

Chief Justice Roger B. Taney, an octogenarian, administered the oath. His hands shook with emotion. He had sworn in many Chief Executives during his almost quarter century in office. But it was not merely the fact that the feeble old man was administering his last Presidential oath that untied his emotions. The author of the controversial Dred Scott Decision and, like President Buchanan, an upholder of the slave system, here he was installing into office a Yankee who had vigorously denounced his decision and was committed to curbing the spread of slavery.

The feeble old man held the Bible as Lincoln declared, "I do solemnly swear . . ." Famous photographer Mathew Brady took a picture. Lincoln stooped and kissed the Bible. Field guns at a distance fired a national salute for the nation's new President. And the Marine Band struck up "God Save Our President."

When Lincoln and Buchanan climbed into the carriage,

they observed custom by Lincoln's sitting on the right, whereas he had been on the left as President-elect en route to the Capitol. A large crowd surged after them, but it dwindled along the way.

It must have been disheartening to the volunteer street-cleaners of a few days earlier to observe the dusty results of this trip on Pennsylvania Avenue. Said the *New-Hampshire Statesman* (Concord):

> The dust was stifling as the procession neared the White House. The President, marshal, and subaltern, the swells and the populace, were alike enveloped in it. One could have written a certificate of good behavior on the back of President Lincoln's coat as he entered the House.

At the White House, Buchanan, who joined Van Buren, Tyler, Fillmore, and Pierce to become the fifth living ex-President, wished Lincoln a peaceful and prosperous administration. "If you are as happy, my dear sir, on entering this house as I am in leaving it and returning home," Buchanan reportedly remarked, "you are the happiest man in this country."

The bachelor bade the new President adieu, went to the home of District Attorney Ould for the night, then left for Wheatland, his home at Lancaster, Pennsylvania.

Lincoln created some excitement at the end of the procession from the Capitol, by kissing all the little girls on the big Republican float. He wound up the afternoon's activities, said the *Washington National Intelligencer,* by greeting several thousand persons who filed by.

While the procession returned to the White House and while Lincoln pumped hands at this informal reception, correspondents were writing their stories for waiting presses. It was "one of the marvels of science of the present day," said the *Daily Illinois State Journal* (Springfield), that Lincoln gave the inaugural address soon after noon on Monday and it was in the hands of millions of readers on Tuesday morning.

This was a big story, yet many newspapers did not play it on the front page, reserved for ads and sentimental fiction. Hammerslough Brothers of Springfield, always with an eye to business, thought "so much has already been said" about the inaugural it was time to turn attention to other important subjects, and first and foremost was—Hammerslough's Clothing House.

Nevertheless, there was intense interest in the newspaper reports of this inaugural, for the whole nation, feeling adrift in a storm, was waiting to weigh every word of its new skipper.

Washingtonians hardly noticed that on this Inaugural Day in 1861 Congress began official operation of the United States Government Printing Office, which was to become the largest printing plant in the world. But they were well aware of another printing plant—the *Washington Evening Star*. They converged on it in such numbers that the "rapid Star presses" could not supply the demand. The trampled *Star* exclaimed on March 5:

> The jam in front of the office was such that door panels, sash and glass, gave way at the first onset, and the incoming crowd, was packed upon the crowd then inside with such force that those who had already secured papers were unable to emerge or make any disposition of their hardly-earned prizes other than to hold them high above their heads out of harm's way of the ravenous host about them. . . . The impatient crowd meantime overran nearly every part of the Star Building in the wild hunt for copies of the paper.

Through the afternoon and evening of Inaugural Day, and in days to come, editors in many cities shaped up their responses to Lincoln's address. Some appraisals were warmly laudatory, some bitterly critical.

"The Republicans are in raptures over it, and the Democrats apparently find little to condemn," a Detroit writer was saying. People "like its straightforward, manly tone," penned a Hartford editor. "He who runs may read it," quoted the

New York Daily Tribune. "It is marked by no feeble expression."

But the *New York Herald* found the address abounding "in traits of craft and cunning. . . . It would have caused a Washington to mourn, and would have inspired Jefferson, Madison, or Jackson with contempt." A Vicksburg writer rated it as a "silly production." And many Southern papers termed it "a declaration of war." The *Daily Chicago Post* quoted the *Richmond Dispatch* as advising that "Every border state ought to go out of the Union in twenty-four hours."

The *Washington States and Union* thought the address suggested that secession was to be killed with white hands "which shall be as spotless after the funeral as before the wake." It prefaced this satire with the expression, "When you pull a gentleman's nose, do it gently."

Before most newspaper subscribers in the nation had read these responses to the inaugural address, indeed before all of the articles were completely written, Washington was putting on the final touch to this historic celebration. As though grasping its last small chance for gaiety, it closed its doors to the rumble of war and had itself a ball.

CHAPTER TWENTY

AFTER THE BALL WAS OVER

After the hand-shaking ended, Lincoln, worn out from a tough day, took a nap, said *Frank Leslie's Popular Monthly* in 1897. Afterwards he had supper with Norman B. Judd, his Illinois political associate, and then got ready for the Inaugural Ball.

Lincoln and General Winfield Scott had tried to dissuade the Committee on Arrangements from having the ball, the magazine explained. Merrymaking was out of order in the trouble-torn country, Lincoln argued. General Scott feared conspiracies and disorder.

But the Committee refused to drop the ball. Among its sponsors, as recorded in the Washington *Evening Star,* were the Secretaries of State and Treasury, the Attorney General, and the Postmaster General, many important members of Congress, including Andrew Johnson, Stephen A. Douglas, Simon Cameron, Montgomery Blair and Edward Everett, and dozens of other distinguished persons—even General Scott.

Tickets were sent to main cities in the North and the South for sale at ten dollars each, the *Washington National Republican* reported. In Washington, many ladies' invitations "have been lost and miscarried," the *Evening Star* announced. To alleviate this miscarriage of justice, ladies were asked to write to committee headquarters for tickets. The *National In-*

telligencer prophesied "there will be a greater display of female beauty than has ever congregated before in this city."

The ballroom had sprung up during the previous two weeks or so near City Hall in Judiciary Square. The contractors had announced they would hire an equal number of men from each of the city's seven wards so as to balance employment opportunities.

"The cavalry and flying artillery, whose barracks are adjoining, give war-like surroundings to the festive building," said the *New York Evening Post.*

The dimensions of the dancing saloon, as given in the *Star,* were about 250 x 60 feet, with the main entrance through the vestibule of the City Hall. Adjoining and running the entire length of the dancing hall was a supper room. Gas chandeliers with eighty burners each were a main feature. Walls were covered with white cambric, decorated at intervals with the American shield. A large American flag hung over the main entrance.

Gentlemen and ladies, decked in their finest, commented enthusiastically about the layout as they arrived. But they did not come in numbers as great as on similar former occasions. *Harper's Weekly* in 1897 put the figure at five thousand. The boycotting of the function by the South and the financial stress of the times were restraining factors. Yet, "the immense ballroom was well filled with ladies and gentlemen, who kept the dancing up till four o'clock this morning," reported the *Washington Evening Star* on March 5.

Among those who attended was an "unknown" who attracted considerable attention. Having lost a bet on Lincoln's election, Edward P. West had paid it by walking some 470 miles from Boston to Washington in ten consecutive days. Alas, he arrived in the District of Columbia at 4:30 P.M. on Inaugural Day, and thus missed the ceremonies. At the Inaugural Ball that night, accompanied by the Massachusetts delegation, he related to those clustering around him how three horses had been worn out by the "Committee of Two" who tagged behind him from Boston to make sure he did not cheat.

A few eccentrics—or a few *other* eccentrics, if you prefer —apparently got into the ballroom. The *New York Commercial Advertiser* mentioned that "a queerly dressed man, with a long shepherd's crook, was on the floor endeavoring to find Mr. Seward."

The big moment was the arrival of Lincoln, accompanied by Mayor James G. Berret, and Mrs. Lincoln, escorted by Senator Stephen A. Douglas. The *Advertiser* said of the new First Lady:

Mrs. Lincoln was superbly dressed in a blue silk, trimmed with point d'Alencon lace, and wore a blue ostrich feather in her hair, which was exceedingly becoming. The President and his attendants promenaded to and fro through the room several times bowing to the right and left in response to the innumerable salutations. He proceeded finally to the dais at the east end of the room.

One writer observed that Lincoln looked less happy than his former rival for Mary Todd's affections, Senator Douglas. The latter, by not having won the Presidency in that day of peril, said the writer, "looked like a person relieved of a burden."

The musicians, mainly drawn from the Marine Band, poured forth excellent music, but, according to some reports, the dancing was mediocre, if not worse. Commented *Frank Leslie's Popular Monthly* in 1897:

The wives of the new Congressmen were not adept in the waltz or the schottische, and the majority of the politicians present remained as ignorant of quadrille steps as was Old Abe himself, and all present acted as strangely toward each other as do the pupils, male or female, in a newly established academy. . . .

Even the marches were slenderly patronized, because even when the President was in these, the guests were fain to become wallflowers and stare at him. And during intervals of music he would be surrounded, so that at one time it looked as if he would be captured by office-seekers; even women enlisting their blandishments in a search after official spoils in behalf of husbands or other relatives. The dancing was soon remitted to the very few young people present, and it was a relief to all the guests when the music of the orchestra announced the march toward the supper room.

The well-furnished festive tables were a main feature of the ball, for it was thought wise to provide Lincoln with an appetizing supper soon after his arrival, since he did not dance. In the center of the tables was a huge pyramid surmounted by the thirty-four state flags.

Plenty of champagne was provided—even though it had to be purchased. Dealers who wanted to supply the Inaugural Ball had been required to send samples, and so many were sent that an economy-minded committeeman suggested the samples would be sufficient without buying any bottles. "But it was soon discovered," the *Washington Confederation* revealed, "that . . . another member had drank a great portion of the samples and carried the rest away. . . . What a pity the spirited samples were spirited away."

After supper, President Lincoln resumed his place of honor on the dais and held an impromptu reception, during which many guests volunteered to introduce themselves. Lincoln soon left for the White House, but it was considerably later before the sound of popping champagne corks and the strains of ball room music died away. Among couples who made a big evening of it were the President's oldest son, Robert, and a young lady from Galena, Illinois.

As Abe, the Rail-Splitter, rode back to his new home at 1600 Pennsylvania Avenue, the head of a great but crumbling nation, he may well have relived not only the events of a momentous day but also some of the events that had brought him there. Did he reminisce about the day Richard J. Oglesby and John Hanks launched him, with some backwoods drama, as the Rail-Splitter candidate? Did he think about the colorful Chicago convention which tossed him officially into the Presidential race? Did he recall the torchlight processions and stump speeches that helped set his bandwagon rolling toward Washington?

Maybe not. With the nation slipping dangerously close to a bloody civil war, perhaps he was pondering the burdensome task awaiting him. Perhaps he tried to peer into the future, which must have appeared as dark as the night about him. Had he been granted that prevision he would have seen Fort Sumter surrendering the following month and brother fighting against brother in mortal conflict. And he would have found himself saying, in December, 1862:

"We cannot escape history. We of this Congress and this administration will be remembered in spite of ourselves. No personal significance or insignificance can spare one or another of us. The fiery trial through which we pass will light us down in honor or dishonor, to the latest generation."

And then he would have discovered himself on the road to becoming Lincoln the Legend as he declared, four years from that first Inaugural Day:

"With malice toward none; with charity for all; with firmness in the right, as God gives us to see the right, let us strive on to finish the work we are in; to bind up the nation's wounds; to care for him who shall have borne the battle, and for his widow and his orphan —to do all which may achieve and cherish a just and lasting peace among ourselves, and with all nations."

REFERENCES

Among newspaper and periodical sources for this book were:

CHAPTER ONE
Century Magazine, June, 1900
Constitution (Washington, D. C.), June 16, 1860
Daily Chicago Herald, May 12 and 16, 1860
Delawarean (Dover), July 21, 1860
Ft. Wayne Sentinel, June 2, 1860
New York Daily Tribune, February 25 and 28, 1860
Norfolk County Journal (Roxbury, Mass.), July 7, 1860
Sandusky Commercial Register (Ohio), November 9, 1858
Weekly Illinois State Journal (Springfield), October 26, 1859 (item reprinted from *Olney Times* [Ill.]); December 5, 1859; January 11; March 7 and 21 (including items reprinted from the *Palladium* [Conn.], *New-Hampshire Independent Democrat,* and *Providence Journal*); March 28; May 2 (item reprinted from *Cincinnati Gazette*) and 16; July 25, 1860

CHAPTER TWO
Albany Atlas and Argus, May 22, 1860
Appleton Crescent (Wis.), May 12, 1860
Constitution (Washington, D. C.), May 17 and 19, 1860
Daily Chicago Herald, May 12 (including item reprinted from *Cleveland Weekly Plain Dealer*), 22, and 23, 1860
Daily Chicago Tribune, May 17, 1860 (item reprinted from *Chicago Press and Tribune*)
Ft. Wayne Sentinel, May 19, 1860
New-Hampshire Statesman (Concord), May 19, 1860 (item reprinted from *Chicago Press and Tribune*)
New Orleans Daily Delta, May 18, 1860
Putnam's Magazine, February, 1909

Republican Farmer (Bridgeport, Conn.), May 18, 1860
Scribner's, November, 1893
Springfield Daily Republican (Mass.), May 16 and 17, 1860
Weekly Illinois State Journal (Springfield), April 18, 1860 (item reprinted from *Chicago Press and Tribune*)

CHAPTER THREE
Albany Atlas and Argus, May 21, 1860
Daily Chicago Herald, May 16, 17, 19, and 26, 1860
National Intelligencer (Washington, D. C.), July 12, 1860
New Orleans Daily Delta, May 18, 1860
Olympia Pioneer and Democrat (Washington), July 20, 1860
Republican Farmer (Bridgeport, Conn.), June 1, 1860
Springfield Daily Republican (Mass.), May 22, 1860
States and Union (Washington, D. C.), May 24, 1860

CHAPTER FOUR
Constitution (Washington, D. C.), May 26, 1860
Daily Chicago Herald, May 15, 18, 19, 23, 28 (including item reprinted from *Springfield Daily Republican* [Mass]); July 23, 1860 (item reprinted from *New York Evening Post*)
National Intelligencer (Washington, D. C.), May 21, 1860 (item reprinted from *Chicago Press and Tribune*)
New Orleans Daily Delta, May 18 and 24, 1860
Olympia Pioneer and Democrat (Washington), July 6, 1860
Saturday Evening Post, August 5, 1899
Springfield Daily Republican (Mass.), May 22, 1860
Weekly Illinois State Journal (Springfield), May 30, 1860 (item reprinted from *Toledo Blade*)

CHAPTER FIVE
Albany Atlas and Argus, May 22 and 28, 1860; May 31, 1860 (item reprinted from *St. Paul Pioneer*)
Bucyrus Weekly Journal (Ohio), May 31, 1860
Cleveland Weekly Plain Dealer, May 23; June 27; July 11, 1860
Constitution (Washington, D. C.), May 22, 24 (item reprinted from *Boston Courier*), and 26; June 2, 5, 8, 22 (item reprinted from *Louisville Journal*), and 25, 1860
Council Bluffs Bugle (Iowa), June 6, 1860
Daily Chicago Herald, May 24, 25, and 28; June 15 (item reprinted from *Buffalo Courier*); July 21, 1860
Floridian and Journal (Tallahassee), June 23, 1860
Ft. Wayne Sentinel, May 19, 1860
Jacksonian (Rushville, Ind.), June 27, 1860
Jonesboro Gazette (Ill.), May 26; June 9 and 23, 1860

Kansas State Record (Topeka), May 26, 1860
National Intelligencer (Washington, D. C.), May 19, 1860
Newark Daily Advertiser, May 19 and 22, 1860
New-Hampshire Patriot (Concord), May 23 and 30, 1860
New-Hampshire Statesman (Concord), May 19; June 2, 1860
New London Daily Star (Conn.), May 19, 1860
New Orleans Daily Delta, May 22, 1860
New York Daily Tribune, May 16, 19, 21 (including items reprinted from the *True American* [Trenton, N. J.] and the *Detroit Free Press*), and 25, 1860 (including item reprinted from *Chicago Daily Journal*)
Prairie du Chien Courier (Wis.), July 26, 1860
Republican Farmer (Bridgeport, Conn.), May 25, 1860
Rochester Union and Advertiser, May 19 (including item reprinted from *Auburn Advertiser*) and 24, 1860
Springfield Daily Republican (Mass.), May 19, 1860
States and Union (Washington, D. C.), May 19, 1860
Troy Times (Ohio), May 24, 1860
Weekly Illinois State Journal (Springfield), May 23 and 30, 1860 (including item reprinted from *Alton Courier* [Ill.])
Worcester Palladium (Mass.), May 23, 1860.

CHAPTER SIX
Albany Atlas and Argus, May 14, 1860
Baltimore Sun, October 16, 1860
Bucyrus Weekly Journal (Ohio), June 14, 1860
Constitution (Washington, D. C.), May 3 and 12; July 10 and 12, 1860 (item reprinted from *State Gazette* [Texas])
Daily Chicago Herald, May 7, 10, 12, and 15; June 25; July 12, 1860
Evening Star (Washington, D. C.), May 7; June 20, 21 (item reprinted from *Louisville Journal*), and 22, 1860
Jonesboro Gazette (Ill.), February 25; July 28, 1860
Manhattan Express (Kan.), June 30, 1860
Mississippian (Jackson), June 7; August 7, 1860
National Intelligencer (Washington, D. C.), October 23, 1860
New Albany Daily Ledger (Ind.), July 27, 1860
New-Hampshire Statesman (Concord), June 30, 1860
New Orleans Daily Delta, May 1, 2, 4, 8, 15 (item reprinted from *Huntsville Democrat* [Ala.]), and May 17, 1860
New York Daily Tribune, May 22, 1860
Philadelphia North American and United States Gazette, May 5 and 10, 1860
Sacramento Daily Union, July 21, 1860
States and Union (Washington, D. C.), May 9, 15, and 22, 1860
Troy Times (Ohio), June 14; July 19; August 30, 1860
Walton's Daily Legislative Journal (Montpelier, Vt.), November 7, 1860

Weekly Illinois State Journal (Springfield), April 4; May 9, 16, and 23; June 13 and 27; July 18, 1860
Worcester Daily Spy (Mass.), May 16, 1860

CHAPTER SEVEN

Albany Atlas and Argus, May 22 (item reprinted from *Boston Courier*) and 30; June 5, 6, and 13, 1860
Bellows Falls Argus (Vt.), June 14, 1860
Bucyrus Weekly Journal (Ohio), June 21, 1860
Burlington Sentinel (Vt.), July 13 (item reprinted from *New York Herald*)
Charleston Mercury (S. C.), September 15, 1860
Cherry Valley Gazette (N. Y.), June 6 and 20, 1860
Cleveland Weekly Plain Dealer, June 6 and 20; July 25; October 10, 1860
Columbian Weekly Register (New Haven, Conn.), October 20, 1860.
Confederation (Washington, D. C.), Feb. 8 and 20, 1861
Constitution (Washington, D. C.), June 1, 6, and 9; July 19, 1860
Daily Chicago Herald, June 11, 13, 22 (item reprinted from *New York Times*), and 28 (item referring to *Milwaukee News* and *Milwaukee Sentinel*); July 16, 1860
Daily Herald (Newburyport, Mass.), May 21, 1860
Delawarean (Dover), October 27, 1860
Democratic Republican (Haverhill, N. H.), September 19, 1860
Dover Gazette (N. H.), June 2, 1860
Easton Times (Pa.), June 30; July 28; August 11, 1860
Exeter News-Letter (N. H.), June 18; August 20, 1860
Fayette and Union Telegraph (Connersville, Ind.), June 22 and 28, 1860
Fond du Lac Weekly Commonwealth (Wis.), June 5, 1860
Jerseyman (Morristown), June 16; September 29, 1860
Jonesboro Gazette (Ill.), June 30 (item reprinted from *Toledo Times*); July 7; August 4, 1860
Kansas State Record (Topeka), May 26, 1860
New Albany Daily Ledger (Ind.), June 14, 21, 22, and 25; July 2, 1860
Newark Daily Advertiser, June 28, 1860
New-Hampshire Patriot (Concord), June 6 and 7 (item reprinted from *Cheshire Republican* [N. H.])
New-Hampshire Statesman (Concord), May 26, 1860; March 9, 1861
New London Daily Star (Conn.), June 12; July 18, 1860
New York Daily Tribune, May 19 and 21, 1860 (including item reprinted from *Albany Atlas and Argus*)
New York Evening Post, May 22, 1860
New York Leader, June 16, 1860
Norfolk County Journal (Roxbury, Mass.) May 26, 1860
Oregon Sentinel (Jacksonville), August 18, 1860

Painesville Telegraph (Ohio), September 20 and 27, 1860
Portsmouth Journal (N. H.), July 28; August 4; October 13, 1860
Prairie du Chien Courier (Wis.), June 21, 1860
Republican Farmer (Bridgeport, Conn.), June 1; July 20; August 24, 1860
Rochester Union and Advertiser, May 22, 1860
Sacramento Daily Union, July 31, 1860
Saint Anthony Weekly Express (Hennepin County, Minn.), May 26; June 9; July 21, 1860
Salem Register (Mass.), February 25, 1861
San Francisco Herald, March 4, 1861
Springfield Daily Republican (Mass.), May 22; June 13, 1860
States and Union (Washington, D. C.), May 14, 1860
Topeka Tribune, May 26; June 2 and 9, 1860
Vermont Patriot (Montpelier), May 26, 1860
Washington Herald (Ohio), June 7, 1860
Weekly Illinois State Journal (Springfield), May 30; June 6; July 4, 1860
Weekly Wisconsin Patriot (Madison), June 30; July 7; August 4, 1860

CHAPTER EIGHT
Albany Atlas and Argus, June 22, 1860
Appleton Crescent (Wis.), August 4, 1860
Bellows Falls Argus (Vt.), September 20, 1860
Binghamton Standard (N. Y.), May 30, 1860
Bucyrus Weekly Journal (Ohio), June 28, 1860
Century Magazine, June, 1900
Cherry Valley Gazette (N. Y.), June 27, 1860
Columbian Weekly Register (New Haven, Conn.), November 10, 1860
Constitution (Washington, D. C.), June 8 (item reprinted from *Indianapolis Sentinel*) and 16, 1860
Daily Alta California (San Francisco), July 3, 1860
Daily Chicago Herald, July 7 and 16, 1860
Delawarean (Dover), October 27, 1860
Detroit Free Press, October 13, 1860
Easton Times (Pa.), June 30, 1860
Fayette and Union Telegraph (Connersville, Ind.), June 28, 1860
Fond du Lac Commonwealth (Wis.), June 6, 1860
Ft. Wayne Sentinel, May 26, 1860
Jonesboro Gazette (Ill.), June 9, 1860
Louisville Daily Courier, October 22, 1860
Manhattan Express (Kan.), June 16; July 17, 1860
New Albany Daily Ledger (Ind.), July 19, 1860
New-Hampshire Patriot (Concord), May 30; August 15; September 5, 1860
New York Atlas, May 20; June 24, 1860
New York Daily Tribune, May 21 and 23, 1860

New York Evening Post, October 8, 1860
New York Herald, June 14, 1860
New York Leader, June 16; November 3, 1860
Painesville Telegraph (Ohio), September 6, 1860
Republican Farmer (Bridgeport, Conn.), August 10, 1860
Springfield Daily Republican (Mass.), May 25, 1860
Tri-Weekly Missouri Republican (St. Louis), October 24, 1860
Union Democrat (Manchester, N. H.), August 7, 1860
Vermont Patriot (Montpelier), May 26, 1860
Weekly Illinois State Journal (Springfield), June 13; July 4 and 18;
   August 22; October 24, 1860
Weekly Wisconsin Patriot (Madison), June 30, 1860

CHAPTER NINE
Baltimore Sun, November 2, 1860
Binghamton Standard (N. Y.), August 8, 1860
Boston Herald, November 1, 2, and 5, 1860
Boston Journal, August 13, 18, and 29, 1860
Bucyrus Weekly Journal (Ohio), September 6, 1860
Century Magazine, June, 1900 (item reprinted from *Alton Courier*
   [Ill.])
Chicago Times and Herald, October 23 and 26, 1860
Cleveland Weekly Plain Dealer, May 23; Oct. 3; November 14, 1860
Columbian Weekly Register (New Haven, Conn.), October 20, 1860
Constitution (Washington, D. C.), May 31; June 12; July 25, 1860
Daily Chicago Herald, May 29; June 2 and 16, 1860
Daily Gate City (Keokuk, Iowa), October 20, 22, and 29, 1860
Delawarean (Dover), October 6 and 20, 1860
Detroit Free Press, October 16, 1860
Easton Times (Pa.), August 11, 1860
Evening Star (Washington, D. C.), May 25, 1860; February 27, 1861
Floridian and Journal (Tallahassee), November 10, 1860
Fond du Lac Commonwealth (Wis.), August 8, 1860
Hartford Weekly Times, October 27, 1860
Jerseyman (Morristown), September 22; October 13, 1860
Jonesboro Gazette (Ill.), August 25; September 1, 1860
Mississippian (Jackson), October 16, 1860
National Intelligencer (Washington, D. C.), October 5 and 25 (items
   reprinted from *New York Times*); August 8; September 4; October
   8, 1860
Newark Daily Advertiser, May 25 (item reprinted from *Hartford
   Courant*); June 4, 1860
New-Hampshire Patriot (Concord), June 7; July 18; October 17,
   1860 (item reprinted from *New York Weekly Journal of Commerce*)
New-Hampshire Statesman (Concord), August 18 (item reprinted
   from *Woodsfield Republican* [Ohio]); October 20; December 1, 1860

New Orleans Daily Delta, May 9, 1860
New York Daily Tribune, May 21; October 24, 25 (including items reprinted from *New York Daily News*), 26, 27, 30, 31, 1860
New York Evening Post, October 6 and 16, 1860
New York Herald, October 24, 1860
New York Times, September 14, 1860
Old Line Guard (Indianapolis), October 20, 1860
Portsmouth Journal (N. H.), September 15, 1860
Republican Farmer (Bridgeport, Conn.), October 12 (item reprinted from *New York Daily Tribune*)
Scribner's, November, 1893
Telegraph (Bradford, Vt.), June 1, 1860
Tri-Weekly Missouri Republican (St. Louis), October 24, 1860
Troy Times (Ohio), July 19, 1860
Union Democrat (Manchester, N. H.), October 2, 1860
Vermont Patriot (Montpelier), September 29, 1860
Weekly Illinois State Journal (Springfield), June 6; July 18 and 25; August 1, 15, and 29; September 12; October 17 and 31, 1860
Weekly Kentucky Yeoman (Frankfort), October 19, 1860
Wizard (South Danvers, Mass.), October 3; November 7, 1860
Worcester Palladium (Mass.), May 23; October 31, 1860

CHAPTER TEN
Appleton Crescent (Wis.), February 23, 1861
Baltimore Sun, November 3 and 12, 1860
Bangor Daily Union (Me.), November 14, 1860
Burlington Sentinel (Vt.), July 13, 1860
Cleveland Weekly Plain Dealer, September 12, 1860
Columbian Weekly Register (New Haven, Conn.), October 27, 1860
Coos Republican (Lancaster, N. H.), October 30, 1860
Detroit Free Press, October 4, 1860
Evening Star (Washington, D. C.), June 20, 1860
Jerseyman (Morristown), August 11; October 13, 1860
Jonesboro Gazette (Ill.), June 23 and 30, 1860
Kansas State Record (Topeka), November 3, 1860
Manhattan Express (Kan.), June 16, 1860
National Intelligencer (Washington, D. C.), October 3; November 12 (item reprinted from *New York Daily Tribune*) and 28, 1860 (item reprinted from *Chattanooga Gazette*)
New Albany Daily Ledger (Ind.), July 12, 1860
New-Hampshire Statesman (Concord), November 24, 1860 (item reprinted from *Boston Post*)
New London Daily Star (Conn.), July 14; August 17, 1860
New Orleans Daily Delta, May 6, 1860
New York Daily Tribune, May 24; July 6, 1860
New York Herald, October 20, 1860

New York World, June 29, 1860 (item reprinted from *Utica Herald* [N. Y.])

Republican Farmer (Bridgeport, Conn.), June 29; November 9, 1860

Saint Anthony Weekly Express (Hennepin County, Minn.) June 9, 1860

Springfield Daily Republican (Mass.), June 30, 1860

CHAPTER ELEVEN

Albany Atlas and Argus, June 6 and 27, 1860

American Eagle (Paoli, Ind.), June 21, 1860

Appleton Crescent (Wis.), July 14, 1860

Bangor Daily Union (Me.), October 20, 1860

Binghamton Standard (N. Y.), July 18; October 10, 1860 (items reprinted from *Toledo Blade, Rochester Democrat* and *Elmira Press*)

Boston Herald, October 31; November 8, 1860

Boston Journal, August 15, 1860

Bucyrus Weekly Journal (Ohio), August 3, 1860

Burlington Sentinel (Vt.), July 6, 1860

Cherry Valley Gazette (N. Y.), June 6, 1860

Cleveland Weekly Plain Dealer, May 16; June 13; July 18; September 26, 1860

Columbian Weekly Register (New Haven, Conn.), November 3, 1860

Constitution (Washington, D. C.), June 1; July 4, 7, and 19, 1860

Coos Republican (Lancaster, N. H.), November 6, 1860

Daily Chicago Herald, July 28, 1860 (including item reprinted from *New York Evening Post*)

Daily Gate City (Keokuk, Ia.), October 16, 17, and 23; November 3, 1860

Daily Omaha Nebraskan, October 26, 1860

Easton Times (Pa.), October 20; November 17, 1860

Exeter News-Letter (N. H.), September 10; October 22, 1860

Fayette and Union Telegraph (Connersville, Ind.), June 22 and 28, 1860

Floridian and Journal (Tallahassee), October 27, 1860

Fond du Lac Weekly Commonwealth (Wis.), August 15, 1860

Ft. Wayne Sentinel, May 26, 1860

Jonesboro Gazette (Ill.), January 14 and 21; July 21; August 25, 1860

Kansas State Record (Topeka), May 26, 1860

Manhattan Express (Kan.), June 23; July 7, 1860

National Intelligencer (Washington, D. C.), July 20; September 20 (item reprinted from *Chicago Times*); October 4 (item reprinted from *Abingdon Virginian*), and 24, 1860

Nebraska City News, August 4 and 25, 1860

New-Hampshire Patriot (Concord), September 12, 1860

New-Hampshire Statesman (Concord), August 25, 1860

New Orleans Daily Delta, May 18, 1860

New York Atlas, July 8, 1860
New York Daily Tribune, April 6; May 25; July 4, 9, and 10; October 24, 26, 27, and 31, 1860
New York Evening Post, October 2, 1860
New York Herald, October 29, 1860
New York Sun, June 26, 1860
Oregon Weekly Times (Portland), September 15, 1860
Painesville Telegraph (Ohio), November 1, 1860
Portsmouth Journal (N. H.), August 4; December 1, 1860
Prairie du Chien Courier (Wis.), June 28; October 18 (item reprinted from *Chicago Times and Herald*); November 15, 1860
Republican Farmer (Bridgeport, Conn.), June 15; July 20, 1860
Rochester Union and Advertiser, October 3 (item reprinted from *Rochester Democrat*)
Sacramento Daily Union, July 13, 1860
Spirit of the Age (Woodstock, Vt.), November 29, 1860
Springfield Daily Republican (Mass.), June 22; August 7 (item reprinted from *St. Paul Pioneer*)
Tri-Weekly Missouri Republican (St. Louis), October 24, 1860
Troy Times (Ohio), July 26; September 6, 1860
Union Democrat (Manchester, N. H.), August 7, 1860
Weekly Illinois State Journal (Springfield), March 28, July 11; October 17 and 24, 1860
Weekly Wisconsin Patriot (Madison), June 30; August 4, 1860
Worcester Daily Spy (Mass.), January 5, 1861

CHAPTER TWELVE
Appleton Crescent (Wis.), March 2, 1861
Baltimore Sun, November 5, 7, and 9, 1860; February 20, 1861 (item reprinted from *New York Express*)
Boston Daily Atlas and Bee November 7, 1860
Boston Herald, November 9, 1860 (item reprinted from *New York Herald*)
Bucyrus Weekly Journal (Ohio), October 5; November 8, 1860
Charleston Mercury, November 10, 1860
Chicago Press and Tribune, November 10, 1860
Chicago Times and Herald, November 2, 5, 6, 8, and 10, 1860
Cleveland Weekly Plain Dealer, December 4, 1860
Daily Alta California (San Francisco), October 7, 1860
Daily Gate City (Keokuk, Ia.), November 5 and 7, 1860
Kansas National Democrat (Lecompton), November 15; December 20, 1860 (item reprinted from *St. Clair Chief* [Mich.])
Kansas State Record (Topeka), November 17, 1860
Louisville Daily Courier, November 10, 1860
National Intelligencer (Washington, D. C.), November 13 and 30; December 1, 1860

Newark Daily Advertiser, May 25, 1860
New York Daily Tribune, April 5, 1860 (item reprinted from *Hartford Courant*)
New York Herald, November 6, 7, and 9, 1860 (item mentioning Bryant, of *New York Evening Post*)
Oregon Sentinel (Jacksonville), December 22, 1860
Weekly Illinois State Journal (Springfield), October 31; November 7, 21, and 28, 1860 (item reprinted from *LaCrosse Union* [Wis.])
Worcester Palladium (Mass.), November 14, 1860

CHAPTER THIRTEEN
American Eagle (Paoli, Ind.), July 26, 1860
Atlantic Monthly, October, 1860
Baltimore Sun, February 23, 1861
Bucyrus Weekly Journal (Ohio), June 14, 1860
Burlington Sentinel (Vt.), December 7, 1860
Charleston Mercury, July 10; September 8 and 13, 1860
Cleveland Weekly Plain Dealer, December 19, 1860
Confederation (Washington, D. C.), February 15, 1861
Constitution (Washington, D. C.), May 5, 8, and 10; June 13; July 7 and 12, 1860
Daily Chicago Herald, May 15; June 7, 16, and 29, 1860
Daily Chicago Post, February 16; March 5, 1861
Daily Gate City (Keokuk, Ia.), October 30, 1860
Delawarean (Dover), August 25; November 3, 1860; February 9, 1861
Exeter News-Letter (N. H.), September 3, 1860
Harper's Weekly, June 2, 1860
Jonesboro Gazette (Ill.), January 28; February 4 and 18; March 10; April 7; May 26; July 21; August 11, 1860
Louisville Daily Courier, October 19 (item reprinted from *Columbus Enquirer* [Ga.]), and 22, 1860
Mississippian (Jackson), July 27; August 10; September 7; October 9; November 9 and 13; December 4, 25, and 28, 1860
New Orleans Daily Delta, April 29; May 8, 11, 13, 18, and 23, 1860
New York Daily Tribune, October 27 and 30, 1860; January 10, 1861 (item reprinted from *New York Weekly Journal of Commerce*)
New York Weekly Journal of Commerce, January 3, 1861
Oregon Weekly Times (Portland), May 16, 1860
Portsmouth Journal (N. H.), July 14, 1860
San Francisco Herald, March 14, 1861
Springfield Daily Republican (Mass.), August 18, 1860
States and Union (Washington, D. C.), February 7, 1861
Weekly Illinois State Journal (Springfield), February 8 (item reprinted from *Chicago Times*); August 8, 1860
Worcester Daily Spy (Mass.), February 21, 1861

CHAPTER FOURTEEN

Baltimore Sun, November 10 and 12, 1860; February 16, 1861
Cleveland Weekly Plain Dealer, November 28, 1860
Confederation (Washington, D. C.), January 29, 1861
Daily Chicago Herald, May 30, 1860
Daily Chicago Post, February 10, 12, 14, and 28; March 1, 1861
Daily Gate City (Keokuk, Ia.), November 14 and 15, 1860
Evening Star (Washington, D. C.), February 2 (including item reprinted from *Norfolk Transcript*), 4, 5, 12, 16, 21, and 23; March 18, 1861
Jonesboro Gazette (Ill.), February 11, 1860
Mississippian (Jackson), September 25; November 2, 1860
National Intelligencer (Washington, D. C.), October 17 (item reprinted from *Richmond Enquirer*); November 1 (item reprinted from *Charleston Mercury*), and 7; December 8, 20, 25, and 28, 1860 (item reprinted from *Charleston Mercury*); February 20, 1861
New-Hampshire Statesman (Concord), December 8, 1860
New York Daily Tribune, October 30, 1860 (including item reprinted from *Portsmouth Transcript* [Va.])
New York Evening Post, February 8, 1861
New York Herald, October 29, 1860
New York Weekly Journal of Commerce, January 3 (item reprinted from *Punch*), and 10; February 21 (including item reprinted from *New York Evening Post*), and 28, 1861
New York World, February 26, 1861
Old Line Guard (Indianapolis), October 30, 1860
Portsmouth Journal (N. H.), October 20, 1860
San Francisco Herald, February 25 and 27, 1861
States and Union (Washington, D. C.), February 14 and 19, 1861
Tri-weekly Missouri Republican (St. Louis), November 6, 1860
Union Democrat (Manchester, N. H.), December 25, 1860
Vermont Patriot (Montpelier), July 28, 1860
Weekly Illinois State Journal (Springfield), December 5, 1860
Wizard (South Danvers, Mass.), November 28, 1860

CHAPTER FIFTEEN

Baltimore Sun, February 15 and 23, 1861
Bay State (Lynn, Mass.), February 28, 1861 (item reprinted from *Cincinnati Enquirer*)
Confederation (Washington, D. C.), February 8; March 1, 1861
Constitution (Washington, D. C.), February 19, 1861
Daily Chicago Post, February 17, 21, 22, 23, and 28; March 6 (item reprinted from *Vanity Fair*), and 14, 1861 (item reprinted from *Cleveland Weekly Plain Dealer*)
Evening Star (Washington, D. C.), February 19 and 20; March 16, 1861
Indiana State Guard (Indianapolis), January 26; February 23, 1861

Lynn Weekly Reporter (Mass.), February 23, 1861
National Republican (Washington, D. C.), February 19, 1861
Nebraska Republican (Omaha), February 27, 1861
Newark Daily Advertiser, February 18, 22, and 26, 1861
New-Hampshire Statesman (Concord), January 19, 1861
New Orleans Daily Picayune, February 13, 19, 21, and 27, 1861
New York Daily Tribune, February 16, 1861
New York Evening Post, February 12 and 21, 1861
New York Weekly Journal of Commerce, February 21 and 28, 1861
New York World, February 18, 19, 20, 21, 22, and 25, 1861
Salem Register (Mass.), February 18, 1861
San Francisco Herald, March 6, 1860
States and Union (Washington, D. C.), February 12, 13, 14 (item re-
    printed from *New York Day Book*), 16, and 22, 1861
Weekly Illinois State Journal (Springfield), February 20 and 27, 1861
Worcester Daily Spy (Mass.), February 16 and 18, 1861

CHAPTER SIXTEEN
Confederation (Washington, D. C.), February 27, 1861
Daily Chicago Post, February 28, 1861
Frank Leslie's Popular Monthly, March, 1897
Harper's Monthly, June, 1868
Harvard Monthly, December, 1885
McClure's Magazine, November, 1894; June, 1895
Nebraska Republican (Omaha), February 27, 1861
Newark Daily Advertiser, February 28, 1861
New York Weekly Journal of Commerce, February 28; March 7, 1861
New York World, February 27, 1861
States and Union (Washington, D. C.), February 25 and 28, 1861;
    March 4, 1861
Worcester Daily Spy (Mass.), January 28, 1861

CHAPTER SEVENTEEN
Confederation (Washington, D. C.), February 8 and 25, 1861
Daily Chicago Post, February 26 and 27; March 1 (item reprinted
    from *New York Times*), 2, 5, 6, 8, and 10, 1861
Daily Illinois State Journal (Springfield), March 14, 1861
Evening Star (Washington, D. C.), February 14, 25, 26, and 27;
    March 1, 2, 12, and 14, 1861 (item reprinted from *Baltimore
    American*)
Harper's Weekly, March 2, 1861
Lynn Weekly Register (Mass.), February 23, 1861
National Intelligencer (Washington, D. C.), November 12, 1860;
    February 13 and 26, 1861
National Republican (Washington, D. C.), February 19 and 25;
    March 7, 1861

New York Evening Post, February 21; March 4, 1861
New York World, February 25, 1861
States and Union (Washington, D. C.), February 28; March 1 and 15, 1861
Weekly Illinois State Journal (Springfield), February 13, 1861

CHAPTER EIGHTEEN
Confederation (Washington, D. C.), March 2, 1861
Evening Star (Washington, D. C.), March 4, 1861
Harper's Weekly, March 9 and 16, 1861
Newark Daily Advertiser, March 4, 1861
New York Commercial Advertiser, March 4, 1861
New York Weekly Journal of Commerce, February 28, 1861
States and Union (Washington, D. C.), March 4 and 5, 1861

CHAPTER NINETEEN
Confederation (Washington, D. C.), February 11, 1861 (item reprinted from *Chicago Democrat*)
Daily Chicago Post, March 5, 7, and 13, 1861
Daily Illinois State Journal (Springfield), March 7, 1861
Evening Star (Washington, D. C.), March 4 and 5, 1861
Frank Leslie's Popular Monthly, March, 1897
National Intelligencer (Washington, D. C.), March 5, 1861
New-Hampshire Statesman (Concord), March 9, 1861
New York Commercial Advertiser, March 4, 1861
New York Daily Tribune, March 5, 1861
New York Evening Post, March 5, 1861
New York Weekly Journal of Commerce, February 14, 1861
States and Union (Washington, D. C.), March 5 and 7, 1861
Worcester Daily Spy (Mass.), January 14, 1861

CHAPTER TWENTY
Confederation (Washington, D. C.), February 28, 1861
Evening Star (Washington, D. C.), February 16 and 20; March 1 and 5, 1861
Frank Leslie's Popular Monthly, March, 1897
Harper's Weekly, March 13, 1897
National Intelligencer (Washington, D. C.), February 28, 1861
National Republican (Washington, D. C.), February 18, 1861
New York Commercial Advertiser, March 5, 1861
New York Evening Post, March 4, 1861

INDEX

ABOLITION, *see* Slavery: abolition and abolitionists
Alabama, delegates bolt, 86
Albany, N. Y., Lincoln in, 279-280
Alcoholic drinks, 46, 50-51, 53, 64, 70, 83, 105, 189-190, 197, 275, 279-280, 286, 311, 314, 331
Allison, John, 30
Anderson, Robert, 259
Arthur, Chester A., 323
Ashmun, George, 68, 72, 110
Astor House, 25, 281
Atlantic Cable, 71-72, 99

BALTIMORE, MD.
    Constitutional Union Convention, 96-97
    Northern Democratic Convention, 88-91
    Southern Democratic Convention, 92
Banners, campaign, 127, 151, 199
Barnum, P. T., 99, 127, 136, 282
Bateman, Newton, 72
Bates, Edward, 42, 52, 306
Bedell, Grace, 118, 275-276
Beecher, Henry Ward, 25, 177
Bell, John, 96, 115, 202
Berret, James G., 330
Betting, 83, 205, 272, 278, 329
Black Hawk War, 103, 150, 271
Blair, Francis P., 42, 68
Blair, Montgomery, 303, 306, 328
Blondin, Charles, 99
Bolt, Democratic convention, 86-88
Books, campaign, 108-110

Brady, Mathew B., 118, 324
Breckinridge, John, 92, 115, 153, 200
Brown, John, 27, 41, 55, 57, 99, 174, 233, 242
Browne, Charles F. *see* Ward, Artemus
Bryant, William Cullen, 26, 124, 127, 154, 221, 281, 300
Buchanan, James, 85, 201, 241, 258, 303, 317-319, 324
Buffalo, N. Y., Lincoln in, 277-278

CALIFORNIA, Indian warfare in, 195
Cameron, Simon, 52, 306, 328
Campbell, Lewis D., 56
Capitol, plot to blow up, 308
Cartter, David K., 61, 64, 69
Cartwright, Peter, 102-103
Charleston, S. C.
    cheers Federal resignees, 220
    Democratic convention, 82-86
Chase, Salmon P., 52, 61, 154, 306
Cincinnati, Ohio, Lincoln in, 267-268
Clay, Henry, 89, 119, 260
Cleveland, Ohio
    Lincoln in, 273-274
    termed "Nigger Town," 231
Columbus, Ohio, Lincoln in, 268-272
Confederacy, 250, 271
Constitutional Union Party, 96-97, 141-142, 202

Conventions, political
   Constitutional Union, 96-97
   Democratic, Charleston, 82-86
   Illinois Republican (1858), 21-22
   Illinois Republican (1860), 17-18
   Northern Democratic (88-91)
   Republican National (1856), 30-31
   Republican National (1860), 35-65, 303
   Southern Democratic, 92
Cooper Union, Douglas meeting, 152
Cooper Union speech, Lincoln, 25-29
Crawford, Josiah, 170-171
Curtin, Governor, 290

DAVIS, DAVID, 48, 59, 301, 305
Davis, Jefferson, 250, 271-272
Decatur, Ill., Republican convention, 17-18
Depression, threat of, 190, 208, 242
Douglas, Stephen A.
   attends Inaugural Ball, 330
   cabinet-maker, 135
   debates Lincoln, 22-25, 109, 240
   defeats Lincoln, 25, 80
   derided in press, 187
   discussed at convention, 82-86
   drinks liquor, 135, 190
   election prospects, 198-199
   height, 117
   inaugural ball sponsor, 328
   nominated for President, 90
   oratory, 156
   play on his name, 115
   popular sovereignty of, 20-21, 24
   ribbed in songs, 126

Douglas, Stephen A.—Continued
   schoolteacher, 196
   visits his mother, 156
   visits Lincoln, 303
Dred Scott decision, 21, 55, 324

ELECTION
   appeal to voters, 208-209
   celebrations after, 216-219
   fraud in, 208
   Lincoln votes at, 209-210
   reported by press, 215
   results, 212-213
Elections, state, 194
Electoral votes, counting, 270-271
Ellis, John Willis, 255
Everett, Edward, 96, 328

FACTIONS, see Split, Democratic
Faneuil Hall, 116, 159
Fell, Jesse W., 32, 106
Felton, S. M., 288
Fillmore, Millard, 209, 277
"Fire-Eaters," 85, 87, 247
Fort Sumter, 259
Fremont, John C., 31, 52, 242
French immigrants, 194
Fusion movement, 202-204

GALLOWAY, SAMUEL, 32
Garfield, James, 323
German-Americans, 41, 194
Giddings, Joshua R., 38, 55, 65, 79
Gist, William Henry, 248
Gougenheim, Joey, 314
Grant, Ulysses S., 300
Greeley, Horace
   boards Lincoln train, 274
   "cabinet" position, 306
   campaign song writer, 124
   in Chicago, 42, 47, 53, 59
   condones secession, 177, 248
   errs in reporting nomination, 59
   impersonated in parade, 151

Greeley, Horace—*Continued*
  Inaugural spectator, 323
  speaks for Republicans, 154

HALSTEAD, MURAT, 48, 61, 67, 108
Hamlin, Hannibal
  vice-presidential candidate,
    63-64
  meets Lincoln, 260
  play on his name, 112
Hanks, Charles, 102
Hanks, John, 17-18, 107, 128, 154
Harrisburg, Lincoln in, 288-292
Harrison, Benjamin, 323
Harrison, William Henry, 45, 66,
  137
Harvard College, 29, 217
Hay, John M., 276
Hayes, Rutherford, B., 268, 323
Heenan, John C., 99
Herndon, William H., 23, 48, 53
Holmes, Oliver Wendell, 154
Homesteads, free, 55, 185
House of Representatives
  discusses Negroes, 223
  guarded by police, 270
  Lincoln visits, 306
  Presidential choice by, 207,
    213
Houston, Sam, 63, 97, 202, 204,
  245
Howe, Julia Ward, 299
Howells, William Dean, 109
Hyer, Tom, 41

ILLINOIS, key convention state, 59
Inaugural address, Lincoln's, 322-
  324
Inaugural Ball, 328-332
Indiana
  key state at convention, 59
  Lincoln in, 264-267
  state elections, 194, 206
Indianapolis, Ind., Lincoln in, 265-
  266
Irish immigrants, 195

JACKSON, ANDREW, 119, 201, 260
Johnson, Andrew, 328
Johnson, Herschel V., 90, 135
Judd, Norman B., 33, 45, 60, 68,
  287, 301, 328

KANSAS
  Lincoln offer to delegate
    from, 33
  in Republican platform, 55
  voters imported from, 211
Kansas-Nebraska Bill, 20-21
Kentucky
  delegate at Chicago conven-
    tion, 47
  Lincoln appeals to, 268
Knox College, 171
Kohn, Abraham, 171

LAMON, WARD H., 291
Lane, Harriet, 302
Lane, Henry S., 38, 62
Lane, Joseph, 92, 115, 181, 200
Lincoln, Abraham
  acceptance letter, 72
  arrives in Washington, 293
  awarded doctoral degree, 171
  beard, 118, 275-276
  biographies of, 100-108
  in Black Hawk War, 103
  burned in effigy, 247
  called "Abram," 110-111
  called "Honest Abe," 78, 113
  called "Old Abe," 111
  casts his vote, 209-210
  in Congress, 20, 188
  Cooper Union speech, 25-29
  debates with Douglas, 22-25,
    109, 240
  defeated by Douglas, 25, 80
  delivers Inaugural address,
    322-324
  education, 101
  escapes "Baltimore plot,"
    291-292
  goes incognito, 291-292

Lincoln, Abraham—*Continued*
  hanged in effigy, 246
  hears of nomination, 64
  height, 69-70, 116, 165
  at home, 19, 64, 68-71, 143,
    164-166, 217, 261-262
  "house-divided" speech, 22,
    108
  at Illinois state convention,
    17-18
  at Inaugural Ball, 330-311
  in Inaugural parade, 317-319
  keeps silence, 177, 240-241,
    265, 282
  leaves Springfield, 262-263
  liquor issue and, 70, 105,
    189-190
  New England trip, 29-30
  nominated for President, 60
  open-door policy, 165
  oratorical ability, 24, 28, 30,
    323
  personal qualities, 32, 59, 73,
    105
  physical characteristics, 19,
    23, 79, 115, 118-122
  play on his name, 111
  prepares Inaugural address,
    260
  presidential candidate, 61
  receives notification commit-
    tee, 68-71
  receives visitors, 164-168
  responses to nomination, 65-
    66
  Second Inauguration, 332
  at Springfield rally, 148
  stand on Mexican War issues,
    188
  stand on slavery, 22, 27, 79,
    173-174, 178, 239-240,
    323
  story-teller, 27, 103-104, 265
  trip to Washington, 262-297
  visits New Orleans, 239

Lincoln, Abraham—*Continued*
  "With malice toward none,"
    332
Lincoln, Mary Todd, 19, 26 170,
  257, 260, 282, 292, 293
  arrives in Washington, 298
  described by press, 70, 171,
    279
  gives receptions, 302
  at Inaugural Ball, 330
Lincoln, Robert, 19, 29, 131, 154,
  217, 260, 301-302, 313, 331
Lincoln, Sarah Johnston, 261
Lincoln, Thomas (Tad), 19, 69,
  164, 262, 282
Lincoln, Willie, 19, 69, 262, 282
Locke, David R., 20
Logan, Stephen T., 48
Longfellow, Henry Wadsworth,
  221, 264
Lovejoy, Elijah P., 144
Lovejoy, Owen, 143
Lowell, James Russell, 124, 154

McClure, A. K., 291
Maryland, Lincoln in, 292
Medill, Joseph, 41, 61
Minute Men, 220, 256
Missouri Compromise, 20
Moody, Dwight L., 260
Morgan, Edwin D., 45, 68
Morrill, L. M., 38
"Mud-sill" theory, 102

Nasby, Petroleum V., *see* David
  R. Locke
Nast, Thomas, 310
Negroes, free, *see also* Slavery
  progress in North, 231-232
  Republican orator, 154-155
  return to slavery, 235-236
  unfair treatment of, 237-238
New England
  Douglas' excursion in, 156
  in Inaugural parade, 319

New England—*Continued*
landslide for Lincoln, 212
Lincoln in, 29-30
New Jersey
Fusion movement in, 202
key convention state, 59
Lincoln in, 285-286
split electoral vote, 212
New Orleans, La., Lincoln's trip to, 239
New York, N. Y.
Lincoln's speech in, 25-29
Lincoln's trip through, 281-284
Republican rally in, 147
Union-Democratic parade in, 150-151
New York State
Fusion movement in, 202-203
Lincoln in, 275-284
Nicolay, John G., 264, 276
Nye, James W., 75

OFFICE-SEEKERS, 168-170, 266, 303-306
Oglesby, Richard J., 18
Ohio
Lincoln in, 267-272
state election, 194, 206
swings nomination to Abe, 61
Oratory, political
Breckinridge, 156
Douglas "visits his mother," 157-159
Lincoln at Cooper Union, 25-29
Lincoln in New England, 29-30
roving orators, 169
Oregon, represented by Greeley, 47

PALMER, JOHN M., 30
Peace Conference, 299, 307

Pennsylvania
delegation at Chicago, 39
Fusion movement in, 202
key convention state, 59
Lincoln in, 272-275, 287-292
state election, 194, 206
Perry, Oliver Hazard, 45
Philadelphia, Pa.
first Republican convention, 30-31
Lincoln flag-raising in, 287
Lincoln in, 287-288
Phillips, Wendell, 174, 175
Phillips Academy, 29
Pierce, Franklin, 245
Pinkerton, Allan, 287, 289-290
Pittsburgh, Pa., Lincoln in, 272-273
Platforms, political
Constitutional Union, 97
Democratic (Charleston), 85
Republican, 55-58
Plots
"Baltimore Plot," 288-290
to blow up Capitol, 308
to elevate Breckinridge, 270
to kill Lincoln during Inaugural, 308
to seize Washington, 288
Polls, political, 58, 204
Polygamy, 55
Pony Express, 99, 214
Popular sovereignty, 20-21, 24, 82, 85, 174
Potter, John F., 49
Press
at Baltimore conventions, 90
campaign newspapers, 110
concerning Democratic split, 92-96
at Democratic convention, 83
Lincoln studies the, 172
reports election, 215

Press—*Continued*
   reports Inauguration, 325-327
   at Republican convention, 45
Prince of Wales, 99, 204, 294
Pryor, Roger A., 49

RAILROADS
   bring inaugural throngs, 310
   excursions from Chicago, 59
   to Pacific, 55
   special Lincoln cars, 262, 280
   trips to Chicago convention, 38-39
Rails, fence
   at Illinois convention, 17-19, 102
   market for, 133
   "railery" by opponents, 134, 206
   role in campaign, 131-136
   split during parades, 144
Rallies, political
   congratulatory, for Lincoln, 143
   crowds at, 142
   Douglas ox roast, 196-197
   length of parades, 143
   at Lincoln-Douglas debates, 22-23
   in New York City, 147, 150-151
   rail-splitters in parades, 144
   in Springfield, Ill., 147-149, 216-217
Rarey, John S., 314
Ray, Charles H., 41
Raymond, Henry J., 53, 68
Republican National Convention, 1860:
   balloting, 60-61
   behind-scenes maneuvering, 58
   chooses Lincoln, 61
   delegates to, 46-48
   Lincoln acceptance letter to, 72

Republican National Convention, 1860:—*Continued*
   names vice-presidential candidate, 63-64
   nominates Lincoln, 60
   notifies Lincoln, 68-71
   opening of, 44
   platform, 55-58
   "reconvenes" in Washington, 303
   wigwam at, 35-38
Republican Party
   first national convention, 30-31
   stand on slavery (1860), 173-174
Rhode Island, Fusion movement in, 202
Richmond, Va., Southern Democratic convention, 91

ST. JOHN'S EPISCOPAL CHURCH, 306
Sayers, Tom, 99, 117
Scala, Francis, 307
Schurz, Carl, 23, 41, 194
Scott, Winfield, 261, 290, 299, 303, 320, 328
Secession, 242-259
   arming, 257-258
   disunion sentiment, 245-248
   Federal property surrendered, 258-259
   seven states secede, 248
   Southern pro-Union sentiment, 244
Seward, William H., 21, 74-77, 154, 290, 293, 306
Shields, General, 103
Slavery
   abolition and abolitionists, 98, 174, 178, 202, 237-238, 240
   enslavement for taxes, 236
   free Negroes return to, 235-236

Slavery—*Continued*
　　freedom through purchase, 43, 230
　　good treatment of slaves, 233-235
　　ill treatment of slaves, 227-229
　　Lincoln's stand on, 22, 27, 79, 173-174, 178, 239-240, 323
　　lynchings, 228
　　market, 224-225
　　political parties' attitudes toward, 173-174
　　property issue, 222-223
　　Republican platform on, 55
　　runaway slaves, 229-230
　　slave trade, 55, 225-227
　　southern viewpoint on, 232-238
　　Underground Railroad, 229
Slogans, campaign, 18, 127, 148, 151, 152, 268
Smith, Caleb B., 63, 306
Smith, Gerrit, 98, 178, 202
Songs, campaign, 124-127
South Carolina
　　first to secede, 248-249
　　Minute Men Movement in, 256
　　three delegates refuse to bolt, 86
Springfield, Ill.
　　celebrates Lincoln's nomination, 68-69
　　celebrates Lincoln's victory, 216-217
　　county convention in, 33
　　holds congratulatory meeting, 143
　　Republican rally in, 147-149
　　state Republican convention (1858) in, 21-22
"Star of the West," 259
Stephens, Alexander, 250
Stevens, Thaddeus, 41
Stevenson, Adlai E., 32, 106

TANEY, ROGER B., 324
Telegraph, 45, 213-214, 273, 291, 293
Texas, delegates at Chicago, 47-48
Thumb, Tom, 99, 127
Toombs, Robert, 176, 247
Trenton, N. J., Lincoln in, 285-286
Tyler, John, 303

UNDERGROUND RAILROAD, 229

VILLARD, HENRY, 41, 164
Virginia
　　postpones secession, 249
　　sponsors Peace Conference, 299

WARD, ARTEMUS, 169, 243
Warn, Kate, 292
Washington, D. C., 41
　　defense of, 316-317
　　Lincoln in, 298-332
　　mayor of, visits Lincoln, 307
　　plot to seize, 288
Welles, Gideon, 41, 306
Wells Fargo & Co., 195, 214
Wentworth, "Long John," 50, 227
Whittier, John Greenleaf, 124, 154
Wide-Awakes
　　campaign role, 137-143
　　at Chicago convention, 39
　　impression on opposition, 138
　　origin of, 138
　　youthfulness of, 140
Wigwam
　　at Chicago, 35-38, 150
　　at Decatur, 17
　　in many cities, 149
"Wildfire," 226-227
Wilmot, David, 45
Wise, Henry Alexander, 256
Women and politics, 23, 37, 44, 83, 144

YANCEY, WILLIAM L., 85, 87, 201